S0-EYO-290

WITHDRAWN
NDSU

MANAGEMENT FOR CHANGE:
THE GARTH HILL EXPERIENCE

To our wives Barbara and Gail;
and to our children:
    Sarah, Alison and Helen;
    Amy and Joshua

MANAGEMENT FOR CHANGE: THE GARTH HILL EXPERIENCE

Stanley Goodchild and
Peter Holly

 The Falmer Press

(A member of the Taylor & Francis Group)
London ● New York ● Philadelphia

UK   The Falmer Press, Falmer House, Barcombe, Lewes, East Sussex, BN8 5DL

USA   The Falmer Press, Taylor & Francis Inc., 242 Cherry Street, Philadelphia, PA 19106-1906

© 1989 Stanley Goodchild and Peter Holly

All rights reserved. No part of this publication may be reproduced, stored in a retrieval system, or transmitted in any form or by any means, electronic, mechanical, photocopying, recording or otherwise, without permission in writing from the Publisher.

First published 1989

British Library Cataloguing in Publication Data

Goodchild, Stanley
  Management for change: the Garth Hill experience.
  1. Berkshire. Bracknell. Comprehensive schools. Garth Hill School
  I. Title. II. Holly, Peter
  373.422'98
ISBN 1-85000-472-2
ISBN 1-85000-473-0 (pbk.)

Typeset in 12/13 Garamond by
The FD Group Ltd, Fleet, Hampshire

Jacket design by Caroline Archer

Printed in Great Britain by Taylor & Francis (Printers) Ltd, Basingstoke

LB
2902
D73
G66

Contents

Acknowledgements   vi

Introduction   1

PART I   THE GARTH HILL EXPERIENCE:
**   AN ENTERPRISING SCHOOL IN THE MAKING**   9
Phase One   In the Beginning   12
Phase Two   Leading from the Front   26
Phase Three Making It Count   45

PART II   AN ENTERPRISING SCHOOL   101
Introduction   103
Chapter 1   School Leadership   109
Chapter 2   School Culture   137
Chapter 3   Management for Change   163
Chapter 4   The Enterprise Curriculum   191
Chapter 5   The Enterprise Culture   213
Chapter 6   Enterprise for the Enterprise   241

Bibliography   267

Index   273

Acknowledgements

We want to take this opportunity of thanking all those who have helped in the production of this book – by typing various stages of the manuscript, reading and commenting on draft material and offering encouragement for the project. Representing the publishers Malcolm Clarkson has been a constant source of support and we thank him for that. Above all, however, we want to thank the staff, pupils, parents and friends of Garth Hill, without whose efforts this book would not have been possible.

Stanley Goodchild and Peter Holly
July 1988

Introduction

This book is the result of close collaboration between two educational practitioners, who together have over forty years of experience in schools.

Stanley Goodchild returned to headship having had a career in local government. His career spans a wide spectrum of activities within the education service; he has held posts at all levels of management in schools and LEA advisory and inspectorial services and, before taking up his present post in 1982 as Head of Garth Hill School, he was Chief Education Officer for Schools in the London Borough of Bexley.

In addition, he has served on numerous national committees, including Education for Capability, Initial Teacher Training Steering Committee (Industry Year), Advisory Committee for Employment (SEG), the TTNS Advisory Board, to mention a few. He has acted as an adviser to numerous organizations and was responsible for setting up the UK 'cell' of the International School-Year 2020 initiative. He has been invited as a guest lecturer by organizations up and down the country, in Europe and in both Canada and the USA, in addition to appearances on both television and documentary films. Last year he was awarded the honour of a Fellowship of the British Institute of Management.

Peter Holly taught for sixteen years in comprehensive schools in the East End of London, Avon and Cambridge and, in 1982, joined the staff of the Schools Council, becoming a team-member of the GRIDS Project and, in 1983, its National Coordinator. The following year he was appointed Tutor in Curriculum Studies at the Cambridge Institute of Education and has since specialized in the areas of evaluation and school development. He has written widely on these and related topics. In 1986/87 he directed the DELTA Project — part of the MSC's dissemination package of the TRIST initiative — and is currently acting as an external consultant for evaluation projects in Northamptonshire LEA and Grampian Regional Authority. A former member of the OECD/CERI International School Improvement Project, he is now, with Stanley Goodchild, a member of the IMTEC School Year 2020 initiative.

It is important to explain the shape of this book.

In **Part I** Stanley Goodchild describes the recent history of Garth Hill School, where he has been Headteacher since 1982. His commentary provides illustrative material of the internal mechanics of the change process in education.

In **Part II** Peter Holly provides an in-depth analysis of the issues arising from the case study in Part One. In doing so, he draws on various kinds of theory to illuminate the practice at Garth Hill. The editorial and production stages associated with this book have been shared jointly by the authors.

While working on the book, three thoughts were uppermost in the minds of the authors:

(i)　The book is about a successful *enterprise* — which happens to be a school. Moreover, change is a constant challenge in organizational life — whether the organization is a school, hospital, church or business firm. It makes good sense, therefore, to share the practice and theory of change in social organizations — across the public/private, educational/commercial, non-profit-making/profit-making divide. It is argued that there are no problems with using organization and management theory arising from practice in the industrial/business sector to illuminate the practice in educational institutions. Equally, it is hoped that the business world could see its way to using the theory arising from the successful practice of educational organizations. Interdisciplinary enquiry is essentially an interactive learning process, within which each partner can both teach and be taught.

(ii)　This book has been put together as an investigation of change management. What are being focused upon, therefore, are management strategies and their effectiveness in promoting change in educational establishments. This book does not represent an attempt to write a complete history of Garth Hill School; while not wanting to make light of previous achievements, the concern here is with events since 1982 and only inasmuch as they provide the backcloth for the exercise of change strategies. It is, essentially, a book about change leadership and it is appropriate that Stanley Goodchild — *the* change leader at Garth Hill — should be one of its co-authors.

(iii)　If this book is to be of practical use, it needs to be of interest to all those other Garth Hills, all those other Stanley Goodchilds. The authors are not offering a blue-print for success. Every school has to find its own brand of success; the chemistry of which is fundamentally school-specific. What the authors are offering, however, are some practical suggestions concerning the ingredients of the 'chemical solution' and one way — the Garth Hill way — of putting them together.

There is evidence that other schools are already following Garth Hill's example. During a recent visit to a comprehensive school in Northamptonshire, Peter Holly was told that the school's 'technology day' had been 'inspired by the work of a school in Berkshire called Garth Hill'. Undoubtedly, the Garth Hill story provides light relief amidst the usual reports of educational doom and gloom.

Given this fact, during 1987, the Garth Hill story hit the national headlines. The *Daily Mail,* 5 June 1987, in a banner headline, proclaimed 'This British school is top in Europe' and the whole-page article beneath the headline sought, in rather emotive terms, to explain its transformation. The article opened in this fashion:

> The Duke of Kent yesterday opened the first high-tech school computer library in the country.
>
> It marked a transformation at a Bracknell comprehensive which has astonished educationalists. From a school no-one wanted it has become the most high powered and technically advanced in Europe.
>
> Garth Hill School has become such a model of advanced technology that television crews from as far away as Japan have come to report its success.
>
> Just five years ago . . . (many) parents did not want to send their children there and the Berkshire Education Authority was considering closure.
>
> (Since then, however,) it has become the sort of model school Education Secretary Kenneth Baker wants to see. Many teachers and politicians say the change cannot be achieved.
>
> Yet parents are queueing up to get their children in the school.

In this same report the *Daily Mail's* Education Correspondent went on to list some of the achievements of Garth Hill. These included: changing the school round 'in about a year'; the new library (where pupils can key into computerized library catalogues across the world to get information and to track down books) which has 18,000 books, many supplied jointly by industry and the County Council; a computer room stacked with all the latest equipment, plus a string of other 'firsts' which the school has achieved:

- the first Prestel International data link in Britain — in the first classroom to be transformed into a working hi-tech office, full of equipment the pupils will have to use when they go out to work;
- the first direct computer link for parents to find out information about the school and their children's progress;
- the first day school in the country to open its high tech restaurant to serve breakfast to pupils;
- nearly £½ million a year pouring into the school from industry.

The reporter was at pains to point out, however, that, alongside its marvels of high-technology, the school can boast an excellent record both in music and sport — with Garth Hill pupils captaining the county's junior rugby and cricket teams — a disciplined atmosphere in the school, reinforced by a smart school uniform, and an above average academic record. Above all,

> five years ago thirty of Garth Hill's leavers could not get jobs, even in a boom town in the heart of the prosperous South East. Last September, not one school leaver was unemployed.

3

The key to success is satisfaction; teacher satisfaction, pupil satisfaction, and parent satisfaction. The article ends by providing some feedback from the school's 'consumers':

> 'I am proud to belong to this school', said 17-year-old Billy O'Riordan, a lower sixth former and student member of the governing body, who hopes to go to London University to study law next year.

> 'The standard of teaching is very good here — the school attracts good teachers and a good atmosphere. There is an expectation that you will do well.'

> 'When I came here the school was so run down. All the window frames had rotted — you could poke your fingers through them. Now they have all gone; it's somewhere you are proud to belong to.'

> 'There's no vandalism here. If you are taught to respect the school you respect its property, too.'

> Deputy head John Kesteven has been at the school since before Mr. Goodchild's arrival too. 'He said we were in for an exciting time and that is just what we have had. Exciting — that's the word for this place.'

The introduction of a Business Manager to the school in September 1987 caused quite a stir in the national press. According to the education correspondent of the *Today* newspaper:

> A top businessman went back to school yesterday to unleash his boardroom skills in *Britain's most enterprising comprehensive.* (our emphasis).
>
> Computer expert Alan Watts began a year-long contract as business manager at Garth Hill School, Bracknell, with a brief to make money from its £50 million assets . . .
>
> But Mr. Watts, a senior executive with computer giant Hewlett-Packard, will take the experiment a stage further and offer firms the immediate benefits of the school's facilities. One plan is to turn the school into a major conference centre with teachers hiring out their services as professional consultants.
>
> Mr. Watts said: 'It's a tremendous opportunity to make great use of tremendous resources.'
>
> His plan includes an annual profit-and-loss report to the parents, who could even end up as shareholders in an independent company.
>
> The appointment will impress Education Secretary Kenneth Baker who sees Garth Hill as a blue-print for the future.

The Times, 8 September 1987, included a similar news item under the heading, 'Business of state education', while both the *Yorkshire Post* and Nottingham's *Evening Post* included a full-page article on the 'Hi-tech lesson' learnt by a team of observers from Nottinghamshire who had visited Garth Hill to receive some advice about how to set up a new City Technology College (CTC).

The *Evening Post,* 9 October 1987, concluded that the success of Garth Hill ('the school that's a business') is largely due to the efforts of the Head, who was quoted as saying that 'I am no longer (foremost) a teacher, I am a company manager.' During a visit to Garth Hill, said the reporter,

> What soon becomes apparent is that Garth Hill's success is . . . (partly due to the) acceptance of the changing role that all head teachers may have to come to terms with in the years ahead.
>
> Stanley Goodchild has a simple but determined philosophy. He runs the school as a business, with himself as managing director rather than headteacher.
>
> He's also a salesman, persuading local and multi-national companies . . . to invest in his school to the tune of nearly £½m a year. He gained his know-how with a management degree from the Open University . . .
>
> Mr. Goodchild then persuaded companies to invest their equipment and support in the school with a direct business appeal, offering publicity, the chance to try out their systems and to train the customers of the future . . .
>
> 'You must give businessmen a return for their investment and make them feel they are making an important contribution. Too many institutions expect industry to give them something for nothing.'
>
> Mr. Goodchild's unique career path has helped him break the psychological mould of seeing himself first and foremost as a teacher.

An accompanying editorial contains the warning that it would be foolish to discuss the style of Garth Hill and its headteacher without 'first studying it closely'. Studying Garth Hill closely is what we intend to do in this particular investigation. Garth Hill has certainly grabbed the headlines. Now we want to not only tell the story behind the headlines but also offer some more analytical reflections on this story — in an attempt to explain the widespread interest in the achievements of this particular school.

Why has Garth Hill been Singled out and Praised for its Effectiveness and its Successful Pursuit of Excellence?

In attempting to answer this central question, inevitably we will cover other related questions such as:

- what are some of the vital ingredients of school effectiveness?
- how important is quality leadership and what are its ingredients?
- what is Garth Hill's recipe for success?
- what will schools need to be like in the twenty-first century?

In many ways Garth Hill is an ordinary school. It is, however, an ordinary school which has done some extraordinary things. In January 1988, during the North of England Education Conference held in Nottingham, Kenneth Baker, Secretary of State for Education and Science, declared that reports from the government's inspectors contained 'a depressing catalogue of mediocrity . . .' According to Mr Baker, too many schools are 'second-rate', characterized by 'low expectations' and thus 'low standards'. Consequently, he said, he now wanted to threaten the 'complacent and the second-best':

> I want to give people the chance to press for excellence. I want to give them the means to demand excellence and I want to create a spur which will oblige all education authorities to deliver excellence.

Garth Hill is one school which has turned its back on mediocrity and, largely through the combined efforts of its staff, its pupils, their parents and the local community, it has traversed much of the same ground now being given the government's stamp of approval. It could be argued that the staff of Garth Hill School have pioneered many of the ideas now being suggested in Mr Baker's brave new world — one of the reasons why the school is currently the focus of so much national and international interest. Garth Hill has been where others are being urged to follow.

When Stanley Goodchild became Head of Garth Hill in 1982, the school was facing something of a crisis. Potentially, however, the school did have some advantages. Situated in Bracknell, Berkshire, Garth Hill is situated in Britain's very own Silicon Valley. A recent paper by the Institute of British Geographers reported on the monitoring of the economic performance of 280 British towns. With indicators being used such as rates of unemployment, house prices and employment in hi-tech industries, the report, entitled *Local Prosperity and the North-South Divide: Winners and Losers in 1980s Britain,* concluded that,

> all the thirty-five highest-scoring places lie south-east of a line which forms a crescent around London from Crawley, Chichester and Winchester in the South to Cambridge, Newmarket and Thetford in the North.

Prosperous places listed in the report included Didcot, Aldershot, *Bracknell,* Reading, Guildford, Andover, Welwyn, Woking and Weybridge. In fact, as the authors commented,

> The South is a broad area of rapid growth, and depends on London for a lot of its growth. Once beyond that barrier, you are in a different world.

Nowadays, the new Garth Hill is admirably suited to its expanding, enterprising 'home' environment; it fits the new, thrusting version of Bracknell. The Meteorological Office is a stone's throw from the school. Local industries include Ferranti (advanced technology and computer systems), Racal (the electronics group), Honeywell (control systems), Avis (car rentals), BMW

(GB) Ltd., ICL (Europe's leading suppliers of information systems), 3M (video tapes and computer discs), British Aerospace (its naval and electronics division), Waitrose (the distribution centre of the food group of the John Lewis Partnership), Hewlett-Packard (measurement and computation systems), etc. Bracknell is twenty-five miles west of London and ten miles from Heathrow Airport; it is equidistant from the M4 and M3 motorways. Formerly designated a new town and administered by the Development Corporation (since dissolved), it has a population of just under 100,000. It is archetypal living for the next century. Housing tends to be modern and clustered in open, leafy developments and the town centre has a shopping precinct — the Princess Square — which is surrounded by ample parking. This new Bracknell has been successfully integrated with the old, even if there is a general feeling of there being 'one too many roundabouts'. Bracknell is also the home of the RAF's Staff College, the motto of which is, rather appropriately, 'visu et nisu' — 'by vision and effort'.

The point remains, however, that it is one thing to *have* potential and another to *realize* it. For Garth Hill to realize its potential, someone had to have the vision and many others had to make the effort. In the first part of this book we will concentrate on describing in some detail these processes of *vision-making* and *vision-implementation*. In the second part, we will draw on this experience to make some general observations of relevance to those involved in helping other schools to become more effective.

It is fitting that the Garth Hill story has been selected by the IMTEC organization to be one of a small group of worldwide case studies of future-oriented change initiatives in education. IMTEC (International Movements Toward Educational Change) is based in Norway and is described as an international learning cooperative. The organization is headed by Per Dalin, who, at a recent IMTEC meeting (held in Soest, West Germany, in June 1988) explained the importance of supporting risk-taking, innovative practice and, in so doing, made the following ten points. There is a need, he argued,

- to take a long-term perspective on the process of innovation;
- to create projects which are new and open-ended and which encourage risk-taking, participative learning and thinking in dramatically new ways;
- to avoid the forces of inertia generated within bureaucratic structures, while establishing a creative framework for innovation;
- to manage the complexities of the change process while stimulating differentiated and more flexible learning arrangements;
- to support innovators and innovation. Changes in education, he argued, are far too slow, mainly because all 'change agents' are viewed with scepticism and are forced to wrestle with the forces of the *status quo*. Forward-looking people, therefore, need to be supported in their risk-taking and linked to sources of sustenance. *Supportiveness* can create the *confidence* to go forward;

- to promote the individual school as the essential unit of change and thus to help and support the staff of a school to define and manage change in their own unique setting;
- to recognize that there is no instant recipe for success in terms of school effectiveness. Attaining 'effectiveness' is a journey over time which involves the growth and integration of a 'mix' of components — a mix (or a 'chemistry') which will be particular to each and every school;
- to appreciate that the debates concerning the structures of schooling are over; *the* emphasis now is on the *quality of schooling* and on *inner reforms* in terms of the quality of classroom processes;
- to understand that, in terms of these inner reforms, the central agents — *the* change agents — are the teachers, who, as classroom practitioners, need help, support and the freedom to succeed.

Dalin's points, as outlined above, provide the terms of reference for this present volume.

Bracknell town centre.
Photo courtesy of the *Reading Evening Post*.

Part I

The Garth Hill Experience:
An Enterprising School in the Making

'Garth Hill is a place where things happen'
                    Head Girl; school prize-giving, 18 December 1986.

Phase One   In the Beginning . . .

Section 1   Stanley Goodchild's Background
Section 2   Background of Garth Hill School
Section 3   The First Day

Phase Two   Leading from the Front

Section 4   The Headteacher as Managing Director
Section 5   Uniform and Discipline
Section 6   Building Positive Attitudes and a Conducive Environment for Learning
Section 7   Links with Industry and the Community

Phase Three   Making It Count

Section 8   Development of Resources and Refurbishment of the School
Section 9   Developing the Curriculum, Developing the Staff
Section 10 Looking Ahead

Part I of this book is an account of Garth Hill School and Stanley Goodchild's role in its development since 1982. According to Goodchild,

> The last six years have been a most exciting and stimulating time and I consider it a great privilege to lead the team of teachers, parents, pupils and the community at large in providing a sound, stimulating and full education for the pupils in our care at Garth Hill School . . . I have found giving this account one of the hardest tasks with which I have been presented, I tell the story with a certain reluctance in the view that it could give a false impression. My brief was to give an account of my role as 'managing director' and that, by definition, focuses on one person. I do not accept, however, that it has been a one man affair. While I happen to be the leader, so many people have had a part to play in the success story of Garth. I could have had all the fantastic ideas possible, but unless I gained the support of colleagues it would all have been in vain. I pay tribute to my staff, pupils, my governors, parents, members of the community and last but not least the education officers and county councillors; without their support my efforts would have proved totally ineffective. When the press come to the school I often find myself the reluctant interviewee; it would be better to have others to do this job. It is the Head, however, who is expected to be the spokesperson. When considering this account, the reader is asked to

remember that it is the 'team' that has made Garth the success it is. We do not know all the answers; we have not found Utopia, but it is hoped that the reader finds our experiences of interest. Having written my account, to make it easier reading, it has been converted into the third person.

In addition to being a most rewarding time, his leadership of Garth Hill has given Goodchild an opportunity to test many of his hypotheses about the Education Service. Goodchild believes that 'The Garth Hill Experience' is not unique, and could be repeated in different forms and scale in many educational establishments; he also believes that the philosophy behind it needs to be practised by those in positions of leadership. Change in education is often an extremely slow process. Strategies used for change in schools have tended to be those of the low risk variety and there has been a feeling that achieving consensus is the all-important process. His experience at Garth Hill has made him question this and he suggests that there is a need to reconsider the strategies used in the process of change in schools, if we are to ensure that our pupils are adequately prepared for life in the twenty-first century.

Garth Hill School.
Photo courtesy of the *Reading Evening Post*.

Phase One

In the Beginning

1 Stanley Goodchild's Background

Before an attempt is made to catalogue the events of the last six years, it may prove helpful to describe a little of Goodchild's own background.

His own education proved problematical to say the least. He missed a year's schooling at the age of 9 because of polio. From that time onwards he found schooling extremely difficult in that he never seemed able to compensate for the complete year lost. He had very supportive parents, however, and attended an enlightened school, East Howe Bilateral, where the Headteacher took a personal interest in individual pupils and their progress. Even in those early days Goodchild had a business instinct and ran a tuck shop behind the Woodwork block, selling lemonade and chocolate. He had negotiated a deal with a local wholesaler and the profits helped to subsidize his pocket money. When the project was discovered by the Headteacher, Goodchild, after a great deal of persuasion on his part, was given the go-ahead to continue so long as he gave a percentage of the profits to the school. In his final year he was made Head Boy. Given the nature of his upbringing (his parents were involved in youth organizations), he wanted to follow in their footsteps. Although the career advice given to him was to go into business, his first love was working with the young and he wanted to become a teacher. At the age of 16, he did start as a trainee buyer in a local department store and, after two months, decided that it was not for him. He then returned to school and attended Bournemouth Grammar School to gain further qualifications. He was delighted when he was accepted at King Alfred's College, Winchester, to follow a three-year teacher training course which he found most rewarding.

In 1964 he took up his first appointment as an assistant teacher of Mathematics and Geography at Chippenham High School for Boys. On his first day he committed the cardinal sin of all probationary teachers; he parked his Morris, an 'old banger', in the place of one of the long-serving members of staff. He was duly given a dressing-down. Under the leadership of Eric Minter, however, he had an extremely good start to his teaching career. He became heavily involved in voluntary organizations and local industry. After three years, against the advice of colleagues, he applied for a Head of Department post. He recalls the interview with some affection. It was in a large staffroom with over fifteen governors present, all trying to ask their questions. The questions about mathematics were so varied and conflicting that he decided to give them a demonstration lesson in mathematics — he was more than surprised when offered the post. The job as Head of Mathematics at Durrington Comprehensive School in Wiltshire was a very challenging one in that the 'O' level pass rate for mathematics was practically zero and, within a year, with the support of colleagues in the Department and of course the pupils, there were dramatic changes in the results, with the pupils in his class all attaining a 'pass' at 'O' level. He was fortunate that, while at Durrington, the Headmaster gave him additional responsibilities which he accepted willingly, along with many extra-curricular activities.

Within a five-year period he had held posts as Head of Year, Head of Faculty, Head of Upper School and had also reapplied for his job during reorganization. In addition, he was involved in in-service training and worked with HMI, Further Education and the Local Authority's Advisory Service. He was particularly keen that the education process (from 5-18 years) should be viewed as a continuum. He worked very closely with the primary schools in the catchment area of the school to ease the transition of pupils from primary to secondary. The Head seemed happy for him to take on a variety of responsibilities, which, at the time were probably 'beyond his station'. With the support of colleagues, however, he enjoyed the experience and found it most rewarding. Until then his sole ambition had been to become a Headteacher, and he was not particularly interested in changing the course of his career. The work he was doing was very similar to that of many Deputy Heads with responsibility for a total section of a school, situated approximately a quarter of a mile from the main administration block. It was unlikely that, at the age of 29, he would gain a headship in the foreseeable future, and he faced the prospect of 'marking time' for a number of years.

In January 1975 Goodchild was invited to apply for the post of County Adviser for Mathematics. After very serious thought he decided to apply and he was appointed as County Adviser for Mathematics and Science in Wiltshire LEA.

At that particular time mathematics teaching in schools was going through something of a hiatus. The so-called modern mathematics phase was gaining momentum and many teachers were confused by the changes. It could be argued that many pupils going through the education system at that time were also confused in relation to mathematics. He remembers going to the Chief Adviser and suggesting that a set of mathematics guidelines should be developed. Although the Chief Adviser was in favour, many educationalists at the time, both in Wiltshire and nationally, felt that guidelines were too prescriptive; there was no great enthusiasm for such documents. By grouping teachers together in their catchment areas, however, working parties were set up and Wiltshire acquired the first full version of Mathematics Guidelines from 5-13. It was a tremendous effort over a period of approximately eighteen months: well over 800 teachers had had a direct involvement in this initiative — truly a team effort. When the guidelines were published, the demand for them throughout the country, and abroad, was unbelievable. The profits made were going back to the County Treasurer, which Goodchild was particularly concerned about, as he was short of finance for further projects. He managed to persuade the Chief Executive to allow the money to come directly to the Advisory Service so that further developments relating to the guidelines could be initiated. As a further development the Steering Group decided to develop sets of assessment cards linked to the items in the guidelines. Once again a business technique had been used to provide finance for further developments. Following this, he took on a general role and was involved in the preparations for the reorganization of schools in the North of the county. He became very much involved in computer-assisted timetabling and ran a number of courses for the county's heads and deputies. An Industry-Education Liaison Group was established in the county in which he was very keen to play a major part. In those days ways were being explored in which industry and education could work together. The first project arising from this involvement was concerned with looking at ways of assessing pupils realistically for the world of work. The Liaison Group members were also looking at sixth-form projects in which industry and schools could work together.

In his previous role as Head of Upper School, he had realized that his chances of fulfilling his ambitions would be hampered unless he obtained a degree. He would have qualified to be seconded to take a degree, but did not wish to be away from the work he was doing for any prolonged time, and when the Open University was founded in 1970, it provided the ideal opportunity for further study. In 1976, a year after leaving Durrington School, he was awarded a BA Pass Degree. During the time he was an Adviser he continued studying for an Honours Degree in Mathematics and Educational Management. He was anxious that his work would not suffer: consequently, much of the studying was done in the early hours, but he had his reward when, in 1980, he was awarded an Upper Second BA (Hons) Degree in Mathematics and Educational Studies. He was even more delighted that he had been able to do it without relinquishing his day-to-day work.

In 1979 he moved on to become Chief Inspector in the London Borough of Bexley, and he was once again fortunate in that the elected members were prepared to support him in a number of unconventional innovations. With the support of the Director and the Council members, the Advisory Service was reorganized to give it 'teeth'. Many of the papers which went to the Education Committee were written and presented by the Advisory Service (which was then still relatively unusual in the UK). The inspectorial role for the advisers was instigated, thus strengthening the service in that particular Borough. After working for Bexley for two years the then Chief Education Officer for Schools took early retirement, and Goodchild was asked to take over that role. Within a year he had reorganized the Education Department, ensuring that it was running more effectively and serving the schools in a more efficient way than had previously been the case.

On Monday 4 November 1981, he was summoned to the Chief Executive's office and invited to consider taking over the role of Chief Education Officer on a permanent basis. That was a memorable day as it was at that point that the story of Garth Hill really started.

As an Adviser/Inspector Goodchild was extremely frustrated on his visits to a large number of schools, many of which were engaged in exciting projects. The source of the frustration was that he felt a little like a butterfly flitting from flower to flower, school to school, never really being able to get involved in any particular school — its problems and delights. He gathered many good ideas concerning innovative practices, but felt incapable of having any serious impact upon the curriculum of the schools — especially those which were perhaps not so successful. In talking to senior staff and headteachers, discussing possible innovations, he was frequently told 'It's all very well for you sitting there, you've never been a Head, you don't know what it's like, you just can't do that unless you have . . .'. There appeared always to be an opting out: '*If only* I had more resources; *if only* I had better staff, *if only* I had this, that or the other, I could . . . but until I have those there's not much I can do'. So many 'if onlys'; while it is not suggested that every head said such things, it was quite common to receive such comments.

It was said earlier that Goodchild really wanted to gain experience as a headteacher and his career pattern had denied him that opportunity. He was now at a crossroads. He knew that if he took the permanent post of Chief Education Officer for Schools he would never have the opportunity to prove whether or not some of his ideas could be put into practice in the school context; if he became a headteacher he would certainly take a drop in salary. On the other hand he wondered whether or not he wanted to be a Chief Education Officer in a London Borough for the next twenty years. When he attended Association of Metropolitan Authorities (AMA) conferences most of his colleagues were talking about early retirement and he felt that at the age of 38 he was a little young for that. Meanwhile, he had twenty-four hours to make up his mind whether or not he was going to consider being the Chief Education Officer for Schools. The Authority had been very supportive of his ideas and it was a great temptation to say 'yes'. He felt, however, that if he went through life without being a headteacher he would have missed a marvellous opportunity. In his opinion there is no better privilege than to be able to play a major part in the development of a young child through to adulthood. He recalls going back to his Chief Executive and saying that he'd decided that he wanted to be a headteacher. The Chief Executive rocked in his chair with respectful laughter and said: 'Stanley, who is going to appoint a Chief Education Officer as a headteacher?' Little did he know but that was the best thing he could have said — it was a challenge which Goodchild was certainly going to accept. His mind was bristling with ideas of the ways in which he could develop a school if only he had the opportunity. The problem now was to get that opportunity to prove his point. Was the Chief Executive going to be right? Was he going to be able to become a headteacher? He knew any application would be viewed with suspicion. If only he could get to the interview stage, perhaps he could convince the panel that his intentions were honourable. He also needed a school which was not in a privileged position; otherwise it would be argued that he was taking the easy option. In the autumn of 1981 he applied for three jobs and he obtained three interviews. One was in Kent, the second in Berkshire and the third in Oxfordshire. He attended the first interview in Kent — it was a disaster. The day before his own interview he had been interviewing for headteachers himself. Consequently, in his own interview, when he felt that the wrong questions were being asked, he started saying things like 'Don't you think you should ask me . . . don't you think you should ask me that . . .' and he could see the job slowly fading away. He was not appointed. The second interview was for Garth Hill School in Bracknell, Berkshire. He made it his practice in all three cases to visit the area prior to knowing whether he had an interview and he can remember standing in the shopping centre of Bracknell, carrying out a survey. 'I'm thinking of moving to Bracknell and wonder if Garth Hill School is the school to which I should send my children?'. The answers he received were varied. Those who had sent their children to the school often spoke about it in extremely glowing terms. The vast majority spoke with great authority and without any real knowledge. Based on its reputation, they explained that there was no discipline, that the pupils who went there were a 'load of thugs', and that many of the shops locked their doors at lunchtime when the pupils came to the town.

He visited the school; its appearance left a lot to be desired, but the qualifications and quality of the staff were very impressive. They seemed to be very genuine and sincere about wanting to do the best for the pupils in their care. The image of the school was far from healthy. Fifty per cent of the pupils from the largest contributory primary school were sent to schools other than Garth Hill. The number on roll was declining rapidly and, in 1982, the projected intake for the following year was ninety. The local further education college had noted the decline and had already mooted ideas of moving into part of the school buildings and eventually taking over the whole site — if and when the school closed. Garth Hill School was occupying a prime site — very near to the centre of Bracknell. Its future, therefore, was most uncertain.

His interview followed the standard pattern: the governors sat round a large table together with representatives from the Local Education Authority. It was apparent that the governors were looking for change; they were particularly concerned with the question of the appearance of pupils; they were also concerned about discipline. The officers were curious to know why he had decided to apply for a headship. They could not seem to understand how he could perceive the move from Chief Officer to headteacher as a responsible one in terms of his career development. The teacher governor on the panel asked the single question, 'Didn't he think that the staff would view him with suspicion?'. His reply was: 'probably they would, but that might be a good thing'.

2   Background of Garth Hill School

Before telling the story of Garth Hill's development since 1982, it is important to understand something of the background of the school and how it had changed since its formation.

Bracknell was classified as a new town and in the late 1940s it took some of the 'overspill' from London. Since then it had grown from a population in 1949 of 5200 to a population in 1982 of 49,300. In recent years much of the new housing developments have been South of the railway line which divides the town into two. The two council estates which Garth Hill serves are Priestwood and Bullbrook which are in the North and were the first to be built. As new homes were built in the South of the town, the children of those who settled in the North moved away — with the result that the decline in school population was shown in the North first.

The North of the town was served originally by Wick Hill Secondary Modern School, and from 1965, Garth Grammar School. As they shared the same site, in September 1969, they were amalgamated and the new comprehensive Garth Hill was formed. At this point the school's population rose to approximately 1800 pupils. Meanwhile a new school, namely Easthampstead Park, was being opened in the South of the town. When this happened, Garth's numbers fell until, in September 1981, the intake was 160 pupils with future predictions of numbers falling to under ninety during subsequent years. Below is an extract from the details sent to candidates applying for the headship in 1982.

Curriculum
For the first three years all children follow a common curriculum consisting of English, mathematics, science, one modern foreign language, history, geography, religious education, music, physical education and art design with the exception of slow learners who need extra help in basic subjects and are organized in self-contained remedial groups and do not study a foreign language. Other pupils are grouped in mixed ability forms but are set in ability groups in mathematics from the first year and language from the second year. There is a capacity for setting in some other subjects at the discretion of the heads of the departments. In the second year those children who are sufficiently able may begin a second foreign language or classical studies. French, German and Russian are the modern languages available. Less able children have additional lessons in English and mathematics. In the third year taster courses are introduced in computer science, design, drama, technical drawing and practical musicianship and dance/gymnastics which can lead to '0' level or CSE courses in the fourth and fifth years. All children have an opportunity to experience courses

in pottery, woodwork, metalwork, needlework and domestic science, in the second and third years, after a first year foundation design course.

A wide range of courses is possible through an options system in the two years leading to GCE Ordinary level, CSE or a combination of the two examinations at 16. English, mathematics and at least one science subject are compulsory. SMP courses are followed in mathematics (modern maths) and Nuffield courses in the sciences. Subjects are chosen from the prospectus after full discussion between parents, teachers and the child. In the sixth form the following are offered to Advanced level:

Art, Biology, Chemistry, Design, Technology, Economics*, English Literature, French, Geography, Geology*, German, History,

Home Economics, Mathematics, Metalwork, Music, Photography*, Physics, Sociology*, Technical Drawing (Engineering), Woodwork.

For those subjects marked with an asterisk, no previous knowledge is expected and these subjects can be studied as a two-year 'O' level course in conjunction with one or two 'A' levels. Academic people take three or four 'A' levels. For pupils who have successfully completed CSE courses there is a one-year 'O' level conversion course in six basic subjects. Typing, Shorthand and CSE commerce are offered in the sixth form link course run with the college of further eduction on our school premises. No commercial subjects are offered below the age of 16.

There are libraries in lower, main and upper schools.

Pastoral Care and Career Guidance

At all stages of school life great emphasis is placed on pastoral care of pupils, each year is guided by a year group adviser and they and their deputies work closely with the heads of faculties and the Career Advisory Service to guide pupils on choices of courses as well as maintaining close links with parents and the Education Welfare Office and other outside agencies.

Parents' meetings are held mainly in half-year groups with form tutors and subject teachers. All parents are encouraged to visit the school at any convenient time. Reports are issued at Christmas and in July and at other times by special request.

There is no school uniform though pupils are expected to conform to a liberal code of dress. Physical education kit is standard and is required. All pupils, with the exception of pupils in remedial groups where homework is set when appropriate, are expected to do homework for one hour per night in the first year increasing to two hours by year 3. Work is recorded in a record book in which there is space for parental comment.

There is no corporal punishment, though guidelines on discipline are strictly adhered to. Failure to complete homework or anti-social behaviour results in detentions with subject staff or year group advisers.

All new entrants to school and their parents are personally interviewed by the head, deputies or senior pastoral staff before joining the school. There are close links with the staff of contributory primary schools. There is an active parents association with a committee elected by parents.

Extra Curricular Activities

The school enjoys a high reputation for music. There is an orchestra, chamber group ensembles, two school choirs and smaller vocal groups. Instrumental tuition is available on a wide range of instruments.

Rugby, soccer, hockey, netball, volleyball, athletics, badminton and swimming are included in the physical education programmes. There is an outward-bound scheme for senior pupils. There are family to family exchanges with France and Germany.

Educational visits, film study expeditions, theatre trips, etc. are arranged regularly for all appropriate age groups. There are currently fifteen school clubs. One major dramatic and/or operatic production and several smaller ones are mounted each year.

The organization of the school was basically of a hierarchical structure with the headteacher at the top of the pyramid, one academic deputy, one pastoral deputy, a senior master, two senior teachers, four chairmen of faculty who were responsible for a group of subjects, and the heads of departments. On the pastoral side, the 'advisers' were in charge of year groups. There were no job descriptions although staff would claim that they knew what their responsibilities were.

From the write-up about the school, it would appear very sound but, at the same time as the interview procedure was underway, an item was going through committee entitled 'Organization of secondary education in Bracknell', which could have had a profound effect upon the development of the school. A passage from this report reads as follows:

Item 7

Organisation of Secondary Education in Bracknell

1 *There is a decline forecast in school population in Bracknell and this report is concerned with the effects of this decline on the secondary schools in the town and with measure to alleviate the resulting problems.*

2 *The major problems are concerned with:*

   (*i*) *The marked decline in pupil numbers in North Bracknell affecting particularly the intakes to Garth Hill.*

   (*ii*) *The numbers of sixth formers which will be insufficient during the 1980s to sustain satisfactorily four separate sixth forms.*

   (*iii*) *The bulge in the projected intakes to Easthampstead Park in the early 1980s.*

3 *The Bracknell area is served by four comprehensive schools, three county and one Church of England (aided) which in the county's development plan are scheduled together to offer thirty-four forms of entry (one form entry equals thirty pupils). In total, twenty-seven forms of entry were admitted to the schools in September 1981.*

4 *The intakes to Garth Hill could be critically low for several years. The redrawing of catchment areas could be considered but such changes in this situation necessarily involve all three county schools. There are no simple*

> *proposals which could lead to a significant catchment area adjustment. It is particularly the case in Bracknell that the schools serve clearly defined communities, each having strong and well established links with the primary schools in their areas could not be brought about without significant disruption for families living in the areas concerned.*
>
> 5 *Bracknell College of Further Education already has the use of four classrooms in other areas of Garth Hill School. The College, nevertheless, remains seriously short of accommodation and discussion has been taking place between the Head and Principal and officers of the Authority with a view to enabling the College to make more extensive use of the school buildings as the school rolls decline. Garth Hill is within walking distance of the College and it is housed in two large building complexities on the same site. Current proposals are that with effect from September 1982 the main Garth Hill Building should house 11 to 16 age groups with the sixth form being housed in the Wick Hill Building and the remaining space there being used by the College for the foreseeable future.*

In addition, at the time of the change of the Head, the issue regarding the school uniform was becoming extremely contentious. Below is a paper prepared for the governors prior to Goodchild's arrival concerning this issue:

1 The decision to abandon school uniform was taken on six main grounds:

    (a) The disappearance of any outfitters willing to stock uniform and the reluctance of parents to be forced into purchases at Jacksons of Reading or Caleys of Windsor. Selling uniform ourselves proved too expensive of clerical time.

    (b) Withdrawal by the county of any grant for special clothing. This has now been made worse by the withdrawal of any clothing grant at all so that the poorer families were and would be unable to obtain any help . . .

    (c) Cost. It is frequently argued that uniform, provided it is merely a preferred colour, is no more expensive than other clothing. However, parental opinion was, and at recent discussions still is, that pupils still require non-uniform clothes for leisure, weekends, holidays, etc.; that at the rate of growth of secondary school children, garments are outgrown before they are worn out.

    (d) Staff time was, and if uniform were to be introduced would again be, unprofitably spent on dealing with the non-conformers of both pupils and parents.

    (e) Pupil's requests, particularly strong from the girls, to be allowed to choose the colours and styles they felt suited them. There was parental support for this as a part of growing up and learning about clothes.

(f)   Uniform is not required and only sometimes worn in contributory primary schools, is not worn in post-16 education; it seems illogical to insist on it for the period 11-16.

2   The arguments in favour of some conformative dress in terms of both colour and style are:

(a)   As an identifying factor in the community at large, but this would require uniform outdoor coats, one colour anoraks or raincoats.

(b)   As a means of promoting corporate unity and loyalty to the school whose uniform they wear.

(c)   As a leveller. As a result of (b) and (c) in 1 above uniform can provide evidence of parental background when considering quality of uniform worn, frequency of replacement, wearing of second-hand etc.

(d)   To assist parents in dealing with adolescent demands for more or unsuitable clothes.

(e)   There is some evidence that the lower school children in years 1 to 2 would like a uniform, though this is not shared by the 14/15-year-olds and fifth year are always a problem as a leaving year.

3   Possible compromises:

(a)   To choose a colour and say that trousers, skirts, sweaters or cardigans may be bought anywhere provided that they are, for example, navy, and shirts or blouses white or blue.

(b)   To establish a uniform for the lower school only initially but it is the older pupils who tend to dress less acceptably because most buy their own clothes.

(c)   To adopt the sports heavy cotton over-jersey with badge in Garth Hill School to be worn with grey trousers or skirts over whatever coloured shirts people have as standard schoolwear. It would look a little American but they are popular.

4   In any event there would have to be prior consultation with all parents by means of a circular letter with a return slip for views. The Parents' Committee have felt unable to make any recommendations, so this would have to be a governors' recommendation.

5   The views of the pastoral staff also have to be considered.

Undoubtedly, school uniform was a smouldering — if not a burning — issue at Garth Hill.

3   The First Day

After the Interview

The day after the interview, Stanley Goodchild was approached by the Press; they were not concerned with his educational views but wished to know whether or not school uniform was going to be introduced. He was evasive and said that he would need to consult with those concerned before such an important decision could be made. Consequently, during the week prior to taking up the appointment, he met with the staff and asked their views about school uniform. Many were in favour, but the general feeling seemed to be that it was hard enough to teach pupils, let alone worry about what they were wearing. There was not a consensus that uniform should be worn. Some of the staff felt strongly enough to write to Goodchild and express their views. Here are some of the quotes:

> I find it depressing to have to spoil my relationships with so many children who are otherwise no trouble. Politically I can see the argument for a uniform now but I would prefer to work with an optional uniform and a very strict code of dress for the others.

> I do believe in the freedom of the individual and the wishes of parents to dress their children in the manner which they can afford — as well as being given guidelines from the school. Some of the staff whose job it will be to enforce uniform are against it because of the trivial nature of the work involved. I am unequivocally against it.

> I can see no correlation whatsoever between wearing a uniform and an improved work ethic. The thought of a uniformed sixth distresses me.

> I am in principle opposed to the introduction of school uniform in this particular kind of school, that far from being a unifying factor it tends to be socially divisive. Of couse, if it is decided to make the children wear uniform I would do my best to back the project.

> The reintroduction of uniform could coincide with a major PR exercise involving staff, pupils and parents and the general public — I would support the move. The agreed policies need the support of all staff and in return the staff must be able to feel that they are supported by all senior members of staff. Uniform need not be more expensive for parents providing we are sensible in our choice so that garments are readily obtained within a reasonable price range.

> The 'pressure' involved in making them wear it is likely to be counter-productive as what actually happens within a school and within the classroom situation is an establishment of the relationships which lead to good learning situations. These are of paramount importance, rather than what pupils are wearing.

> I am in favour of anything to improve the image of either pupils or the

school fabric itself. I also feel that now is the time for any changes as we have worked through our bulge and the numbers are now right for the school image improvement.

I feel that the attempt should be made but I believe that it will have to be a gradual process and my suggestion would be that new first years 1982/83 will be expected to wear school uniform and that for the present the rest of the school should be encouraged to do so if they wish. Finally may I say that parents inside and outside our catchment areas would be even more impressed if the standard of behaviour and academic attainment was improved as well as the appearance of the pupils.

I would be keen to enforce such a uniform if I were sure the introduction of uniform would be concurrent with an improvement with the school decor in general, in general standards of cleanliness inside and out, its greater control over the movement of pupils about the site as winter especially can still bring a great deal of mud into corridors and classrooms alike.

I support its reintroduction. Whether we like it or not, local parents are inclined to judge the school by the appearance of the pupils leaving it.

These quotations summed up the mixed feelings of the staff.

The first morning
After taking up the post, on the very first morning, Stanley Goodchild met a group of four parents who were adamantly against reintroducing school uniform, as in their opinion, it was tantamount to an invasion of individual rights. He knew that the uniform issue needed to be resolved, and resolved swiftly. He felt, however, that he needed to take a good look at the school before he decided what measures needed to be taken. He wandered around the building and was depressed at the state of the fabric and the apparent acceptance of this 'down-at-heel' environment by his staff. For example, in the staff room, daylight could be seen through a wall constructed out of wooden sections; many of the desks and chairs around the school were covered in graffiti as were some of the walls; glass-panes, when broken, had been replaced by hardboard. The furniture in the classrooms was in a state of disrepair; radiators in the main hall were missing; very few paths around the school were intact and a great deal of mud was being tramped into the school; many blinds were either non-existent or in shreds; in one part of the school he considered the outside wall to be unsafe — it was in sections made of wood and the whole thing was rotten; in the toilets, the sanitary-ware was badly chipped and broken, there were no locks on the doors, and the walls had the usual array of graffiti. The floors were dirty and certainly did not look as if they were well swept. On the approach to the school there were no signs to say where the entrance was; in fact the entrance looked

like the back door. Inside the front door was a quarry-tiled lobby (red tiles) and the reception window was approximately eighteen inches square and at a height suitable for a 6 or 7-year-old. To talk to the receptionist you needed to bend right down and stick your head through the hole. If there was a school uniform, it consisted of denim jackets and jeans with a variety of hair styles about which something will be said later. Indeed, many of the older pupils looked threatening to any teacher or visitor to the school. Some of the classrooms adjacent to the dining hall had wooden partitions as walls; it was very difficult to teach in them, especially just before and after lunch when the school's canteen staff were preparing and clearing up the midday meal. The outside of the building certainly needed a good coat of paint. Much of the netting around the tennis and netball courts had been vandalized and looked rather shabby. When he approached the Maintenance Department of Shire Hall he was told that many of the items he mentioned had not been repaired recently because they had been repaired well over a dozen times previously and then immediately vandalized. It had been decided, therefore, not to waste any more ratepayers' money. The school, which was on a split site, appeared to be badly designed; in one of the buildings there was no through corridor — pupils had to go outside twice and face the elements when travelling from one end to the other. Beneath the Head's office there was an exceptionally large bicycle shed which was very dark and dingy and an ideal place for such activities as bullying and smoking. Interestingly, however, some of the staff did not seem to notice the unkempt condition of the school.

First impressions

By breaktime on the first morning Stanley Goodchild had come to the conclusion that something urgent had to be done about the decor of the school. Drastic action was required. He decided to meet with some sixth formers after break on that first morning. Immediately after the bell there was a knock at the door and the first student appeared; he stood there in his full regalia of denim jacket, jeans, chains and crosses around his neck, ankles and wrists. He had an intriguing hairstyle of several colours, 'just like a cock's plume'. Goodchild's was undoubtedly a prejudiced reaction. His first impression was 'What kind of lout do we have here?' The student entered the Head's office, sat down and proceeded to talk about the 'A' levels he was doing; his homework was also mentioned. He spoke very politely and the Head's opinion of him changed rapidly. The student explained the complexities involved in getting his hair to stand up on end; that he had to spend many hours with soap and gel to achieve the effect. He also demonstrated how he could either have it sticking up or lying flat and the Head was quick to tell him which he preferred. The Head wondered if other peoples' first impressions were similar to his own.

Perhaps in the same way that his first impression of that young man was that he was something of a lout, others outside the school might well feel the same and start making generalizations about the pupils and the school — Garth Hill. By lunchtime the Head was beginning to wonder what he had taken on and whether he could really make the changes that he wished. On the whole he felt the staff had high expectations of him — the new Head — but were very set in their ways. It was very apparent that, however good the school was in terms of its academic or social achievements, unless the people outside believed in the school, it would be difficult to make any progress. Before the school could hope to attract the help of industry and the community generally, it needed to gain its own confidence and that of the immediate community which it served. It was very depressing to talk to some of the pupils who had such a low opinion of the school which they attended. With such a view how could they hope to achieve their best? Generally speaking morale was at a low ebb. The Head felt that the only way he could make changes and make them rapidly was to create pressure from outside the school by responding to the worries and concerns of the local community.

Priorities for development
Given that the school was under threat of closure, by the end of the first day Goodchild could see very clearly the needs of the school. These could be summarized as follows:

1   To develop a clear list of aims and key tasks for the school, which could be used as a guide for the future success of the school. To give the school an identity and a role in the local community. It was necessary to raise the morale of both staff and pupils and parents alike and create a sense of belonging.
2   To raise the expectations of both staff and pupils, thus improving standards of education in the broadest sense. There was a general feeling of acceptance of the status quo rather than any resolve to strive for greater things.
3   To develop a strategy for changing attitudes in both staff and pupils — thus laying foundations for further developments, especially in the curriculum.
4   To develop a better environment through an emphasis on interpersonal relationships and skills.
5   To produce a strategy to provide better resources, encouraging greater investment by both the local education authority and industry.
6   To create the basis for a management structure which would incorporate proven management strategies. It was one thing to decide the needs of the school and quite another to initiate the necessary changes. The greatest problem concerned the staff; would they appreciate the extent of the crisis and would they, as a team, be able to react quickly enough in order to save the school from closure and the FE College taking over the site? Goodchild knew that he had as little as eighteen months in which to prove that the school was viable and worth saving. With the threat of closure hanging over the school, immediate action was required — but would the staff be prepared to make the effort? Stanley Goodchild knew the nature of his brief — to turn the school around.

Leading from the Front

4   The Headteacher as Managing Director

Stanley Goodchild's earlier work as an inspector convinced him that the way to run a school effectively is to run it as a business in which the Head takes the lead as the managing director: so often, in his view, Heads are teachers and administrators rather than managers. In his many talks as an inspector, he often used the saying, when is a Head not a Head? Answer, when he still thinks he's a teacher. So often a headteacher has feelings of guilt and a perceived conflict between his role as a teacher and his role as a Head. Goodchild can remember sitting in front of a Head who was proudly telling him that he taught sixteen periods a week out of forty. After a pause Goodchild explained that he thought that such a teaching-load was totally inappropriate; if he was teaching sixteen periods a week then, in actual fact, he was an overpaid scale 1 teacher. Of course, a Head must be totally committed to teaching and to the learning of the pupils; but, as Head, through good management, he facilitates good teaching by others and ensures that the pupils have effective learning programmes. So, as Head and managing director, right from the start, managerial techniques were used in initiating or developing change within the school. No-one in the school seemed to have targets or objectives; there was little vision; crisis management was the order of the day with the senior staff dealing with the crises as they arose.

Cleaning up the school
Even the caretaker was not completely sure what was expected of him; in the first week he sat in the Head's office and explained very proudly that he felt the standard of cleaning was good and his cleaners were most effective. Indeed, he said, if they did a good job and had finished the work, they could go after one hour instead of working the two allocated. Goodchild explained that he felt the school was very dirty and untidy and that the Authority was paying for twice as many hours as they were receiving, which was totally unacceptable. Signing in and signing out procedures were instigated. The caretaker explained that, as a

result of such restrictions, he was sure that his staff would all resign on the spot. Goodchild explained to him that, if that should happen, it was just as well they went, as he would only need to employ half as many to receive the same amount of cleaning done previously. In fact, when the procedures were introduced only three cleaners chose to leave the school. Instantly the amount of cleaning in the school doubled. Cleaners were given a sheet on which they were asked to report any damage which appeared immediately they found it. The staff were also asked to do the same.

To make the cleaning staff feel that they were an integral part of the school, they were all provided with cleaning overalls and Goodchild met with them once a month to talk about their problems and successes. This proved to be very successful, although much of the discussion was concerned with the lack of equipment they had to clean the school. This was yet another problem which had to be resolved. The cleaning of the school, however, was a priority, not as an end in itself, but in terms of its contribution to the general image of the school.

Directive leadership

Although it was not necessarily his preferred style of management, in those early days, when not all staff members seemed to appreciate the extent of the crisis, Goodchild had to be very authoritarian — in the sense that he did not have time for decisions to be made by consensus. Other urgent issues were in need of action. The Further Education College, realizing that the school was going to resist any more encroachment, became more pressing in terms of the plans for expansion. The Head knew that they had to turn around the declining intake within a few months if Garth Hill was going to be able to make a claim on the accommodation which had been previously declared as surplus to requirements.

Public statements were made in the local press about the school's expansion scheme; consequently, the Authority was rather hesitant in making the final decision that the Wick Hill building should be handed over to the College. Goodchild's objective in the first term was to prevent such a decision being made. He was confident, from the first day, that they would be able to win back many of the pupils who had been sent to other schools because of Garth Hill's poor image. The numbers game was vital. The proposed FE reorganization plan could not go ahead if the pupil population exceeded the accommodation available in the main building.

Meeting the parents

Stanley Goodchild, in that first term (the summer term, 1982), decided to lay the foundations for future developments. He decided, for instance, to meet every single parent of the pupils in the school. Ideally he would have liked to have met them individually but that was not possible. He did, however, meet them in groups of ten to twenty, and held sixty evening meetings within a six-week period. This meant that on many evenings there were two or three meetings. In this way he managed to meet with parents and representatives of the community and local industry, asking them how they felt about the future development of the school. A number of parents did not turn up and he made a point of visiting homes and asking them directly if they cared about the education of their children — this move proved quite a shock to the system. The proposals that emerged were taken to the staff and the changes began rapidly.

5   Uniform and Discipline

The two real issues which surfaced in the meetings with the parents were those of discipline and uniform. Concerning school uniform, there were 800 families in favour and thirteen against. Given this overwhelming support for its reintroduction many of the pupils thought they were going to be forced into uniform and were planning protests and petitions .

The saga of school uniform
An interesting event then occurred. The press had been following the uniform story and the local papers reported the result of the survey of parental opinion. This attracted the attention of the national papers and, the day after the issue was reported locally, Goodchild had reporters from all the popular tabloids on his doorstep asking for more details and wishing to interview pupils. In fact, interest was also shown by both BBC and ITV newscasters wishing to write or produce news items. Goodchild realized that he could use the media to the advantage of the school in a most effective fashion. During the preparation of the television items, the news-team asked to interview two pupils in favour and two pupils against the introduction of a uniform. Goodchild provided the two in favour and said they could speak to anyone else they liked. In retrospect, this might sound a rather over-confident stance to take, but knowing that he had 800 families in favour of school uniform, it seemed worth taking the risk. To his amazement, and that of the reporters, they found it very difficult to find any pupils who were prepared to speak against the school uniform. Moreover, the pupils were now realizing that the world out there was interested in Garth Hill in a very positive way. This episode seemed to be the beginning of a change in attitude on the part of many of the young people in the school. Pride in, commitment to, and identification with, their school was beginning to grow and they now had something in which to be proud. As it happened Goodchild had to find a pupil to talk against uniform to provide a more balanced picture of the situation. Consequently, it seemed that the story about 'the parents putting Garth Hill students into school uniform' became a national talking point for a week in June 1982. In the eyes of the community and local industry, the wearing of school uniform meant that, almost overnight, as it were, the school became respectable and disciplined. Although in the educational world it is acknowledged that the connection between school uniform and student

The new uniform.
Photo courtesy of the *Reading Evening Post*.

The 'old' and the 'new'.
Photo courtesy of the *Daily Mail*.

behaviour is unproven, it is perceived by the community in much more simple terms. The school now had a foundation of respectability on which to build.

Smartening up the school's image
Concluding the story of school uniform, the first day of the autumn term 1982, proved interesting to say the least. Goodchild received numerous accounts from parents of those students who had previously been coming to school with hair of various colours and dressed in all sorts of regalia, putting on their school uniform and wondering if anyone else was going to wear it. There were stories of pupils peering out of their front doors just to see who was coming along and whether they were wearing uniform; and when they saw others doing so they stepped out and came to school. In fact, on that first day, there were only three pupils who were in unacceptable dress. The telephone did not stop ringing, bus drivers ringing to say how the pupils had changed and how polite they were;

shopkeepers calling up and saying what a delight and how polite the children from Garth Hill School were; old age pensioners and all sectors of the community were ringing up to congratulate the pupils of the school not only on what they wore, but on their politeness. By the end of the first week one of the local department stores presented the school with a cheque for £500 saying that the children had miraculously changed in attitude and no longer were they so worried about shoplifting during the lunch hour. The pupils may not have changed at all, but the way they were perceived by the community certainly had.

It was agreed with the parents that fifth year pupils would not have to go into school uniform, as they only had two terms to go from the September before, possibly, leaving school. It was also agreed that the sixth form should remain out of uniform. Both these groups, however, were told that, from September, no denim jeans, coats or any other articles of clothing of that type were permitted. The sixth form pupils were probably the most resistant to such changes and Goodchild decided that, apart from such basic requirements as the ones mentioned above, he would leave them alone.

Staff dress
During the initial meetings with parents, some took the opportunity to raise all sorts of matters. Uniform, as already mentioned, was a highly charged subject. In addition, the Head was asked whether or not he was going to do anything about the unsuitable dress of some of his staff. He explained that this was a professional matter which he would obviously bring to the attention of his staff. The expectation at Garth Hill is that all staff will dress formally and, in those early days, there was one member of staff who dressed as if he was on a university campus. By discussion the matter was resolved. Indeed, during the meetings with parents, Goodchild explained that if they had any criticisms the school wished to know of them; because, if the criticism were justified, or any misunderstandings had occurred, the school would want to put things right. Some staff found such statements very threatening and felt that the Head had laid them open to all sorts of complaints. These fears proved to be unfounded and the school's stance helped to bridge the gap between the parents and the school. Indeed, the strategy released staff from being on the defensive and therefore lessened any stress the staff may have been experiencing.

Grooming the sixth formers for responsibility
Stanley Goodchild was anxious to develop 'traditions' in the sixth form. He felt that, for many years, Garth Hill had mimicked the further education colleges by allowing pupils to attend in any dress. They certainly looked very different from the rest of the school and certainly did not look as if they belonged to a school at all. After the first year, in 1983, a prefect system was introduced; a certain percentage of the sixth formers were elected as prefects after discussion amongst the staff. Previously, the school had operated a system whereby if people were needed to carry out certain functions, then the staff asked for volunteers. This was now different in that the sixth formers were not asked if

they would like to be prefects — they were elected. They had the choice of opting out, however, although to date no-one has chosen that option. Goodchild was surprised — and pleased — when, in 1986, he was approached by some of the sixth form pupils, who asked whether they could introduce formal dress, i.e. dressing as if they were going to the office. Goodchild promised them that he would consider the matter, but it did not take him long to agree with their suggestion. It is also interesting to note that, although there was no official uniform in the sixth form, one had developed — mainly red jumpers and ties. With the sixth form going into formal dress, however, Goodchild was advised by a number of his colleagues that the sixth form would then dwindle. In fact, it has done far from that and is expanding quite rapidly.

The sixth form is seen as an integral part of the school and is used a great deal in the implementation of various schemes. More recently, they have helped, together with the main school, to raise nearly £5000 for the Royal Berkshire Hospital Cancer Appeal. Every year an old age pensioners' party is held when the elderly in the neighbourhood are invited to come to the school. They are wined and dined and then given an evening of entertainment, including an annual pantomime. The sixth form is encouraged to be challenging and critical in debate and has a Union which meets regularly, after which points raised are discussed with the Head and senior staff and future arrangements negotiated.

Pupils with self-reliance and initiative

Garth Hill has encouraged its pupils to use their own initiative and a very good example of this was when one of the sixth form pupils wished to do some voluntary service in Africa prior to going to university. She had to raise £1700 and was very enterprising in writing to companies for financial support, running a pet show at the autumn fair and the grand finale was when she organized a challenge to one of the non-stop records in the *Guinness Book of Records*. The weekend was a memorable one. The record-breaking attempt was started by the Right Honourable Gordon Palmer, Berkshire's Lord Lieutenant. The pupils made a tremendous effort and the event lasted just over twenty-four hours. Although they did not break the record, they had a tremendous amount of fun and the necessary money was raised. These are the qualities which are required in the leaders of tomorrow. Other young people in the sixth form decided to run a fashion show for a local charity. They managed to persuade Dorothy Perkins (who do not normally participate in such activities) to lend them the clothes; they set up the 'cat-walk' and arranged the publicity. It was a tremendous effort and it was all organized by a group of young people. The main organizer was a fifth former.

Discipline

Self-reliance, initiative and self-discipline — on the part of the pupils — have all been encouraged during Stanley Goodchild's time as Head of the school. He is also a believer in a firm, but friendly, approach to school discipline, and has been able to build upon traditions which were already well established in the school. For instance, if any person visits a classroom, the pupils are expected to stand automatically. This is something which the school feels is very important. If a person enters the Head's office he stands to welcome him or her; he argues, therefore, that the pupils should stand when a person enters the classroom.

Another aid to discipline is the conference room, which had been established previously. If a child has been disruptive in a lesson, rather than he/she stand outside the room and receive the reward of not having to do anything, he/she is sent to a conference room where there is always a senior member of staff and an appropriate programme of work prepared by each subject department. The child works on his/her own and is unable to be disruptive; nor is the class disrupted. In addition, the person who is sent to the conference room receives a detention which is arranged at the end of school.

6 Building Positive Attitudes and a Conducive Environment for Learning

Sporting achievements

The attitudes the pupils had towards their school were in the process of changing. It was important to capitalize on the momentum which had been created over the issue of uniform. The members of the Physical Education Department were anxious for their teams to be entered for numerous local county championships; it was decided, however, to try to involve everyone else by setting up a house system. Four houses were created named after famous people who lived in the area. These were Fielden, Lawrence, Brownlow and Haversham.

Although the school was divided on a horizontal basis for pastoral matters, it was felt that the House system should be used solely for sporting and after-school activities. Each house was given a colour and every pupil could identify others in their house by the colour of the stripe in their school tie. Brothers or sisters coming into the school would be placed in the same house. The surge in interest in sport was phenomenal. It was not unusual to see teams on the playing fields at 8.00 a.m. practising for forthcoming matches against other houses within the school. Sports day took on a new meaning because the pupils had an interest in every event; they were keen to support their house in every race rather than only those in which a friend was competing. This increased interest in sporting activities, however, presented an immediate problem. The playing fields, although extensive, were under water for ten months of the year and could not be used to any great extent. The cost of draining the fields was going to be prohibitive, and it took eighteen months to persuade the Local Education Authority to carry out this work. After that point, however, for the first time, they were in use throughout the year. This problem did not stop the enthusiasm of the young people and, in the first year, they won the majority of tournaments they entered. The great sporting highlight of 1983 was when Garth Hill's under-19 basketball team (girls) reached the national final. This was considered an outstanding achievement in that only two of the girls in the team were over 16-years-old. The media took a positive interest in the school's progress and the final, which was held at Havant, was attended by three or four coachloads of pupils from Garth to cheer on the team. The great attention paid to sporting activities presented a further problem for the management of the school in that the Physical Education Department was poorly resourced and a considerable sum of money had to be spent — just to provide basic equipment. It was considered to be very important, however, and the money was found.

Rewarding student progress

In the early days Goodchild was very conscious that he was seeing pupils for things that they had done wrong and had not really seen many for positive reasons. A merit system was introduced, therefore, which meant that, if a child did some very good work in a particular subject, he/she was awarded a merit by his/her teacher which was countersigned by the year group adviser. When three merits were gained a commendation was automatically received which meant that he/she had to attend the Head's office — commendations always being awarded by the Head. This is somewhat like collecting 'trading stamps', but the eight pupils in each year who received the most commendations received a limited edition school badge which was highly prized. In addition, the merits and commendations were awarded for effort rather than attainment and were therefore in reach of all pupils, whatever their abilities.

The school as a living environment

If the pupils were going to have any sense of pride in their school something would have to be done about the environment in which they lived and worked. If the staff were going to create good discipline it had to be based on a careful balancing of sanctions and rewards. Rewards would be in the form of resources; new furniture, new improved facilities like lavatories, carpeting, and new buildings; plus access to the school for pupils in breaks and lunch hours. Generally, the aim was to create a sense of community and ownership amongst the pupils and staff. The vandalized furniture and equipment had to be removed quickly. This was done within the first two days of Goodchild's arrival at the school. Within the first week the majority of the graffiti-covered desks had disappeared — to be replaced by new ones. He is very reluctant, however, to explain just how this was done.

It was no use providing the new equipment if it was going to be damaged. At the time, the Head was much criticized by the staff for spending money on furniture and equipment (rather than books), but Goodchild realized that, unless they had a pleasant environment, pupils would not take any pride in, or feel any respect for, the school and its resources. It was very much a 'back to basics' approach. According to Goodchild, resources and equipment constitute 'the basics'.

Given that considerable sums of money were being spent, it would be a sensible question to ask 'where did the money come from?'. Having been a Chief Education Officer, Goodchild was very familiar with the financing of schools and was able to read the County's budget book with understanding. Two examples show how he was prepared to use this acumen to help the school.

The toilets used by the pupils were in a very sorry state of repair; many of the seats were missing, the stoneware was cracked and graffiti was much in evidence. The pupils were brought together to discuss whether or not they were happy with the cloakroom situation. They were not. They had already seen some of the changes that had taken place and they were given an undertaking that, if they felt able to look after the cloakrooms, replacements would be found and repairs carried out. The 'contract' was agreed and the toilets and damaged basins were replaced; and, five years later, there has been no need to replace or refurbish them.

Goodchild feels that it is important for every new Head who is appointed to be inducted into the inner workings of the Local Authority. Budget books, for instance, are often written so that the laymen cannot understand them. Generally, the school appeared to be uncared for in terms of its fabric and much of this was due to the fact that mud was tramped in from the water-logged playing fields. There were very few paths around the school, and this added to the problem. When Goodchild tried to obtain money from the Local Education Authority there was none obviously available, although the officers were prepared to put it on the list of minor improvement bids for the following year. However, a considerable time was spent searching the budget books and a 'vote' entitled 'paths' was found. The officer who was responsible was initially reluctant to acknowledge its existence but after much negotiation and discussion and a face-to-face interview he accepted that it existed. Goodchild then asked if there had been any requests for money from the 'vote' but the officer was not prepared to discuss this. It emerged, however, that there were no bids for the £9000 and so the total sum was requested. After some very lengthy negotiations, Goodchild was allowed to spend the £9000 which enabled him to build a series of paths, greatly alleviating the problem of mud around the school.

School assemblies

When he arrived at the school, Goodchild felt that a greater community spirit needed to be developed among the pupils as a whole. Where one existed, it was in the year groups; the decision was made, therefore, to build on this level of activity. Goodchild immediately installed a system of assemblies and personally led an assembly with the Lower School and the Upper School once a week. Attending these assemblies became one of his highest priorities; they became the focal points in his week to be attended at all costs. It was not necessary for him to actually conduct the act of worship, but it was important for him to be there and to address the school. It is absolutely vital in any school, Goodchild argues, for the headteacher to have a high profile amongst the pupils and for him/her to be seen daily around the school. Goodchild considered it a compliment when, early on in his time at Garth Hill, a pupil said to his parent. 'The trouble with the new Headmaster is that he keeps popping up all over the place'. The assemblies lasted for twenty minutes and became the vehicle for the creation of a deeper community atmosphere. Every third week a member of the clergy came to take the act of worship and, on the other two weeks, it was a member of the staff. This was a voluntary activity, but a good cross-section of staff took turns in conducting the assembly. Goodchild would always deal with the notices and talk about the achievements of the school and, if necessary, give youngsters a reminder of the things which were not being done which should have been done. The pattern of assemblies meant that, every week, every pupil had an assembly with the Headteacher, a year assembly, a house assembly and two form assemblies. In recent years the main assembly has been enhanced by a pupil from the school introducing the session with a musical item. This has done a great deal to provide atmosphere for the occasion and has helped to instil confidence in the students who are learning to play an instrument. Goodchild believes that, if a school is strong on the sports field and in musical activities, it is well on the way to being a school of excellence on the academic side as well.

The sound of success
As far as the music in the school was concerned, Goodchild was fortunate in that there was a well established tradition of music in the school, although not all pupils were able to participate. From his arrival Goodchild promised parents that the school would provide a tutor for any instrument their children wished to play. If the school was going to do this, however, the staff concerned would expect total commitment from the children. Once again, the problem with music was that it was poorly resourced and, over the last five years, large sums of money have been invested to improve the situation. Consequently, music has flourished and every child in the first year is a member of the choir and is expected to take part in the first concert of the year. The school has two orchestras, a Balalaika Orchestra (the only school Balalaika Orchestra in the UK) and last, but not least, a swing band. When Goodchild arrived at the school the brass section was rather weak. He explained that as he was invited to the School Proms held at the Albert Hall annually, now that he was Head of a school, he hoped that it would not be long before he heard the name of Garth Hill being announced as one of the participants. After five years they have not yet reached the dizzy heights of the Albert Hall, but Goodchild is sure that the swing band will soon reach the required standard. In 1987 the school has felt it appropriate to hire the local Wilde Theatre to hold the annual musical concert, a move in the right direction.

Setting the tone by setting the aims of the school
Another aspect of the management of the school which needed attention was the establishment of a set of aims. Garth Hill had no clear written aims and objectives and, in his first term, Goodchild ensured that a list of aims was set

down which could be used as a set of guidelines. These aims read as follows:

1   To provide a broadly-based curriculum which is flexible, relevant and interesting, and appropriately geared to the pupils' stages of development and the technological age in which they live.

2   To foster awareness of the 'ever-expanding frontiers' of knowledge and to encourage the concept of learning as a valuable and life-long process, in order to meet not only their present needs and interests, but also to prepare them for the future demands of a challenging society and world.

3   To provide pupils with the opportunities to gain the basic general skills, standards and qualifications demanded by employers, examining bodies, colleges and universities; to inform them about the world of work and enable them to make well-informed and appropriate personal career choices.

4   To develop pupils' skills in a wide range of areas of experience; intellectual, linguistic, numerical, physical, practical and creative. In particular, to enable the pupils, within the limits of their capabilities, to become articulate, fluent, confident communicators in all forms of oral, aural and written English, and to encourage a love of reading and an enthusiasm for all the literary arts.

5   To provide the right working conditions, educational opportunities, stimuli and encouragement, to enable each individual pupil to work to their fullest capacity, achieving their potential in all areas of prescribed or chosen study; to foster a respect for both endeavour and excellence; to develop a capacity and enthusiasm for personal effort and for individual enquiry and study; to encourage an appreciation of, and respect for, the view and opinions of others.

6   To attempt to influence 'for good' the personality, character and attitudes of our pupils, with the aim of assisting and encouraging their development into sensitive, well-balanced, self-disciplined, morally responsible adults, able to meet the challenges of adulthood as individuals, parents, citizens and workers.

7   To demonstrate concern for the total welfare of each individual by the adoption of a 'pastoral care policy', which actively seeks to integrate young people into the community as individuals worthy of esteem, and to support and assist them in achieving their full potential, in terms of academic, personal, social and vocational opportunities.

8   To develop a happy, caring and well-ordered community in which staff and pupils can live and work harmoniously together and relate positively to the wider community beyond the school.

The staff handbook and record books

These aims were published in the new staff handbook. This document was an innovation in itself. The average length of service of the staff was in excess of twelve years and most of the rules and regulations according to which they worked were conveyed by word of mouth. These customs and conventions were unwritten 'laws' and caused problems when trying to change systems and improve them as and when necessary. A staff handbook, then, was one way of signalling that changes were afoot. While it was deemed to be totally unnecessary by many staff, at least it laid down the basic policies and provided for consistency — of rhetoric, if not performance.

Staff record books

All staff, including Goodchild, are expected to produce a weekly record of work covered with various groups, plus homework set. This is seen by Goodchild on a weekly basis first thing on a Monday. Whenever possible the Head follows up a set of the record books, either to give teachers praise, or just to talk about particular projects in a specific subject. The information provided is extremely useful when dealing with parents who wish to know the details of their child's homework. It makes it more difficult for misunderstandings to occur.

Leading from the front

In those first few months of Stanley Goodchild's leadership at Garth Hill much effort was put into tidying up the school and many staff members helped with the painting. In order to show that they meant business, the Head and his wife spent the summer holidays painting the main entrance and the front corridor. The front foyer, previously paved with quarry tiles, was carpeted so that anyone coming to the school would be received into a warm welcoming area and a number of departments agreed to produce a display for the front entrance. This meant that anyone coming to the school would not only be able to recognize where they were, but also immediately sense the caring atmosphere of the school. The Highways Departent agreed to erect signs showing directions to the school and, once visitors were in the school grounds, where to find the reception area and car parking facilities.

All these things are important for the image of a school. So often one approaches a school and there are no signs to show which door to go in or where to find the reception area; this is not very welcoming for a visitor. At the end of the summer term the graffiti had disappeared, as had the vandalized furniture. Another important development had taken place when the county accepted that many of the exterior walls would be replaced and an emergency programme had been set up to replace totally two floors of window sections during the summer vacation. It was demonstrated under health and safety regulations that if they were not replaced the pupils would be at risk. It had also been agreed that there would be a rolling programme over a number of years replacing all rotten sections. During the summer term a window frame had fallen from an upstairs window on to a pathway below. Luckily no-one was injured but it did give a warning that something had to be done very rapidly. There were many more things which needed attention which the school and the Local Authority still had to face. In truth, however, during that term the officers of the Authority had been most supportive in trying to help put the school back on its feet.

As far as the Local Authority Officers were concerned, Goodchild knew that some of them viewed him with some suspicion and he spent the first term talking with them, asking their advice about how they thought the school should develop. One of the strengths of Garth Hill School is the positive support it receives from both the Authority's Officers and the members of the County Council. Goodchild involved each of these groups in the development plans. A slogan, which he used from the beginning, was 'involvement generates commitment'.

Taking the school into the community
Also in the first term, apart from setting out the aims of the school, a glossy brochure was produced containing information for parents according to the requirements of the 1980 Act. Again, he was criticized by a few members of his staff who claimed that the money spent on the brochure should have been spent on books. To avoid such a criticism, therefore, he persuaded a local company to help defray the cost. He used this opportunity to explain to his staff that 'it's all very well spending money on books, but if we've got no pupils to read them there's not much point'; the promotion of the school in public relations terms was very important. At this early stage the idea of marketing the school was alien; and not fully appreciated by some staff. It was hoped, however, as time went on, that they would see the benefit of adopting such a strategy.

Some staff were also apprehensive when Goodchild announced that, in the following October, the school would be open for interested visitors from the community and industry to walk round and see the work being done at the school. This horrified some staff as they felt once again that he was forcing them to be exposed to possible criticism. Goodchild explained that their fears were unfounded; that he was very impressed with their dedication and their conscientious approach and all he could ask of each of them was to give of his/her best and to display in their classrooms and teaching areas the high standard of work they were doing with pupils. Some staff did not agree, however, and this created a certain amount of anxiety. While time would tell whether or not their fears would be realized, Goodchild was quite confident that it would be a resounding success. During autumn 1982 their community open days took place and although some of the staff were apprehensive about how the community was going to view their contributions, every department without exception, pulled out the stops and produced a magnificent range of exhibits, demonstrating the range of work generated within the school. In fact, during that first year, approximately 3000 people visited the school from various sections of the community and the teachers received nothing but praise. Local newspapers gave a great deal of coverage of the open days and many VIPs attended. Goodchild has suggested that the staff surpassed themselves — indeed, surprised themselves — at the standard of the exhibitions. While many visitors came out of curiosity and went away impressed with the quality of the work being exhibited, the great spin-off was that staff actually went and visited their colleagues' departments to see what was going on. For the very first time staff were able to visit departments and talk about cross-curricular matters, thus laying the foundations for future developments. Goodchild was keen to introduce other 'public' events and ceremonies.

In order to try and develop a 'tradition' within the school, a prize giving evening was introduced. Previously, all fifth year pupils leaving the school were given their certificates in the Headteacher's office. The new prize giving evening was used not only to present such certificates, but also to give progress prizes to youngsters in every year group. The significance of progress prizes, as opposed to attainment prizes, is that they can be achieved by any pupil as the award of them is based on personal effort. As funds are extremely limited, to overcome the problem the school provides prize winners in each year with a basic £2 book token to which parents can give additional funds to buy a specific book. The evening, which is held towards the end of the autumn term (so that those at university can also attend), is a very formal occasion which is chaired by the Chairman of the Governors. The Head gives an annual report, the Music Department provides a number of musical items and a guest of honour presents the prizes. On such occasions the guest of honour is usually someone who has a personal connection with the school, not a national celebrity. Indeed, guests of honour over the last five years have included the Chairman of the Bracknell District Council, the Chief Executive of Berkshire County Council, the Chief Executive of PCAS and the Director of Education. It is very pleasing to note that, each year, a larger percentage of school leavers return for this very special occasion.

Special occasions like open days and prize givings helped to reinforce Garth Hill's improving image. The outside world was coopted in support of the school's development plans. Indeed, the success of Garth Hill since 1982 has been greatly enhanced by its links with its external 'partners' — the local community and industry.

7 Links with Industry and the Community

As far as industry was concerned, Stanley Goodchild was determined to forge fresh — and revitalising — links. He invited himself to as many meetings as possible of the various local organizations such as the Chamber of Commerce and the Town Watch Committee. He visited many companies in the town and was invited to be a member of the Schools Industry Partnership in which, previously, the school had not taken part. He visited all the main companies in Bracknell, asking them what they felt about the school. Before doing so, however, he made sure that he was due to speak to those of some influence within the companies. As far as the community was concerned, he became a member of the Age Concern Committee, the Crime Prevention Panel and many other organizations. His aims were unashamedly twofold: not only to take part in community and industrial life but also to promote the name of Garth Hill School. As far as the governors were concerned, he made sure that he met with his Chairman of Governors frequently; he wanted to be sure that he was taking the governors with him as far as the new developments were concerned. Indeed, he need not have worried on that front as the views of the governors were very similar to his own and they were happy with the ways in which he was proposing to develop the school. Concerning the parents, as well as the evening meetings mentioned above, he wrote numerous letters to them, explaining what the school was hoping to do and asking for their views. As the President of the Parent/Teacher Association, he impressed upon them just how important their role in the school was going to be. As mentioned above, from the day Goodchild was appointed he always kept a very close contact with his Chairman of Governors and involved the Board in all aspects of the life of the school. He sees them as a great support rather than a hindrance and all the developments within the school have been discussed at length. They are encouraged to come into the school as often as possible; in fact, they take turns in leading an assembly. Industrialists, as well as parents, are governors of the school. In fact, probably 50 per cent of the current Board are parents and 40 per cent are industrialists (these are not two discrete groups). The governors are involved in all interviews and Goodchild looks to them as his Board of Directors to whom he is accountable. The Parent/Teacher Association of Garth Hill, which has now been renamed 'The Friends', is also encouraged to play a major part in the life of the school. Not only are parents welcome without appointment, but they play an active part in such places as the library, the uniform shop and the book shop. Indeed, the latter is worthy of special mention. This is a walk-in shop where children buy reading books and writing instruments. It is totally managed by parents who deal with finance, stock control and other administrative matters. The uniform shop is also completely controlled by parents with their own account and stock. It was built with the help of the suppliers of the uniform; it is a lucrative concern. The latest project is that the school is hoping, with the help of parents, governors and the local community, to build an Olympic size swimming pool. A company has agreed in principle to provide the capital and the school will cover the running costs when the pool is rented out to other organizations (when it is not being used by the school or the main investor). The company who are providing the capital will have access to the pool at regular times for their own employees. To help raise some of the money for this project the parents have taken over a car park in Bracknell every Saturday where shoppers can park for 30p a time. It does not seem much, but within a year they have raised approximately £3000. This is a typical example of the enterprising spirit of Garth Hill and its parents.

Mini-enterprise schemes

Indeed, this enterprising spirit has spread throughout the school. The sixth form was featured recently on Thames Television in relation to the Young Enterprise Scheme. The school felt extremely privileged as the ten minute programme went out at peak time and showed the sixth form pupils setting up a company to produce notice boards. The film showed the youngsters meeting in a local company's board room and making policy decisions about the company. It also included coverage of production, marketing and sales. As it is a qualified company, members of the public can invest in its shares but by the end of the year the company has to go into liquidation. Nevertheless, the experience gained by the young people is most valuable.

Stanley Goodchild encourages people from industry to visit the school and, on one occasion, a District Manager of a well known High Street bank came to talk to the pupils; he was so impressed with two sixth formers that he invited them for interviews. Neither had more than a CSE grade 4 when entry into the bank normally requires at least two 'O' Levels. On this occasion, however, the manager decided to employ both on the strength of their personalities and initiative and, after a few months, he made it clear that they were some of the best recruits he had had for many a year. As a result of that experience, this particular bank is reviewing its national admission policies for future recruits.

An open door policy

Since Stanley Goodchild's arrival at Garth Hill, the school has practised an open door policy. Consequently, the school receives a wide variety of visitors from international dignitaries, such as the Minister of Education of Bulgaria, to interested members of the public. The school never says 'no' and will always accommodate those who wish to see around the establishment. Whenever posible, as Head, Goodchild fulfils this role of guide and public relations officer. Eventually, however, he hopes to appoint a person who will accept this responsibility. Students are used on special occasions, but this is an exception rather than a rule (thus avoiding too much disruption to their education). The volume of visitors to the school has had a very positive effect. No longer can special provision be made for the visitor, so the pupils have to be on their best behaviour all the time. In any week there can be a television crew, several journalists and a bevy of educationalists all touring the school and asking very searching questions.

Even before a Business Manager was appointed, the school was let out to various organizations. To avoid any damage the school had to have assurance that they were bona-fide organizations and had to provide a third party liability insurance which was stored in the school's safe. By carrying out this simple precaution, damage has been kept to a minimum. Now Garth Hill is thinking of letting out its premises on a more commercial basis. The week has been divided up so that organizations which cannot afford to rent accommodation are not squeezed out and are still able to use the facilities. It is extremely important that the members of the immediate community of the school feel that they have access to the many facilities.

Arising from its close links with the local community, the school has good contacts with the police; there is a constable assigned to the school who acts as one of their tutors in social and personal education. The pupils meet with the police from year 1 to talk about community matters, and this has had beneficial effects on the pupil's understanding of the role of the police in the community.

At his interview, Stanley Goodchild had stressed the need for 'management' at Garth Hill. On his arrival at the school, he emphasized the importance of not managing 'by the textbook' and firm leadership. According to the coverage of the early days of his headship in the local press, Stanley Goodchild had 'taken a firm hold of the reins' and had 'already firmly committed himself to his new role'. He was, said the reporter, a firm believer in discipline and high standards, believing in the value of working hard and playing hard. The return to school uniform, the redecoration of the school and the encouragement of competitive sport were all mentioned as initial targets, the foundations for development. Goodchild also stressed the need for a partnership between the school and the parents; he argued that it was essential to listen to the parents and to create 'the community in the school, the school in the community'. Above all, however, from the beginning, Goodchild understood the importance of creating an 'alliance' between the school, the local community (including the parents) and the local press. He saw this as the way to halt and, indeed, reverse the downward spiral of falling rolls and falling reputation. From the outset Goodchild took the opportunity of using the local press to build up the image of Garth Hill School. Every step of the uniform story was covered and the sports pages were full of Garth's achievements. The headlines included such items as:

'Garth Hill Basketball Team Sweep the Board'
'Kart Team Success'
'Garth the Invincibles'
'Sporting Garth Hill'
'Julie receives England nod'
'Boys set off on rugby tour'
'Excellent sporting record'
'Trampolining: National Success'

The emphasis on non-traditional sports (trampolining, go-karting, BMX bicycling, boys' and girls' basketball, etc.) was an interesting one. There was also much talk of fund-raising (fairs, sponsored events, etc.), but not only for the school. Local (and national) charities were the beneficiaries of the school's endeavours. The NSPCC, Age Concern and the Royal Berkshire Hospital's Cancer Care Appeal all benefited from the fund-raising efforts of the pupils and teachers.

All these emphases — educational achievement, disciplined endeavour, school uniform, sporting achievement and charity work — were all endorsed by the Head in his addresses given at successive prize-givings:

we must ensure the pupils gain the best possible education that we can provide . . . and that is exactly what we intend to do. (16 December 1982)

A Bracknell headmaster has pledged his intention to leave no stone unturned in his fight to get pupils' employment and good career prospects. (15 December 1983)

Significantly, for the future development of Garth Hill, however, the talk now was of employment prospects, building a 'bridge between education and local industry', the opening of the computer centre, technological links and information and computer technology. Within an eighteen-month period, the school (and its fortunes) had not only been turned around, but also had laid the foundations for its further development. As one of the local papers heralded, the school was already going 'from strength to strength'. And, in so doing, it was creating a sense of values, an ethos.

Making it Count

8 *Development of Resources and the Refurbishment of the School*

During Stanley Goodchild's first term at the school, he convened a staff meeting and told them about the plans for redeveloping the school in terms of building a new staff room, a library, a drama studio, science laboratories and a restaurant. Overall, he said, Garth Hill would become a school of excellence. As many staff told him afterwards they thought that Goodchild was in the land of make believe and 'on cloud nine'. But time would tell. The other part of Goodchild's message to the staff concerned the importance of information technology (IT).

The school needed its own identity and, being situated in a high-tech area, it seemed to him that computer techology ought to become the school's shop window — its distinctive quality. Had the school been situated in another geographical area, then it may well have been some other aspect of the school and its curriculum that was highlighted.

Computer centre
The suggestion that the school should save sufficient money to build a computer centre received mixed reactions from staff. Given that many departments were very short on the basics of teaching — text books and other such resources — the ideas did not receive universal acclaim. In 1982 computer centres were still comparatively rare; and the Head suspected that many of the staff did not realize exactly what a computer centre was or its potential across the curriculum. They agreed, however, that they would help raise £24,000 for such a centre. There was a new found pride in the school; plans were made to achieve the financial targets. Governors, parents, staff, all became involved in various fund-raising activities. The group to be most congratulated, in fact, were the pupils, who arranged an 'activities afternoon'. This involved all sorts of sports, including: how many goals can you score?, a marathon, hockey matches, and a BMX bicycle track built by the pupils. They also invited the BMX

British champion as the star guest, which obviously attracted the press. Each of the events was sponsored and the whole afternoon proved a great success. After ten months, however, the school had raised only £12,000 and some people were getting quite despondent. Nevertheless they decided to go ahead and build as much of the computer centre as they possibly could. The money covered the building of benching; it also enabled the school to buy the VDUs, but only four computers. From the front of the room, the computer centre looked very impressive, with all its VDUs in place. But there were still many blank spaces

'England calling . . .'
Photo courtesy of the *Reading Evening Post.*

— where the computers ought to be. The school had a problem — how were they going to capitalize on all the hard work that everyone had put into the fund raising activities? The Head visited several libraries in London to find out what was happening in the near future and he discovered that Prestel were launching their first European link, their first direct dataline to Europe — in fact, to Sweden. He telephoned the people at Prestel and said to them: 'I understand that you are launching your European link from a hotel in London'. When they acknowledged this as being the case, he suggested that that was rather an unimaginative thing to do, and that it would be so much more exciting to come to the school and combine their launch with the launch of the school's computer centre. Within twenty-four hours they 'phoned him back saying that it was a marvellous idea, and, yes, they would like to do their launch from Garth Hill School. He then telephoned Acorn Computers and told them about the event and explained to them that reporters (and cameras) from national television would be attending, together with some personnel from the European press, and that it would be impressive if the launch could be on a BBC machine. Acorn were delighted and rapidly came down to the school to see the venue. When they entered the computer centre their faces dropped; in puzzlement, they asked why the school was involved in such a scheme yet had so few machines. It was explained that they only needed one, and that they had, in actual fact, four machines. The people from Acorn felt that, as the launch was going to have so much publicity, this was not good enough and so, overnight, the school was presented with eighteen computers and an Econet system, with all the trimmings. Many parents will remember that week because they had a very short time to install the machinery and, on one particular evening, the helpers worked through the night until 4.00 or 5.00 a.m.; the centre was ready for the launch. As promised representatives from the national media attended the opening ceremony and Garth Hill School 'booked' a camping holiday in Sweden using the first direct link to Europe. Acorn were extremely pleased with the day; so was the school. They now had a very sophisticated computer centre available to the pupils, instead of, as previously, one 380Z computer and a great deal of wire. The event was reported on both BBC and ITV and in many of the national newspapers. The school realized that, overnight, they had gained a commodity to sell — and a market which could be exploited — for the benefit of the pupils. During the next few months the school had many other offers to supply equipment, but, what was needed, was a carefully planned strategy. Many visitors came to see the computer centre and Acorn gained a great deal of kudos from the exercise. Moreover, the school now felt that they ought to exploit the reputation they were gaining and decided, after consulting industry, to establish a business office.

The business hi-tech office

This was intended to be a room where children could experience using the machinery and equipment they would find in a modern office. They managed to adapt two rooms by knocking them into one, and consulted many people in industry and the DES about what should be included in such a room. They had no difficulty in finding equipment for the room; it was set out with modern furniture and such equipment as a dedicated word processor from ICL, a digital mini computer, and a photo copier. In fact, there were something like eighteen stations, all providing different experiences for the young people. It was at this time that Hampshire LEA was launching its double-certificated Business Information Studies course and Garth Hill was invited to act as a pilot school — through the auspices of Ben Kelsey, then the Adviser for Business Studies for Hampshire. Financial help also came from the Manpower Services Commission — through the TVEI programme — and, when the room was finally launched, it contained approximately £65,000 worth of equipment, provided by various companies. Once again something of a splash was made of the official opening

A weather check.

Learning keyboard skills.

Project work.
Photos courtesy of the *Reading Evening Post* and the *Daily Mail*.

and the school was delighted when Lord David Young accepted the invitation to officiate. Once again, this launch received a great deal of publicity in the national and international press; it was a further 'UK first'.

Following the launch of this room Garth Hill was beginning to receive many visitors not only from this country but also abroad through the Central Office of Information. The school also received delegations from Eastern bloc countries as well as Western ones. And for every single visitor who came, the pride of the school grew.

The 'Apple office'
The computer centre was mainly being used as a general purpose room and had been set up so that teachers, who had no previous experience of operating computers, could use the facilities. The computers in the school were not being used to make programmers but as aids to teaching and learning. The hi-tech office, on the other hand, was used as specialist accommodation for those studying business and information studies. Soon after the opening of this hi-tech office, Apple said that they wanted to put a business office into the school and provided £150,000 to build a purpose-built centre housing eighteen 512K machines. This room was launched by Geoffrey Chandler who was then the Director of Industry Year (1986) and he used the occasion to launch the national project. Once again a great deal of care was taken in preparing for the launch, ensuring that it was well covered by the national and international press.

The Times Network Systems

At that time the school was developing the Times Network System; this was an electronic communications system, comprising electronic mail and databases which enabled schools and educational institutions to communicate with each other at a very cheap rate. In its infancy Garth Hill School was used as a test bed for the scheme and many of the facilities that it provided were developed at the school. When the system was launched nationally in April 1986 it was decided that this should happen from Garth Hill School and once again it attracted the national media, who were becoming used to visiting the place. TTNS is now used universally in primary, secondary and further education for databases and also electronic mail.

'Is this a message back from Japan?'
Photo courtesy of *The Times*.

A computer link for parents

Following the launch of TTNS, many parents felt it would be extremely useful to be able to log into the school to find out what their children were doing. For example, it would be useful to know what was being said in the latest newsletters or what homework was going to be set for John or Mary. With help from parents and staff, a parent database was set up and a local company agreed to provide the modem at a highly discounted price. The database enabled parents to send absence notes, to find out their child's homework timetable and be generally in touch with the school. This also attracted a great deal of international attention and was yet another acclaimed 'UK first'. If the school was to attract large sums of investment from industry, it needed to keep a high profile. Consequently, every six months, a UK first was launched from the school — to keep it in the public eye.

By the end of 1986, forty five camera crews had visited the school, as well as scores of dignitaries from all over the world.

Microlive — from the school
The producers of a well thought-of BBC television programme called *Microlive* decided that the school warranted an outside broadcast programme about computer education. For a week in 1985, therefore, something like eighty technicians and ten BBC outside broadcast vans descended on the school in preparation for a half-an-hour live outside broadcast about Garth Hill School. There was a great deal of excitement and the BBC crew were extremely cooperative in allowing the pupils to explore the ways in which outside broadcasts are operated. Most of the week was spent preparing for the live broadcast. In fact, so much material for the programme was found that it was extended from thirty to forty-five minutes. Then at 7.00 p.m. on a Tuesday evening, the main school hall was transformed into a studio for the actual programme. Not only were dignitaries invited but many parents were able to attend together with their children. The only 'technical' hitch occurred when the recording of the programme (for a repeat showing the following week) went

Linking home and school.
Photo courtesy of the *Reading Evening Post*.

A hive of activity.
Photo courtesy of the *Reading Evening Post*.

awry. There had been a misunderstanding between the outside broadcast van and the BBC headquarters and the first part of the live showing was not recorded onto tape; so when the programme was finished, the first part had to be done again. Despite this hiccup, it was a memorable occasion for all concerned and the programme did the school a great deal of good in the sense that it added to the growing interest in the development of Garth Hill School and helped to establish the school's reputation as a national leader in computer and information technology.

Worldwide interest
How did Garth Hill come to be an acclaimed leader in Europe? Therein lies an interesting story. A Japanese delegation visited the school and were extremely impressed by what they saw. When they returned home, they decided that they wanted to make a Panorama-type documentary about the school and its approach to information technology. They sent a film crew all the way from Japan to do a week's filming of the school; the first few days went very well, but after that point they wanted to film everyone and everything. When asked why this was necessary, they explained that it was a long way to come for retakes. The half-hour programme went out on all twenty-nine channels in Japan. The story-line, however, was that all schools in the UK were like Garth Hill, that Japanese schools were falling behind in the use of computers in education and

Filming for Japanese television.
Photo courtesy of the *Reading Evening Post*.

that something needed to be done about it before they fell too far behind. The story goes that two European MPs were sitting in their hotel in Tokyo watching TV and were surprised to find themselves watching a programme about a school in England called Garth Hill — subsequently they raised questions in the European Parliament. Consequently, Garth Hill School became well-known throughout Europe. The school received a huge postbag from Japan; the staff tried to answer all the questions and thought they had done a good job, only to find that they had to answer a second wave of questions.

With the school being so well-known throughout the world companies began to queue up to invest in Garth Hill.

Investing in Garth Hill

During the last three years the school has attracted between £250,000 and £500,000 a year in investment and equipment. How are people persuaded to invest in Garth Hill School? It operated very much as a company; the staff decided what their needs were before approaching any organization for support. Stanley Goodchild then did a certain amount of research in London to find out the state of the companies which could provide the equipment required by the school. He would find out what their assets were and how much profit they had made over the last two or three years; obviously if a company was making a loss it would be a waste of time to approach its directors. Having researched the company very thoroughly, Goodchild would then find out the names of the decision-makers and invite them to visit the school, saying that they had something to offer each other. Goodchild would send them some of the press cuttings concerning the successes of the school. Each consequent visit to the school consisted of a tour, a good look at the pupils in action and a discussion concerning the school's plans. The school would have already worked out a proposal and this would be presented to the visitors. It is no good asking for money without a well-defined project in mind. They would be shown a video of the school and lunch would then be served. The hope was that the visitor would be prepared to 'sign the cheque' before he/she left the school. Goodchild would always stress that the school was a shop window and a comparatively cheap form of advertising. Every project was initiated in different ways. When considering one particular project, three companies were invited to tender for this opportunity to invest in the school. The project aimed to put twenty-five personal computers around the school networked for administrative purposes and an investment of over £100,000 was required. Three companies in the UK declined to back the venture, saying that it was unrealistic. Goodchild then wrote to the European Director of the chosen non-compliant competitor saying how disappointed he was that the UK branch of the company did not share the vision of the school. He was invited to meet with him and as a result of this meeting, IBM joined the list of investors in Garth Hill School.

In the business of finding investors for schools, Goodchild argues that 'you should never take "no" for an answer, but at the same time make sure you do your homework'.

The rebuilding programme

Garth Hill's reputation had to be rebuilt; so did much of the school itself. From 1982 to 1987 the rebuilding programme was making steady progress. The school was in a very sorry state when Goodchild took over and the first phase of refurbishment was completed when much of the damaged furniture and fabric had been replaced. Nevertheless, the design of the school still left much to be desired. It was important to consolidate the school on one site and a deal was struck with the FE College. The latter gained a building from Garth Hill and Garth Hill, now concentrated on the one site, gained a capital building programme. The local authority agreed that it would be better to adapt the existing building than find a completely new site. It was demonstrated to the powers-that-be that FE and the LEA would have a good deal if the accommodation required by the school in the Wick Hill building was to be replaced on the main site, leaving the original accommodation for the College as planned when Garth had falling rolls. This decision provided the ideal opportunity to redesign the school and to make it an effective seven form entry school (with an annual intake of 210+ pupils). The first phase of this building programme was to move the staffroom from its existing position to the cycle sheds — soon to be rebuilt. When this was mentioned to the staff there was initial uproar. The Head assured them, however, that if they did not like the final result then it would be used as a classroom and the staffroom would be put elsewhere. Many of the staff had unpleasant memories of the old cycle sheds and felt that it was a retrograde step to have the staffroom built there. When this was done, however, all the staff, without exception, felt that it was a far better room than they had had previously and all was well. This enabled the builders to convert the old staffroom into a corridor and they used the rest of the space to build a reprographics room. This was a vital resource for good, facilitative teaching and for the production of high quality learning materials. The rest of the space was used to develop a new suite of home economic rooms which was desperately needed.

Resourcing the curriculum

The reprographics room proved to be a key area. It was stocked with sophisticated machinery which enabled teachers to present work sheets and other materials of a very high standard to the students. The school agreed to go into partnership with Roneo and two machines were installed, one a straight-forward duplicator and the other an offset litho with collator. Every department was provided with a key which incorporated a copy-count. This meant that every sheet of paper which went through the machines was debited to one department or another. The interesting thing about the adoption of the key system was that it highlighted a 40 per cent wastage factor in terms of previous practice.

The home economics suite

The home economics rooms were carefully designed and nothing but good quality equipment was installed in them. They are now used as a showpiece for the rest of the county and, because of the high standard of facilities, both boys and girls have been attracted to choosing this 'option'.

As a general point Stanley Goodchild was very anxious to see that any equipment or furniture that went in to any of the new rooms was of high quality. He would put quality before quantity. He believed that quality resources were more likely to be well looked after. The home economics rooms were built at the same time as a new corridor which ran the length of the building; a development much appreciated by the pupils.

The hi-tech library

The next phase was the building of a new library and drama studio. The school was determined that any library built would be of the order of a hi-tech one and that industry would have a big part of play in its design. A great deal of time and effort, then, were spent on planning the library which was designed by the architect from the local education authority. He had vision and many original ideas. For example, the link corridors, which were factory made, and which were copied from Heathrow's Terminal 4, were cheaper to erect than a flat roof on poles. The new corridors are very futuristic and add to the tone and atmosphere of the school.

His Royal Highness opens the hi-tech library.
Photo courtesy of the *Reading Evening Post*.

As far as the library was concerned, not only did it have provision for 18,000 books, but also had computer terminals which could be used to access many databases throughout the world. The library had a security system; if a

Royal interest.
Photo courtesy of the *Reading Evening Post*.

book is taken out of the library without being checked out, then a buzzer sounds and the door locks. It is important to note that most of the finance for the school has been gained from industry, i.e. from national and international companies. Local companies are not prepared to give to one school and not another, the reason being that a company's employees will have children in the local schools and the company needs to be seen to treat all schools equally. To try and get local companies involved, however, Garth Hill invited them to invest in the library in £100 units which bought a certain number of books. In this way sufficient monies were found to equip the library comprehensively. As far as the terminals are concerned, they have a system for searching for titles and

An explanation is provided . . .
Photo courtesy of the *Reading Evening Post*.

this can be operated from anywhere in the school, not only in the Library. They have the capacity to log in to DIALOG, BLAISE, PROFILE and the Times Network System which is extremely useful in acquiring information. They are able to tell, for example, if a book is in the school library, the Berkshire library or a library in the UK — at the touch of a button. The Garth Hill library constituted another UK first and the staff were delighted that, in June 1987, it was opened by His Royal Highness the Duke of Kent.

Two recent additions to the library are the Doomsday Project, which the pupils have found most interesting, and also the World Reporter which allows pupils to search for various topics in the daily newspapers published over a period of four years. All these electronic sources of information have appeared in the nick of time for pupils studying for GCSE and with projects to complete.

The drama studio

The drama studio, which is part of the same complex as the library, is a 'black box' fitted out with the latest electronic mechanisms for lighting, all controlled by a BBC computer. Garth Hill believes that drama is an extremely important part of the curriculum as it helps to develop the esteem and self-confidence of the pupils. The 'black box' has been designed so that it can be used as a theatre, as a music hall or as a meeting place for up to 120 people. Once again, all the equipment which has been installed is of the highest order.

The drama studio has many additional uses, such as a TV centre. Companies are able to use it, when it is not being used by the pupils for making in-house videos. The Music Department has also found it very useful for small concerts.

The restaurant

During the building programme, the old dining hall which was a U-shape and extremely difficult to supervise, was completely gutted and the area was redesigned to become a school restaurant. The title is very important, Garth Hill does not have a school canteen or dining room, but a restaurant. The furniture within it is of the 'MacDonalds' type although the food served is not. Pupils have access to the restaurant from either inside the school or outside and it opens at 8.00 a.m. for breakfast and closes in the afternoon at tea-time. It serves a variety of foods and is a popular meeting place for both staff and pupils. Every day there is a 'special' which is extremely good value and the whole operation is run on a self-financing basis.

Breakfast time at Garth Hill.
Photo courtesy of *The Times*.

Going to work on an egg.
Photo courtesy of the *Reading Evening Post*.

The new complex, the library and the drama studio, had been so designed that there is a direct link through to the restaurant and the main hall — thus providing a self-contained unit which can be hired as a conference centre or for other functions.

The Business Manager

To maximize the use of these and other facilities, in September 1987, the school appointed a Business Manager — another 'UK first'. His role is to exploit the school's resources when they are not being used by the pupils. The significance of the link between the restaurant and the main hall now becomes obvious; when the hall is let out for a conference, the restaurant can also provide a high quality three-course meal, thus giving the school another opportunity for revenue.

Getting down to business.
Photo courtesy of the *Yorkshire Post*.

The Business Manager has produced a business programme to enable the resources of the school to be hired by outside organizations and companies. Moreover, the Business Manager is being used to encourage the existing teaching staff to obtain consultancies from industry, which enables them to increase their salaries quite considerably. In order to ensure that they have 'saleable' skills, the Business Manager has also arranged in-service training sessions to equip the teachers with the necessary skills for them to lead training sessions. This 'perk' is an attraction for school teachers of excellence in Garth Hill's bid to be a school of excellence. The Business Manager is looking at ways of encouraging distance learning and, by using electronic communication direct to companies, will be able to provide instructional materials in the use of such equipment as word processors. The launch of the library, the restaurant and the

An early start.
Photo courtesy of the *Yorkshire Post*.

role of Business Manager each attracted the national press which is very important when marketing the school. When involving the press, however, there is always a danger that it is a double-edged sword and any untoward events will also be published. In the interests of the pupils, however, it is considered that this is a risk worth taking.

9   Developing the Curriculum, Developing the Staff

TVEI: Resourcing the curriculum
It is important to mention Garth Hill's involvement in TVEI. Berkshire had not been accepted in phase 1 of the pilot scheme, but its bid was accepted second time around. Consequently, Garth Hill, together with the other schools in Bracknell, was nominated and became a pilot school.

TVEI has been usefully introduced as follows:

Technical and Vocational Education Initiative
The Background
TVEI was launched by the Prime Minister in the House of Commons on 12

Source: AMMA Report to Members No. 15

November 1982. Seven million pounds was to be made available to fund the initiative. The finances, however, were to be controlled by the MSC, who also laid down the objectives and the criteria which had to be met in order to obtain funding. The intention was to establish a small number of pilot projects for the 14-18 age range which aimed to produce a new type of four-year course that had a distinctive technical and vocational bias. The fund guidelines for LEAs to make their bids were not available until January 1983 and the deadlines for submission of projects was 4 March. In early April the projects were chosen — all to start in September. This allowed less than a term to appoint staff, evolve detailed plans and implement curriculum development and in-service training.

The pilot projects were hardly under way before the second phase of TVEI was announced. This time many more LEAs were to be involved and a ceiling of £400,000 p.a. was laid down for each participating LEA over the five-year phase. The deadline for submission was 12 December 1983. Forty-six successful applications were announced on 3 February 1984; one LEA later withdrew. Berkshire was one of these 'second-round' authorities.

Pupil Participation

Pupil participation in the scheme is:
* voluntary
* open to all abilities
* and to boys and girls equally.

In each LEA, the scheme aimed to recruit 250 pupils in each year. In many LEAs far more than 250 pupils took part in the programmes, and resources were used to benefit many more. In September 1983 4000+ pupils in fourteen LEAs followed over 500 'new' courses.

In September 1984 an additional 12,000+ pupils joined the scheme.

The Programme

At 14, pupils follow a four-year programme of general, technical and vocational education. They may leave or enter the scheme at 16 or 17.

Each scheme includes:
* work experience
* regular assessment and counselling
* courses of technical and vocational subject elements which relate to potential local employment opportunities
* access to national recognized qualifications i.e. 'O' levels, CSEs,. RSAs, CGLI, B/TEC
* final record of achievement.

NB: Seventy per cent of the pupils' timetable should consist of general education; 30 per cent should comprise technical/vocational studies.

What is Different?

Some LEAs have based their approach on an emphasis on high-technology:
Courses available include:
* control and modular technology

* electronics
* microprocessor control
* robotics
* information technology

Others have used broad occupational groups like MSC's Occupational Training Families to identify vocational areas.

* community care
* food industries
* transport services
* retail and distribution
* administrative, clerical and office studies.

According to the *Times Educational Supplement,* 14 October 1983, TVEI was the means of translating the 'MSC dream' into 'curriculum reality'. In this article (which was circulated to interested staff at Garth Hill), the general criteria laid down by the MSC for local TVEI schemes were listed as follows:

1   girls and boys should normally be taught together and care should be taken to avoid discrimination and sex stereotyping;
2   programmes should provide four-year curricula designed to prepare the pupil for particular aspects of employment and for adult life in a changing society;
3   they should have clear objectives and encourage initiative and problem-solving ability;
4   they should have a general and a technical/vocational element but the balance can vary;
5   these elements should be broadly related to potential job opportunities;
6   planned work experience should be an integral part from the age of 15;
7   courses should be capable of being linked effectively with subsequent training/educational opportunities, and
8   there should be regular assessment and careers counselling with all students and their parents receiving periodic written assessments.

Garth Hill quite naturally exploited this new source of revenue and much of the MSC funding received in 1984, together with investment from industry, went towards helping to equip the hi-tech office. TVEI was interested to skew the curriculum towards the more technical/technological subjects, but Garth Hill, having already taken that line, did not need to change direction. Those in the school, however, benefited in two ways: firstly, they received further finance over a period of five years and, secondly, they were able to work closely with the college in providing additional options in electronics, catering and technology.

1986 was Industry year; given its emphasis on links with industry, Garth Hill received much attention — starting with a lead article in the *Times Educational Supplement* (entitled 'In business', 17 January 1986). In the article it was claimed that Garth Hill:

is being considered by the national and educational press as a leader in Europe in the field of information and computer technology . . . This has come about as a result of the school's continual awareness of its role within the community and its strong links with parents, industry and commerce. Industrialists do more than provide financial support for the school; they provide training for staff and pupils, and as industrial tutors, accept both pupils and staff for work experience and offer valuable technical support.

This pioneering use of industrialists as tutors (helping with careers advice and simulated interview experiences) led to one of the locally-based international companies, Hewlett-Packard, offering the school a work shadowing scheme, designed to help 'A' level students make the right career choices.

Central to Garth Hill's links with industry are its involvement in both TVEI and the Young Enterprise Scheme. According to the *Times Educational Supplement* article:

Since September 1984 the school has been a member of a TVEI consortium in Bracknell, comprising two other comprehensive schools and the local college. Thanks to TVEI, for the first time the staff have been able to enjoy a properly resourced in-service training programme which equates to that of industry. Pupils who follow TVEI courses are assigned to an industrial tutor. 3M have linked with Garth and provide a team of three tutors who meet all the pupils on a regular basis covering a wide ranging programme.

The pupils play an active part in the Young Enterprise Scheme and working with 3M, Ferranti and Lloyds Bank, the school was represented at the national final last year. Also local business men and women organize evenings of mock interviews at companies, making the interview procedure more realistic.

Also in January 1986, the NUT's *Secondary Education Journal* carried an article by Stanley Goodchild, entitled 'Garth Hill: Following industry's path', which contained the following passage:

Working with industrialists
The school was honoured in 1985 by winning a National Techmart Award for its technologically-oriented links with industry. The school has made a special point of involving industrialists with as many aspects of the life of the school as possible. In addition to ensuring that local industry is well represented on the governing body, the school encourages projects which foster the partnership between school and industrialists.

No wonder that when, in 1988, there is so much talk of 'compact schools' (i.e. schools closely linked to local business, industry and employers), people are looking for advice to the school with the experience of such arrangements — Garth Hill.

Laying the foundations of the curriculum

Providing guidelines

In his first term at Garth Hill, Stanley Goodchild had initiated the process by which a number of curriculum documents were put together in order to satisfy the demands of the 1980 Act. These 'guideline' documents contained curriculum aims and plans for their delivery. At that point, the method used was for the Head to write a paper, ask for staff comments and, when comment was received, it was amended until a final version became established. The timescale was limited and the discussions and consultations were not as full as Goodchild would have wished in normal circumstances.

Organizing the learning situation

In 1982 most subjects were taught in mixed ability groups. As an inspector, Goodchild had had very mixed feelings about this form of teaching as it was known to be very successful *if* the class organization was appropriate. However many teachers claimed to be using mixed ability teaching, their practice was varied to say the least. Very often mixed ability teachers were teaching children as homogenous groups. At Garth, staff had the choice of continuing to teach in mixed ability groups, provided that the classroom organization was compatible, that is it contained a mixture of individual, group and class teaching. In the event, this led to most subjects, apart from those in the humanities area, being taught in sets after the first year.

Interviewing the staff

Indeed, during that first term in 1982 the work had to be tackled on several fronts. Debate was required involving the pupils, the staff, the governors, the parents, industry and the local community. As far as the staff were concerned, during that term, the Head interviewed each member in an extended session, talking with them about their own career aspirations. He was surprised that, in many cases, staff members had not seriously thought about their own career development. Some had done so. The average length of service of members of staff at the school was over twelve years and many had started their careers at Garth Hill and stayed there. All these considerations helped Goodchild to come up with a strategy which would need to be instigated during the course of the following year.

Staffing matters

The staff had to be dealt with in a very understanding and sympathetic way. For some staff change was too rapid and certain initiatives were somewhat threatening; they could not believe that the school was going to be turned around so rapidly and questioned whether or not the Head had his feet on the ground. Alternatively there were a considerable number of staff who viewed his arrival as an opportunity to implement changes which they felt were well overdue. Their problem, however, was that they were really impatient and wanted to know why it 'couldn't be done yesterday'. Goodchild explained to the staff that he intended to 'put the school on the map'. In the first term a weekly newsletter was instigated, which was sent to the local press. As a result they had an abundance of information which they could print and very seldom did a week go by without Garth Hill School being mentioned. Goodchild made sure that much of this 'news' came from the departments in the school. He was particularly keen to build up the sporting side of the school's activities. Consequently, as far as the members of the PE department are concerned, he explained that he hoped they would rectify the situation (in which competitive sport was at a premium) and that, although it was hoped to win as many tournaments as possible, the important thing was to take part. This went down well with the pupils and the staff concerned; they were prepared to work extremely hard towards this particular goal. This is a good example of Goodchild's approach; which involves target setting and the establishment of a challenging set of expectations. He made it very clear to the staff that there was going to be a great deal of hard work ahead of them and that, if they wanted the school to succeed, then everyone would have to travel ten miles instead of one. He explained that because of the situation in which the school found itself, he was going to have to be fairly ruthless, although he assured them that 'no-one will be walked over'. He mentioned, however, that if they had any concerns they were to let him know and to come and talk them over with him. If the new philosophy of the school was totally alien to them, then he emphasized that he would be understanding. As the staff did not have a major say in the choice and the appointment of the new Head, he would counsel them if necessary to resolve the 'conflict' by either helping them to understand more clearly the objectives of the school or, in the nicest possible way, helping them to find an alternative job. He instigated an in-service training system which he ran himself for those who wished to apply for jobs elsewhere. This course included help on the completion of application forms and the acquisition of interview techniques. This was all done not in the spirit of 'I want some of you to go', but by means of a positive approach, in the knowledge that whenever there is a change of Head some staff become unsettled and want to leave.

It was important in those early stages that new posts were created, but he was hampered somewhat in his plans, mainly because of the redeployment problem which he appeared to have inherited at the beginning of the term (but which, by the September, had disappeared) and the fact that the school was facing severe falling rolls. To be able to inject new blood into certain areas of the school he needed to create vacancies; on the one hand, no-one would be made to feel unwanted, but, on the other hand, if people felt they wanted to move he would help them in whatever way he could.

Saving jobs, earning loyalty
When Stanley Goodchild arrived at the school in April 1982, fifteen teachers were due to be redeployed. As a result of the rapid turn-around in the school's fortunes and the increased interest in the school all those posts were saved. Although for a time the school was still considered to be overstaffed, all the

projections were that there would be a rapid increase in pupil numbers, thus indicating that all the staff would be required. Given a combination of factors which involved the reintroduction of school uniform and the high profile stance taken up by Goodchild and the school in the summer term, the community at large were now behind Garth Hill and willing the school to do well. Survival is often determined by pupil numbers.

Changing attitudes

In order to take the school forward, however, embedded attitudes had to be 'unfrozen'. This concerns the question of how those at Garth Hill managed to change attitudes and, in so doing, change direction within the school. It was obvious from the events surrounding the uniform issue that one of the most powerful factors in influencing rapid change is the creation of pressure from external sources. During the first year any vacancies which arose were left vacant. At the end of his first year (i.e. July 1983) there were seven vacancies which had not been filled, which enabled Goodchild to look at the total staff resource and identify the key posts which were needed as 'catalysts' for change. When he made it clear to his colleagues that any post above a scale 2 would be advertised nationally, this created a certain amount of disquiet as the custom had been for people to be promoted from within the school. He made it clear, however, that he only wanted to appoint the best and, if someone within the school was the best, he/she would be appointed. 'Best' was defined strictly in relation to the post in question. In the event, of those seven posts, all seven went to outside applicants. This was unfortunate but the posts were in areas where there was little expertise within the school. It can be imagined, however, that they either had to turn out to be 'super-men' and 'super-women' or the existing staff would voice their disapproval. It was a calculated risk, but one worth taking.

Making key appointments

One of those key appointments was for careers education and guidance. When Goodchild was an inspector he felt that this area of the curriculum was always given low priority and yet it should be central to the total school curriculum and is certainly one of the key positions. The post of Head of Careers education and Guidance was advertised and, although there were many applicants, an appointment was not made as a particular type of person was sought. The school re-advertised the post and there was delight and some relief when a person was found who not only had teaching experience in this curriculum area, but also had industrial experience. This one person had an important impact on the school; she completely changed the attitude of many staff about careers education and guidance. Previously, the school had had little work experience for pupils. Within a year, however, all the fifth year pupils (nearly 200 of them) had at least a week of work experience and the links that she created for the pupils were extensive. She was also instrumental in making sure that local industry and commerce was actively involved in the school in many different ways. For example, not only were the work experience opportunities set up, but also the concept of industrial tutors was introduced. These were people, mostly managers from industry, who allocated a number of hours per week to come and work alongside the teaching staff in the classroom, especially in careers education and guidance, but also in other areas of the curriculum. One of the first 'shadowing' schemes was set up, whereby pupils shadowed senior managers in the local companies. As part of this scheme, one of the sixth formers shadowed the Managing Director of Hewlett Packard. She was picked up every morning in a Rolls Royce from her home — the neighbours thought her family had won the 'pools' and the event caused a great deal of discussion locally. The pupils certainly gained a great deal from the shadowing scheme. The latest venture involving industry was work experience consisting of two weeks in Milan. Twelve sixth form pupils, having followed a survival language course, have worked in Italian companies. The school feels that it is extremely important to develop links between various European companies; Italy was picked as it is very different from the more usual French or German connections.

Another key appointment was a person as Head of Computers Across the Curriculum whose sole objective was to see that computers were being used effectively in all subject areas. This appointment was made because so often, at that time, Heads of Computer Studies found it very difficult to relate to computers across the curriculum and could be very protective of the skills that he/she had acquired. Computers become 'land-locked' and compartmentalized. It is accepted, however, that in recent years this has changed. Indeed, at Garth Hill, the post is now fast becoming redundant as the use of information technology is part of every scheme of work in every subject.

In the early days, then, these key appointments were used as catalysts to get staff to rethink both content and approaches. Goodchild was very fortunate that he took on an extremely well qualified and good staff in 1982. However, there needed to be an input of new ideas. The fact that these new people had to be introduced did not mean that the rest of the staff were incapable of thinking up new ideas, but at times, every organization needs fresh blood. It is noteworthy that at the time of writing there are now more internal candidates who have received promotion than those who have been appointed from the outside.

Managing the school and changing the structure

Another early development within the school was the setting up of a senior management team, which comprised the Head, the three deputy heads and the two senior teachers. These 'managers' had not been used to working as a team and it took some considerable time for them to work together successfully. They had always had very specific roles and therefore for some the suggestion that they should rotate responsibilities came very hard. They now work on the assumption, however, that every member of the senior management team is in preparation for taking up a headship and, therefore, over a three-year cycle, they receive experience of the majority of the management roles that a head would need to perform. The changes required in setting up a management team to work in this new style were quite threatening to some members of the group as they had well established, defined roles and to change these meant going into the unknown. In addition, by working as a team, a certain amount of their autonomy appeared to have been lost. Even at this senior level, therefore, there was a certain amount of resistance to change. Initially, the management style of Goodchild was very much that of a 'despot' (his own word) as change had to be rapid to secure the future of Garth Hill School. Before talking about the changes in the staff structure and the development of the school, it is important to explain the original set up. Below the Head there were the three deputies and two senior teachers, and four chairmen of faculty who were responsible for a group of subjects. Then there were heads of departments and other scale posts below that. There were no written job specifications and people did what they felt was required of them in their particular positions.

This needed to change. Following the Head's interviews with individual members of staff, job specifications were introduced for heads of department. This was a general specification which was the same for all heads of department. Following this, every other scale postholder was issued with a job specification following consultation with the particular head of department and scale postholder. Year group advisers were also given job specifications. The most difficult group to deal with was the chairmen of faculty as their job was not fully understood. Each member of the senior management team was given a job description and so was the Head. Each member of staff now had a baseline from which to work. It is interesting to note that on the whole the job specifications were very much welcomed. Many teachers find specified 'job tasks' reassuring and confidence-building.

In 1988 the structure has gone one stage further. No-one in the school has more than seven colleagues reporting to him/her (as is the common practice in industry). Each of the three deputies has a maximum of seven heads of department reporting to him/her in terms of day-to-day management. Each deputy has executive control of his/her own and only needs to refer to the Head when an issue is outside the defined policy of the school. The phrase 'you have to do this because the Head says so' is taboo. The structure of delegation ensures decisions are available at great speed. Every job is structured as part of staff development. The total structure of formal meetings is shown in figure 1.

Figure 1: *Organisational Chart*

Note: This illustrates the relationship between the main working groups and does not include the many *ad hoc* groups of teachers which meet for specific reasons.

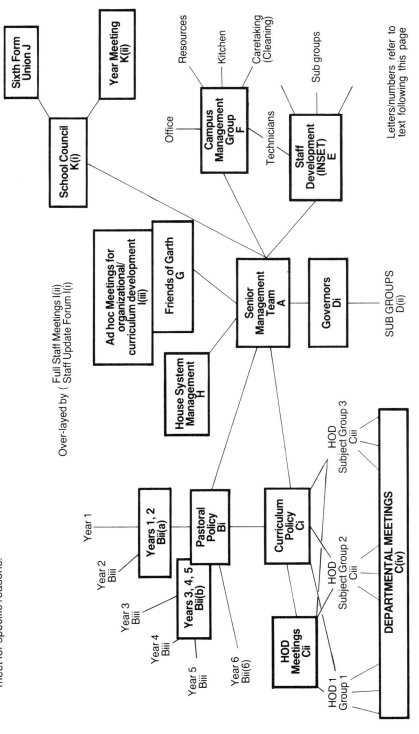

Management Structure — Garth Hill School
Note the Headteacher title was changed to Principal in 1987 in line with other
European countries. Also year group advisors were changed to heads of year.
The Principal is *ex-officio* at all meetings.

A   SENIOR MANAGEMENT TEAM
    Chairman: Principal
    Attendees: 3 Vice Principals, 2 Assistant Vice Principals and others at/by
    invitation.
    Frequency of meetings: Fortnightly.
    Key functions: To consider all policy decisions relating to management of
    the school, both in terms of curriculum and pastoral.

B   (i)   PASTORAL POLICY GROUP
    Chairman: Vice Principal responsible for Pastoral Policy.
    Attendees: Heads of Year 1-6, the Vice Principal responsible for lower
    school, the Assistant Vice Principal responsible for years 3, 4 and 5, the
    Assistant Vice Principal responsible for Sixth Form — (years 6 and 7).
    Frequency of meetings: Once a month.
    Key functions: To consider the overall school policy relating to pastoral
    matters. Issues will be raised in this group which span the whole school.

B   (ii)   PASTORAL SUB GROUPS
    (a)   Lower School
    Chairman: Vice Principal responsible for Lower School.
    Attendees: Head of Years 1 and 2.
    (b)   Upper School
    Chairman: Assistant Vice Principal responsible for Upper School.
    Attendees: Heads of Years 3,4 and 5
    (c)   Sixth Form
    Chairman: Assistant Vice Principal responsible for Sixth Form.
    Attendees: Nominated Sixth Form Tutors
    Frequency of meetings: (a) (b) and (c) — weekly.
    Key functions: To deal with day to day operational matters relating to the
    pastoral matters.

B   (iii)   HEADS OF YEAR MEETINGS
    Chairman: Head of Year
    Attendees: Form tutors
    Frequency of meetings: Monthly
    Key functions: To deal with day-to-day pastoral matters relating to the
    role of Form Tutor.

C   (i)   CURRICULUM POLICY GROUP
    Chairman: Principal
    Attendees: Three Vice Principals and other staff by invitation.
    Frequency of meetings: Fortnightly

Key function: To review curriculum development, management and innovation.

C (ii) HEADS OF DEPARTMENT MEETING
Chairman: Principal
Attendees: Heads of Department, members of Senior Management Group
Frequency of meetings: Half-Termly
Key functions: To manage the academic curriculum of the school.

C (iii) HEADS OF DEPARTMENT — Three Sub Groups
Chairman: Vice Principal (Subject groups 1, 2 and 3)
Attendees: Heads of Department who are members of each group.
Frequency of meetings: Half-termly
Key Functions: To manage individual departments and to initiate cross-curriculum activities. Also to monitor and promote the education of the pupils within the given subjects.

C (iv) DEPARTMENTAL MEETINGS
Chairman: Head of Department
Attendees: Members of Department
Frequency of meetings: At most weekly
Key functions: To ensure the proper management of the department in all respects.

D (i) GOVERNORS
Chairman: Chairman of Governors
Attendees: Elective Governors, Principal and Bursar
Frequency of meeting: Termly
Key functions: As specified in the Articles of Government but in general to oversee the management of the school

D (ii) GOVERNOR SUB GROUPS
Chairman: As nominated
Attendees: As nominated
Frequency of meetings: As and when necessary
Key functions: As prescribed by main body of governors

E STAFF DEVELOPMENT (INSET)
Chairman: Vice Principal
Attendees: Representatives from senior management, Heads of Department, Pastoral, teachers on main salary scale and newly-appointed colleagues.
Frequency of meetings: Monthly
Key function: To monitor needs of staff and to plan the in-service training programme including specific in-service training days.

F CAMPUS MANAGEMENT GROUP
Chairman: Member of the Senior Management Team
Attendees: Representative from non-teaching staff

Frequency of meetings: Fortnightly
Key functions: To consider matters relating to the support services comprising catering, administration, technicians, caretaking and cleaning and lettings.

G   FRIENDS OF GARTH HILL SCHOOL COMMITTEE
Chairman: An elected parent
Attendees: Friends of Garth Hill Committee
Frequency of meetings: Half-termly
Key functions: To develop and initiate a programme ensuring that parents play an integral part in the life of the school.

H   HOUSE SYSTEM MANAGEMENT TEAM
Chairman: Vice Principal
Attendees: House leaders
Frequency of meetings: Half-termly
Key function: To manage the house activities within the school

I   (i)   STAFF UP-DATE FORUM
Chairman: None
Attendees: All staff
Frequency of meetings: Twice weekly
Key function: To facilitate the need for staff to exchange information about pastoral matters both relating to pupils and colleagues.

I   (ii)   FULL STAFF MEETINGS
Chairman: Principal
Attendees: All Staff
Frequency of meetings: Half-termly
Key function: The main grid is overlaid by staff meetings. The agenda of each can be influenced by any of the meetings being held.

I   (iii)   AD HOC STAFF MEETINGS
Chairman: Various
Attendees: By invitation or self selection
Frequency of meetings: As and when required
Key function: To deal with specific issues of organization and curriculum development. These are disbanded once the objectives have been achieved.

J   (i)   SIXTH FORM STUDENTS' UNION
Chairman: Elected by students
Attendees: Sixth-formers
Frequency of meetings: Monthly
Key functions: To discuss matters relating to life in the Sixth Form.

K   (i)   SCHOOLS' COUNCIL
Chairman: Principal
Attendees: Year representatives and staff as appropriate
Frequency of meetings: Half-termly

Key functions: To give pupils a formal voice in the organizational structure.

K   (ii)   YEAR MEETINGS
Chairman: Head of Year
Attendees: Representatives from forms
Frequency of meetings: Half-termly
Key functions: To give pupils a formal voice in the organization structure.

Note: This is *only* the formal communiction structure. Probably as important are the more informal, individual discussions which take place daily.

During the summer term the Head produces a list of key objectives and tasks together with suggested time deadlines (these are reviewed termly). A key task is above and beyond the routine responsibilities of a member of staff and has to be capable of being measured. Each member of the senior management team then produces his/her list, followed by heads of department and heads of year. By the end of the summer term the set is complete. The progress of these lists is monitored on a termly basis. They are discussed with senior management and the Chairman of the Governors. Next year the system will be extended to all staff. Those involved thought it was yet another task rather than a way of regulating work; this view is changing, however, as the advantages of setting objectives are becoming apparent. An example of the Principal's (Head's) key tasks are shown below; they are available for all staff to peruse.

KEY TASKS FOR THE PRINCIPAL 1987/88

1   Initiate and implement a revised overall curriculum strategy:
   (a)   To produce a discussion paper for consultation — 9.87
   (b)   To initiate a procedure for implementing the agreed strategy — 2.88
2   Restructure the organization to achieve:
   (a)   No individual has more than seven reportees — 3.88
   (b)   Each senior staff member has clearly defined delegated responsibilities and the authority to carry them out — 1.88
   (c)   Complete the procedure for members of staff to have individual staff development interviews — 7.88
3   (a)   Outline the objectives for the Business Manager — 12.87
   (b)   Monitor the work on a monthly basis.
4   Local Financial Management:
   (a)   To prepare for the pilot scheme — 1.88
   (b)   Implement the pilot scheme according to the Authority's guidelines — 7.88
5   Establish the new framework for the sixth form together with the new range of courses — 3.88
6   Ensure that the IBM system is implemented and the appropriate staff trained to use same — 7.88
7   To prepare the Governors for the new procedures relating to the Education Bill 1986 — 10.87

8 Organize the new procedures for election of parent and teacher   3.88
   governors
9 To initiate a further dimension to Friends of Garth Hill, namely   12.87
   educational evenings

Bidding for Financial Support — The Internal Process

Every department was asked to produce an annual report under certain headlines.

HANDBOOK ITEM 27
DEPARTMENTAL REPORTS — 1986/87

The purpose of the Departmental Report is to provide Heads of Department with an opportunity to give a brief but constructive appraisal of the work of the Department during 1986/87 and to outline ways in which they feel their department could work even more effectively to the benefit of the pupils. Ideas may have implications for the timetable, members of the department and resources. These will be the subject of discussion with senior management during October/November but colleagues can be assured that, as long as they are within the general ethos and aims of the school, all that is possible will be done to support these endeavours. However, it must be remembered that, in the end, we have to work within the resources provided and it is for each head of department to optimize the use of these resources. We should be always seeking to raise the expectation of our colleagues and to ensure, whenever possible, job satisfaction is improved.

Comments in the report will be used in the Planning Programme for 1988/89 and should cover the following sections:

(a) Resources: Staff — contribution of, utilization of, job descriptions. (Acknowledgement should be given to the positive contribution which individual staff have made to the department and school in general. This should be discussed with members of staff concerned.)

                     Accommodation — Utilization of ....

                     Equipment — Utilization of, health of stock, stock control ....

       Time allocation on the timetable — Strength and weaknesses as it related to the department in 1986/87.

(b)   Subject Organization   —   Subject organization for the various age and ability groups making special emphasis of any new development in 1986/87.

(c)   Curriculum policy and approach —   In this section one should include an analysis of examination results over the past five years.
Please tabulate statistics in the format used in 'Information to Parents' booklet.

(d)   Special events during the school year 1986/87 within or involving the department.

(e)   Comments and recommendations for department resulting from experiences in 1986/87.

(f)   Your key departmental objectives (goals) for 1987/88 including financial and resource implications. These should be compiled taking into account those produced for 1986/87.

(g)   In what area of work during the last year do you feel the department has been
    (i)   most successful?
    (ii) least successful?

(h)   Are there any constraints on the work of the department? How might they be removed?

(i)   What training/experience would be of particular value to you and your colleagues in the department at this time in assisting with your work/the development of your careers?

These notes are only meant as a guide and the topics mentioned are in no way exhaustive.

IMPORTANT (a)-(d) should be mainly factual. Subjective comment can be included in (e)-(i).

If you require any further information, please do not hesitate to let me know.

Thank you for your cooperation.

Stanley Goodchild

The basic task was to say whether they had achieved their goals during the previous year and what they were hoping to do in the future. These reports proved to be very important because no money is issued to any department as a matter of right. Each report is discussed within an individual interview with the appropriate deputy head and an action plan results. This is presented to the Head and the plan is activated. It also provides evidence which can be used in presenting departmental bids for support. All departments are required to make bids under three headings, namely 'essential', 'highly desirable', and 'desirable'. If a department is unable to justify expenditure then the money is not released for the department (except to satisfy the basic requirements of stationery, exercise books etc.) If a department puts forward an imaginative scheme to develop the subject, however, then the money would be provided even if it amounts to well over £50,000. Over the last five years this has meant that departments have developed at very different rates. In the early days the departments with the ideas got the money and the rate of progress in those areas was therefore far greater. Although it was not done for this reason it did create peer pressure and it meant that departments who were slow in coming forward with ideas were forced to think again. Goochild made it clear that, should there be any criticism about the lack of resources within a department, the onus would be fairly and squarely on the head of the department (rather than the Head). While, in the early days, there was little delegation and the Head's name was used as the reason for doing things, this has progressively not been the case and greater devolution of responsibilities has been encouraged.

Ringing the Changes

In addition to bringing new people into the school it was important that those members of staff who had been at Garth for a long time and had done a good job, had the opportunity to accept new challenges. Colleagues were given, therefore, the opportunity of considering a new set of responsibilities. An example of this was a 'seven staff move' — made in September 1987. It was as follows:

The person who had set up the careers service and done such an extremely good job became the Assistant Head of Sixth Form; the Assistant Head of Sixth Form moved to become Head of Art; the Head of Art moved to assist the new careers person and also had responsibility for general displays around the school and one of the Heads of Year moved to be Head of Careers. At the same time, one of the Chairman of Faculty moved into the Head of Year slot. This meant that there were now only three Chairmen of Faculty instead of four and these were made Directors of Study — to assist the Deputy Heads in their responsibilities. The whole structure of the school is established on the understanding that all members of staff are trained for the next move; the Directors of Study, therefore, are trainee Deputy Heads, whereas the Deputy Heads are trainee Heads, etc.

Staff Development

Staff development is extremely important in the school and staff are encouraged to spend a period of time on attachment to local industry. Local industrialists have also run school-based in-service training and a system has been devised whereby many companies make available one or two places for staff of Garth Hill to attend business conferences and training sessions. This has proved to be a very welcome offer as it has enabled staff to attend courses which would normally be well out of the Local Authority's price bracket.

The latest in-service training project at Garth Hill is to train treachers in making the most of the latest technology that is available in the school for their specific use. To enable the school to do this, money has been given under the government's Grant Related In-service Training (GRIST) proposals, thus allowing teachers to spend a day in 3M, a local company, for in-house training. Not only do they learn new skills but also have the experience of working in a business environment. Other staff members have received training within the school by an industrialist.

Changes in the Structure

Reviewing the curriculum

The latest phase of the school's five-year development programme is a curriculum review in which a new set of aims is being devised.

New Aims relating to Curriculum Review (1987)

1 to establish, and constantly to review, our approach to students' learning so as to create an educational atmosphere in which each student can achieve the highest level of her, or his, ability;
2 to provide each student with a challenging programme in which each subject area, while valued in its own right, will also form one element of a coherent balanced curriculum;
3 to relate all the experiences and opportunities provided by the school to the preparation of students for employment, continuing education, responsible citizenship and the enjoyment and satisfaction of a full life;
4 throughout the curriculum, to highlight the applications of technology to the teaching situation;
5 to build the 'pastoral curriculum' on the natural care and concern of parents for their children, and to develop an effective partnership between the teachers and the parents aimed at ensuring that each individual student develops her/his talents to the full;
6 to ensure that local business interests and those of the community at large are thoroughly involved in keeping the curriculum up to date and relevant to the students' aspirations and the demands of working in an adult life.

Now that the school has been restructured, each aim, although it has a cross-curricular dimension, is mainly associated with one particular section of the school, i.e. aim 1 deals with the management role of the school by the senior management team; aim 2 is mainly concerned with departmental curriculum development; aim 3 is to do with careers education and guidance and social and personal education; aim 4 is the use of technology across the curriculum, thus relating to all departments; aim 5 is concerned with the pastoral side of the school, specifically the role of the form tutor; and aim 6 is to do with the school's links with local industry and commerce. During the autumn term (1987) the structure was agreed and departments and other sections of the school are now involved in implementing the strategy.

Over the last five years all subject areas have been given an initial scan to see whether their inclusion in the curriculum can be justified. In the sixth form, as well as offering 'A' level courses, GCE courses, CPVE and TVEI courses, a series of business modules have been introduced. Each of these modules has proved to be very attractive to students and also very practical. They include such areas as word-processing, business French, and technology with business. Each of these courses leads to a national qualification.

Over the last five years, the staff at Garth Hill have been involved in two major 'rethinks' of direction, both centred on staff conferences. The first was held on Monday 28 February 1983, and was entitled 'Curriculum Review — The Starting Gate'. Each member of staff was given a set of background papers which contained the following introduction presented by Stanley Goodchild (see over). Also included was a statement of the aims of the conference:

STATEMENT OF AIMS OF CONFERENCE
The conference will enable staff:

— to exchange information between faculties and departments about the current curriculum at Garth Hill School, for example with regard to syllabuses and schemes of work currently being used, methods, resources, aims and objectives, recent developments and initiatives, hopes and intentions for the future.

— to review the current curriculum in relation to the statement of general school aims contained in the school handbook.

— to propose specific new developments which would be worth considering in greater detail in the future, for example by existing working parties and committees, or by a working party especially convened for this purpose.

— to work towards agreement on the general form and use of the written statements about schemes of work which are to be drawn up by each department during the next few months.

The programme contained five elements:

(i) a welcome session during which the aims and format of the conference were clarified;

(ii) a small group session to review recent and current work;

(iii)   case studies from other schools;

(iv)   more group work to outline directions and proposals;

 (v)   final session; discussion of the next steps.

In the booklet handed to all staff members were the following 'thoughts' papers (to inform their discussion), culled from various sources:

- Aims of Garth Hill School — as contained in the brochure for prospective parents.
- Resistance to change.
- Organizational health.
- Some basic beliefs which underpin the working party system.
- What responsibility does the remedial department have to those subjects from which it withdraws pupils?
- 'Inter-departmental liaison'.
- The main findings of *Fifteen Thousand Hours*.
- The relationship between social education and the work of individual developments.
- 'All departments have a responsibility to the Teaching of English'.

Examples of these papers along with the introduction, are included below.

Introduction to Staff Conference 'The Curriculum Review'

It is hoped that this, our first staff conference will prove to be of benefit to all those taking part, and that from it will come an abundance of ideas for the future development of the school. Garth Hill will only develop from strength to strength if we, the staff, work together as a team. Whenever the staff of a school sits down to discuss aspects of school life or the curriculum there is a real danger that the results will damage the confidence of some staff and destroy relationships between others. The inevitable frustrations of the classroom take the centre of the stage and anger and anxiety can become dominant emotions. Junior staff complain of lack of support of senior staff; senior staff criticize the ineffectiveness of junior ones. I am most anxious that our afternoon together should not be wasted in this way and I should like to set the tone by saying that I believe that all the teaching staff at Garth Hill School work hard according to their abilities to achieve what are largely common aims. We are not entirely successful and we never will be, but that is a healthy state of affairs. The object of our discussion is to improve our knowledge of each other's views and needs so that we can support each other more effectively, and if necessary to make changes in our practices so that we can have more influence over children's work programmes, attitudes and behaviour.

I should like to take this opportunity of thanking Robin Richardson (Berkshire Education Advisory Service) for the major part he has played in the planning and organization of the afternoon. His help has been most valuable and greatly appreciated. Our thanks also go to my two headteacher colleagues from Oxfordshire, Mr. John and Mr. Grubb, who although extremely busy have agreed to join us for the afternoon to share some of their experiences in their own schools and to answer questions. We are also pleased to have with us Fred Ranson, the School's Advisory Officer. Thanks also to Mrs. King and her staff for what, I am sure, will prove to be a most enjoyable afternoon tea.

Attached to the programme are a number of discussion papers from various sources which I hope will help us in our thinking over the next few months. They are meant only as background reading and not necessarily indicating topics to be discussed. It must be stressed that the afternoon is just the beginning of a long process when it is hoped that each of us will play our part in reviewing some aspects of the total curriculum. I am sure that if we approach the discussion in a positive way we shall have a profitable and rewarding afternoon and that we shall achieve some of the improvements that we all hope for in the months that follow. Remember, a healthy organization is one which recognizes that there is always room for improvement.

Headmaster

ORGANIZATIONAL HEALTH

A secondary school exhibiting organizational health is one in which:

1   All members of staff know and work towards agreed objectives, both social and educational, using agreed plans.
2   All decisions relating to school matters are made by or near the sources of information relevant to the problem regardless of position in the school hierarchy.
3   The principal, deputy principal and heads of department accept and recognize their responsibilities for the growth and development of their subordinates and also for the creation of team-spirit, both within the school as a whole and within each department.
4   Communication throughout the school is relatively open and trusting. Information travels in all directions, not simply from the Principal's study downwards. Teachers are not afraid to speak their minds. There is freedom from threat and coercion both physical and psychological.
5   There is a great deal of discussion and argument amongst the staff directed at tasks or problem solving: there is relatively little energy wasted in clashing over interpersonal difficulties.
6   There is a management ethos (operating from the Principal's office but accepted and recognised by all) of helping each person in the

school (pupils' included) to maintain his integrity and uniqueness as a person while at the same time being integrated fully as a member of a team.

7   There is a built-in provision for self criticism via weekly staff meetings or team meetings, or by people outside the school as resources and as a means of feedback to enable groups and individuals to learn from their own experiences.

8   There is a continuous re-examination of the bureaucracy to ensure that the school does not become a prisoner of its procedures.

'ALL DEPARTMENTS HAVE A RESPONSIBILITY TO THE TEACHING OF ENGLISH'

'If reading comprehension is to be significantly improved then every subject teacher in a secondary school must assume responsibility for developing all those skills that are needed by his pupils to read intelligently the material he presents to them. Reading should receive increasing attention from all teachers at each successive stage of education.'

'Specialist teachers too often believe that children need only be fluent readers to cope with their subject.'

'Pupils, unable to read selectively and to summarise the information cannot possibly cope with project work except to copy verbatim from the books they are consulting.'

'Writing should come out of normal classroom activities and not from artificial stimuli.'

'Subject teachers, instead of just complaining to English colleagues about spelling, should co-operate in implementing an agreed policy of language across the curriculum.'

'All secondary schools should have a policy for the development of language across the curriculum.'

THE ABOVE ARE FROM 'THE BULLOCK REPORT'

A summary specifically of Chapter 12 of the Bullock Report

Before a child is 5 he has made more rapid progress that he will make in any other five-year period in the fields of learning about his environment and of language, and the two processes are completely interdependent. What is advocated is that this interdependence should be maintained.

To achieve this we must convince the teacher of history or of science, for example that he has to understand the process by which his pupils take possession of the historical or scientific information that is offered them; and that such an understanding involves his paying particular attention to the part language plays in learning.

Perhaps in a rather simplistic way we can see this interdependence as being easily maintained in a junior school where a teacher is responsible across subject boundaries — in a secondary school the specialized curriculum makes it far more difficult.

'In general, a curriculum subject, philosophically speaking, is a distinctive mode of analysis. While many teachers recognise that their aim is to initiate a student in a particular mode of analysis, they rarely recognise the linguistic implications of doing so. They do not recognise, in short, that the mental processes they seek to foster are the outcome of a development that originates in speech.'

The importance of expressive pupil talk is not recognised in many subject areas. Similarly subject demand is for transactional writing rather than for expressive writing (perhaps the most natural form of communication).

In reading 'Subject teachers need to be aware of the processes involved, able to provide the variety of reading material that is appropriate, and willing to see it as their responsibility to help the pupils meet the reading demands of their subject.'

Subject teachers should also be ready to help with the modes of recording which their individual subject requires.

The teacher must be conscious of his own use of language.

FOOD FOR THOUGHT?

'as children talk or write . . . in a mathematics lesson, or in the playground when they are sorting out the rules of a game of marbles, they are doing mathematics. It is not just that language is used in mathematics: rather it is that the language that is used is the mathematics.'

. . . 'English and maths which seem to us to be the key subjects. We cannot help but be disturbed, both by the mediocre standards of spoken and written English among children leaving our schools, and by the low standards in the fields of mathematics which are (so it seems to us) wrongly accepted as inevitable for far too many pupils.'

(PREFACE 15-18 REPORT OF THE CENTRAL ADVISORY COUNCIL FOR EDUCATION.)

Taken together, these papers indicated a 'core' agenda. The emphasis was on the strengthening of the school as an organization; and, given this orientation in terms of organizational cohesion, various interrelated themes emerged:

- interdepartmental liaison, information exchange and collaboration;
- the nature of resistance to change in organizations;

- broad-based (whole staff) involvement in change initiatives;
- the school's organizational health (i.e. effectiveness);
- the staff as the school's major resource;
- the need for team-building;
- cross-curricular developments;
- the acknowledgement of collective responsibilities, for example,
  — social education
  — skills associated with 'English' and 'maths'
  — supportive education
- the affective power of the school as a social organization;
- the importance of whole staff/whole school review for developing the whole curiculum;
- the identification of development needs and priorities;
- the articulation of an action plan;
- implementation of the changes (as identified) within the department's structure;
- moving forward from the 'starting gate', across and within departments.

It has to be acknowledged, of course, that this emphasis on whole staff review and development work occurred alongside more individualistic, innovative, entrepreneurial endeavour within the school. Indeed, the individualistic and the (inter-staff) collaborative approaches can both be seen as reactions against the 'boxed', compartmentalized nature of the departmental structure. Peter Holly (in Reid, Hopkins and Holly, 1987) has talked about the characteristics of 'The Learning School'. He has argued that the learning school has four basic, inter-related features:

- the aim to facilitate and maximize the learning of all the pupils;
- the acceptance of the importance of the continuing learning of individual teachers and, therefore, their professional development;
- the elevation of teachers learning together — in collaboration, i.e. staff development — for the development of their school;
- the understanding that the Learning School has to 'learn its way forward'; it has to be adaptive, responsive, and flexible, yet dynamic and pro-active.

In 1983, Garth Hill was striving to become the learning school. This first conference must be placed in context. During Stanley Goodchild's first year at Garth Hill it was important that the views of teachers were known and, in addition to the individual staff interviews, this one-day conference was a good vehicle for ascertaining their ideas and opinions. Consequently the most important aspect of that day was the fact that staff were asked to write down the things which they felt needed attention and the responses were then collated. The aim was to implement as many as possible of the staff's suggestions which were in line with the overall policy of the school — this helped to improve the organization and enable staff to feel that they had views to which the management of school was prepared to listen. The ideas presented, as shown below, were very varied. Some were concerned with individual aspirations and those of departments; others were concerned with the general health of the school. Some were a statement of approval or disapproval of what was happening in the school at the time. Taken together, they formed a very comprehensive list. Some of the ideas constituted minor changes; others proved more fundamental, for example a 'staff briefing' was initiated which involves the holding of a staff meeting before school for ten minutes twice a week; staff have an opportunity to express any concerns they have about pupils or give any notices which they feel are appropriate for other staff to hear.

Another example of a change originating in the list was the 'CDT' circus in which, during the first three years, pupils of all abilities received the same allocation of time for a rotating programme of experiences in craft, design and technology — including home economics. In terms of provision for less able pupils, the staff have still not found the ideal solution. The 'extra English' and 'extra mathematics' have disappeared and *parallel teaching* has been introduced as a pilot scheme enabling pupils with learning difficulties to spend some time within the mainstream curriculum, but receive in-classroom support provided by a second teacher.

CONFIDENTIAL TO ALL STAFF
SRG/BT   14 March 1983

Staff Conference
Curriculum Review — Monday 28 February 1983

Attached please find a copy of a list of suggestions put forward by colleagues at the end of the Conference.

May I take this opportunity of thanking you for your contributions. I feel that with very few exceptions they were ideas which complement the general direction in which the school is moving and I hope that over the new few months many of the ideas will be implemented. I must give a word of caution to those who expect instant action. It is anticipated that many of the suggestions will be incorporated as various aspects of the school organization and curriculum are reviewed. It is very clear from the responses that urgent attention needs to be given to the development of a Special Needs Department and this I think appears to be the highest priority.

I was very pleased with the way colleagues entered into the spirit of the afternoon and I feel that the conclusions were extremely positive. A sincere thank you to everyone concerned.

CONFIDENTIAL

CURRICULUM DEVELOPMENT

1   Departments to look critically at their aims and objectives and the content/structure of their syllabuses to meet the changing demands/values of society.

2   More planning to coordinate out of school music and drama/dance activities. More coordination with craft departments about provision of sets and costumes for productions.

3   Revision of faculty groupings (Mr John's ideas) — subjects in faculty to be more compatible.

4   Along with departmental reviews look at the possibility of self-assessment and evaluation schemes.

5   Provision for leisure education, for example, gardening, outdoor activities, fishing, nature trails, local hiking involving local history, country code, agriculture etc. Lectures by visiting speakers on various hobbies and leisure pursuits.

6   Formation of Performing Arts Faculty incorporating Art, Drama, Music and Dance.

7   I'd like to see mathematics as a wider subject rather than just an examination subject — How? I'm not sure.

8   Change to be made in pupils' method of selecting options.

9   I especially want to see a goal to aim for, for all less able language pupils — whether it be a proficiency certificate or Mode 3 CSE, which would hopefully result in all pupils carrying on their language studies to a level suited to their ability.

10 Some external examination syllabuses are inhibiting — can we look around for different boards, which relate more to children's present day needs?

11 Vocational education across the school.

12 Encouragement should be more widely given for quiet pursuits.

13 Have provision for 'O' level candidates to do craft — otherwise they may become stale.

14 Requirement for all 'O' level and CSE candidates to take at least one craft or practical subject, i.e. art, woodwork, TD, PE, metalwork, building studies, pottery, design, parentcraft, dress, home economics.

15 Setting up of a curriculum working party.

16 *Curriculum interrelationships* — for example, graphs to be taught in Maths by the time they are needed in science.

17 Careful and cautious appraisal and consideration of changes which will improve the opportunities offered to the children so that they are each encouraged to realize and strive towards their full potential.

18 Intensive language course?

19 Exchange of classes with school abroad.

20 Move away from SMP maths to a more 'mixed' syllabus *OR* early 'O' level entry in maths so that the transition from SMP to traditional 'A' level pure could be smoother. It is wrong that so much time is spent teaching basic algebra to sixth year students.

21 Return to 'A' level pure and 'A' level applied as two subjects.

22 Reintroduction of Latin — aid to vocabulary development and as a 'discipline'.

23 Reintroduction of European studies onto CSE curriculum.

24 To introduce a working party to look at curriculum on the same basis as Wheatley Park.

25 Development of business studies orientated courses in years 4-5 to be offered as options at end of year 3.

26 Modern languages within the curriculum.

27 Secondary/primary school liaison.

28 As regards the top ability groups it might be advisable to study all syllabuses on offer and to choose the most appropriate to this day and age. This applies obviously to the top 20 per cent — 'O' and 'A' level courses. This study of courses and syllabuses on offer might also be used for lower ability groups, e.g. Use of Chamber of Commerce.

29 Leisure afternoon/double lesson — extra curricular activities.

30 No loss of minority subjects.

31 Correct courses for CSE/'O' level pupils.

32 Not all our non-'O' level pupils should follow CSE.

33 I would like to see a permanent curriculum Review Body composed from all aspects of the subject range, with neither the Head nor Deputies as chair people, to make recommendations to the School Body for amendment, approval and implementation, leading to a reworking of the timetable on a fairer basis to reflect the curriculum as it should be.

34 Consider the teachers' desires as to what they teach.

35 Rationalize lessons of a non-specific nature, i.e. handwriting, form periods, CHP, non-prepared extra English. Consider motivation and vocational training. Basic foundation courses to be revitalized.

36 A curriculum review body should be set up (perhaps comprising two departments plus Chairman of Faculty) to look at board areas of inclusion in the curriculum. A paper from this should be returned to faculties/departments for discussion, then back to the review body. When a broad consensus has been reached — faculties and departments consider what input might be made by them. At this stage the division of the day and apportioning of time and subjects might be reconsidered. I think that open dialogue is of extreme importance.

37 Leisure pursuits must be catered for more fully by all abilities. Sailing, climbing, drawing and painting, car maintenance, home maintenance, camping etc., etc. A lot of children leaving will probably have in the future a reduced working week or have no job at all. It is important they have additional interests.

38 Provision to be made for leisure activities for children who may

not get a job when leaving school, for example, fishing, gardening, have a school greenhouse run by children. To incorporate this, the number of 'padded' lessons could be reduced, i.e. extra maths.

39 All subjects need injections of what non-school-world has to say about our priorities and efficiency.

40 How does the study of learning and methods in educational research get turned into knowledge and adaptions among teachers?

41 That change occurs to place more emphasis on basic skills development across the curriculum for the individual pupil. Further, that this basic skill development be linked to diagnostic testing and be unambiguously placed under the direction of an individual and/or a department.

42 Development of a specialist Careers and Guidance Department under the management of a senior member of staff.

43 More thought given to subjects taken by girls. Why do so few take science/maths/crafts?

SPECIAL NEEDS (REMEDIAL/GIFTED)

1 The philosophy of remedial work in our school. Its practical application as regards content and teaching methods. To construct a suitable structure for remedial work. More discussion on remedial teaching materials.

2 We need a properly staffed and funded Remedial Unit. We have suffered from 'ad hoc' timetable filler staffing for years. How many staff at present are proper remedial-trained staff?

3 Remedial teaching in all subjects and do we know what difficulties other people have to face. Review handwriting.

4 Equal provision for 'high fliers' as for remedials.

5 Structured remedial teaching in science, involving possible withdrawal of pupils from lesson. This will involve more coordination between English department and other departments.

6 Concern for 'high fliers' as well as remedials.

7 Development of a more meaningful timetable/curriculum for remedial classes.

8 Gifted children, provision for, identification of, etc.

9 A *real* remedial programme which *actually* tests, assesses, extracts, withdrawals etc.

10 Provision of professional consultations regarding remedial teaching approaches across the curriculum.

11 Development of *spoken* and *written* skills across the curriculum.

12 More help with remedial classes, for example, dealing with reading, writing difficulties, etc.

13 Some provision made for gifted children.

14 Gifted children at least ought to have the same provision as remedial.
15 There is a lack of analysis of and provision for the remedial needs of children in mixed ability classes. Similarly for children of special abilities.
16 Provision for pupils with special needs in *all* years of school.
17 Explore possibilities of 'extraction' from classes as a remedial technique.
18 Train someone in *true* remedial techniques — diagnosis/treatment for the above.
19 Remedial mathematics required. I would like to see more children being considered for going 'up' or 'down' during their first two school years. Too frequently a number of pupils are "put up" at the beginning of the third year who are then far behind the rest of their set.
20 Is 'extra maths' useful or is it to fill in the timetable of Lower School pupils?

*(see below)

TIMETABLE

1 Fewer teachers in contact with first years — teachers voluntarily teaching an extra subject within their interests.
2 Timetable constructed from points of views of *aims* first — not means.
3 Each department to have one period when *all* members free to discuss and plan department business.
4 'Parentcraft' should be taught to all pupils (boys and girls) during their time in secondary school.
5 The pattern of free time during the week can make a difference to one's ability to cope.
6 A closer look at the timetable, its influence on the curriculum and vice versa.
7 Time allocated for head of department role to be a priority.
8 Look at the role of the form teacher and the influence of the form teacher on the group.
9 Look at *exactly* what certain pupils are involved in during a week — what is actually hapening to them. Similarly for individual teachers — IMPORTANCE OF CONTACT RATIO.
10 Revise shape of timetable if possible so as to allow greater lengths of time p.m. for music, art, matches, etc., and other cultural and leisure activities.
11 Review of timetable needed with particular attention to continuing a balanced curriculum in the fourth and fifth year. This might mean reducing the options to include a greater core, plus alternatives to CSE.

12 Less teaching periods — say four a day to enable teachers to thoroughly plan lessons, set up equipment, mark work and be fresh to give their best.

13 Review of time (number of periods), when and how arranged for:
(a) Home Economics
(b) Nutrition and Cookery
(c) Parentcraft

14 I would like to see a block of time given to each year for their 'Games' sessions. This would be for the *whole* year and would make team practices and training far easier, especially as many of our lunch-times are now taken up with house matches, and I would rather maintain fixtures after school than substitute in practices. The individual PE lessons need not be grouped with the 'Games' session.

15 Have longer lessons but no double lessons. This would incorporate most of the subjects when single lessons are offered. Lower ability children find it difficult to concentrate on double lessons. Have a seven-period day with longer lunch hour.

16 Restructuring of the timetable. The present eight-period day is rather onerous both to pupils and staff. The last part of the day could be timetabled for leisure and cultural pursuits or optional subjects.

17 The teaching day be examined with respect to length of periods (all 45 minutes — seven per day?) and duration of day.

18 Examine possibilities of alternative timetable — 6 — 10 day etc.

19 Revision of timetable.

20 Pastoral time must be given on the timetable at the most appropriate time of the day and specific time for EWO, social services contact.

21 Changes in timetable. More consultation between subject teachers and those in charge of timetable regarding the actual time allocations for that particular subject.

22 The size of classes in 'O' level sets is often highly disproportionate — for example, English and maths sets up to 32, and languages for example very low. The resultant work load is not obvious on paper! After an eight-period day, such effects as marking thirty-two pieces of work become severe.

23 What about one double lesson of leisure activities. Take children off TT.

24 More thought given to TT and options.

25 More pupils to take crafts (use bright pupils).

26 'Continental Day' — Registration/Assembly   9.00-9.15
Period 1   9.15-9.50
Period 2   9.50-10.30
Break

Period 3	11.00-11.40
Period 4	11.40-12.20
Lunch	
Registration	1.00-1.15

Inter-school and community activities.   1.15-3.30
House matches, Duke of Edinburgh award,
extra languages, work experience, fieldwork,
cultural.

27 Remedial specialist appointed for years 3-5.
28 Teachers should not be asked to teach subjects that they do not want to.
29 If setting or banding, then no member of staff should be asked to teach more than one lower group unless he specifically asks to.
30 If setting or banding, each teacher gets one top set for every bottom set.
31 If time is set aside for an activity it should be carried out, not cancelled (e.g. assemblies, house matches carrying on into form period, lessons etc.).
32 Compulsory oral tests in every year — *timetabled*.
33 Extension of common core and reduction of options.
34 Technology must be made available for all on the timetable, from the lowest ability to highest qualified sixth-former.
35 A provision be made for a 'rural studies' style of course for years 4 and 5 — lower ability pupils.
36 What about one double lesson of leisure activities? Take children off TT.
37 More thought given to timetable and options.
38 More pupils to take crafts (i.e. *bright* pupils).
39 Uneconomical size of classes to be reviewed.

MANAGEMENT *and* COMMUNICATION

1 Hierarchical structure simplified.
2 More discussion, fewer *fait accomplis,* on issues of general concern.
3 List of all suggestions on staff notice board, for example:

Suggestion	Action (if any)	Date
1. ????????????	Instituted	5 May 1984
2. etc.	„	

4 Every teacher to produce a summary of the work they are doing and their method of teaching and a typical report of a lesson they take. To be done by a questionnaire or by own devices (limited format) and a copy of all given to each member of staff.
5 Not a pyramidal hierarchy of management — some really good ideas come from scale 1 teachers.
6 Review all admin procedures with a view to giving staff more time for conversation, debate and forward planning.

7   A working party should be set up to report on how communications can be improved within the school, particularly with regard to the decision-making proposal.

8   Thought should be given to the amount of time and pressure demanded by certain tasks, in addition to the everyday demands of the profession.

9   How do we ensure that we have sufficient time in which to *do* and *prepare for* our basic (and most important) role of teaching?

10   The possibility of a horizontal 'power' structure as opposed to the pyramid situation where everyone knows what everyone else is attempting.

11   Emphasis should be placed upon the communication of developments to all members of the staff so that the picture is not one of only those in the related working parties, SMT etc. having a clear idea of the situation

DEPARTMENTAL AND SCHOOL LIAISON

1   Inter-departmental meetings (perhaps of curriculum day groups) to consider changes.

2   Some form of interdepartmental liaison should be set up to discuss relevant curriculum matters such as overlap between subjects etc.

3   Greater liaison between departments, i.e. possibilities for getting to know function/what they actually do.

4   Relationship between subject/pastoral staff — there frequently seems to be a gap.

5   Possibilities for further discussions of this kind in that junior staff tend to be ill-informed and rarely — if ever — have the opportunity to make themselves heard — working towards greater democracy.

6   Specific opportunities should be given for departments to discuss their curriculum development, prior to a wider discussion on the same theme amongst the *whole* staff.

7   Greater liaison between departments, i.e. possibilities for getting to know function/what they actually do.

8   Better communication — especially to heads of department.

9   Communication between departments to standardize common aspects, for example, units, stages of development — graph construction.

10   For the head to work closely for a period with each department, to make proposals and support change for the better as a result of this newly gained knowledge. (As carried out in one of the case studies.)

11   Examine possibility of greater interdiscipline, cooperation/uniformity.

12   Headmaster to regularly join a department for a complete day(s)

and, at end of such period, meet and discuss with department.

13   Better interdepartmental understanding of each others needs and problems.

14   How can sideways communication between departments be vigorously encouraged?

15   Primary school contacts should be developed further.

16   I would like to see more departments being given the opportunity to visit other schools — to see how departments in other schools are organised, to see a fresh approach to the subject and to view resources.

17   More time to be available for a group of teachers (teaching the same subject) to visit other schools together to discover/discuss other methods, details of syllabus, etc.

STAFF DEVELOPMENT

1   Desperate need for language staff to be offered short courses or secondment to a foreign country. This increases stimulation of individual and enthusiasm for subject.

2   Need for more secondments.

3   More in-service training for staff regarding:
   (a)   own subject matter;
   (b)   pastoral care.

4   More time, less irrelevant pressure — the opportunity to do better what one is doing in teaching terms.

5   Look at roles of staff. Clear definition — job specifications needed.

DISCIPLINE and PASTORAL (specification)

1   *Time:* for YGAs. There is never time to plan ahead, to see the children privately.

2   Proposal for appointment of a Special Needs coordinator to recognize and run a 'throughout the school and throughout the curriculum' department for the least able children.

3   There are too many conflicting standards exemplified with present lunch-time systems to complete a socially acceptable moral standard throughout the school.

4   Pupils (boys and girls) *should* provide their own protective clothing, that is aprons or overalls for all practical lessons.

5   Greater control and standardisation relating to standards of presentation, etc.

6   An appraisal of tutorial time. Should it be structured, should it be put aside for remedial teaching/teaching for gifted pupils.

7   *Vertical Tutor Groups* i.e. forms containing a range of pupils in different years rather than just one age group.

SIXTH FORM and SIXTH YEAR (specification)
1 Sixth form, sixth year courses.
2 Must we accept all pupils who wish (or whose parents wish) them to return to school? We have a number of undesirable sixth form pupils wandering around the school misbehaving . . .
3 Complete revamp of non-'A' level sixth form curriculum.

RESOURCES (specification)
1 Resource needs. Help to teachers in the preparation of resources is far too limited for adequate teaching of many subjects. Non-teaching time is insufficient for administrative catch-up, let alone preparation and marking.
2 Ancillary help in HE rooms for cleaning cookers, fridges, etc., also for laundry — to give teachers more time for teaching commitments.
3 Some ancillary help (voluntary — parents) to help in departments with filing, etc., to give teachers more time (also help with duplicating).
4 In the end we have to stand up in front of a group of children and take a lesson, then another lesson and so on. How we do this depends on the time we have, facilities available and the structure of the day. I hope at some time we can come to some decisions which are *specific* to this.
5 Blinds or curtains (better) for Mathematics Department so that OAP and other technical resources can be used for mathematics. So far, it's strictly chalk and talk.

*Special Needs
21 Special needs coordination.
22 What are we to do with our bright pupils, and what are we going to do with our 'please let me leave school' pupils?

MISCELLANEOUS
1 *TIME* is needed to discuss various school activities, preferably before and after the event.
2 Attempt to produce a list of general priorities for staff.
SRG/JLL
MARCH 1983.

The second staff conference — given the title 'Curriculum Review: The Second Phase' — was held on Monday 8 February 1988. It was exactly five years on and the themes remained much the same. While the context had changed somewhat — 'Baker Days' had arrived and the school now had an INSET Committee to organize the staff deliberations — the talk was still of a 'healthy organization' which was 'one that recognizes that there is always room for improvement'. If anything, however, the work was now more focused. The aims of the school had been redrawn and unpacked for the staff (as exemplar material) and the staff were encouraged to come up with performance criteria with which to judge success (or failure). Two new emphases have appeared in the discussion:

- the centrality of the learning process in the classroom — the effective curriculum;
- the importance of evaluation and assessment in the investigation of various aspects of the school, including the quality of teaching and the effectiveness of learning outcomes.

Undoubtedly, exploration of these linked dimensions will be the shape of Garth Hill's future for some time to come.

10   Looking Ahead

Strengthening the Curriculum

The school's high profile has not only acted as an incentive for industry to invest in Garth Hill, but also helped when recruiting new staff. For example, in 1986, the school was able to recruit a Head of Modern Languages of very high calibre. Before her arrival, modern languages in the school for a multitude of reasons, was not a shining success story. To remedy the situation, the school had just introduced modern languages for pupils of all abilities starting in year 1; this was not well received either by staff or pupils. Within a year of the start of the new Head of Department, the popularity of her subject had grown to such an extent, and there were so many students wishing to study either French or German (or both), that the school has had to solve some major timetabling problems. The subject is now very popular and highlights the most important resource of any school — the quality of the staff. Through her own vision and initiative, she has created a turn-around in the fortunes of her department very similar to the way the school has changed round over recent years. Undoubtedly, this process of strengthening the curriculum by attending to its constituent parts will be extended in the years to come. Certainly, after five years, Stanley Goodchild's job at Garth Hill is not yet complete, but the young people attending the school, their parents and the community that supports it, generally feel that Garth Hill is an integral part of their lives. The pupils are encouraged to have high expectations of their achievements and therefore achieve far more; however, at the same time, they are realistic in terms of what they are able to achieve. They have not only developed academic but also social skills. Teachers who work at Garth Hill School are under tremendous pressure because they are expected to realise these high expectations. Garth Hill, however, is probably the best resourced school in the country. Yet it is important to attract more resources, never to be complacent and to always seek to improve standards throughout the school.

When the latest phase of the school's development began in 1982, it was very dependent on the Headteacher. This is no longer the case in 1988. The mould is set and the school is very much in the hands of a local partnership involving the staff, governors and parents. The Head believes that the new Garth Hill School has come of age. He started by having to be somewhat authoritative and now the school is controlled, on a daily basis, by the team of the senior management. The local education authority has felt involved in the development of Garth Hill School and whenever there has been one of the six monthly 'UK firsts', not only have the education officers been invited to the school but also the County Council members. It has been very important to invite them to share in the success story, as it has helped in gaining their continuing support.

The school is now involved in Local Financial Management (LFM) and has recently appointed a Bursar and Office Manager. The newly-appointed officer works closely with the Business Manager in ensuring that the resources of the school are maximized, both in matters relating to the school day and when they are not being required by the pupils of the school.

More widely, Garth Hill now has friends from all over the world. In order to maintain the high level of involvement of industry and commerce, the school has needed to keep a very high profile and has received many visitors — up to ninety in any one week and this has added a tremendous burden upon the Head personally and also the staff in general. It has been necessary, however, and is a cost which has had to be paid. But the investment by the staff has paid rich dividends in terms of the goodwill and support of the friends of Garth Hill — and there are many of them.

Over the last six years, then, Stanley Goodchild has 'run a tight ship' at Garth Hill. In many ways he has been the school — especially in the eyes of those outside Garth Hill. But a school is so much more than one person no matter how powerful or influential that person seems to be. The school is now beginning to discover itself and the staff members have taken up the reins of change. Garth Hill is undoubtedly entering a new phase of its development and the person most affected by this transformation could well be the Head himself. He hopes that he will have to adjust to a situation in which 'his' ship is being sailed by the crew.

Garth Hill: The Technological School

No doubt Garth Hill will continue to build on its real strength — information technology, the use of this technology across the curriculum. Garth Hill is a unique school in so many ways, but, in curriculum terms, its uniqueness lies in its well-established emphasis on 'technology'. It is, and has been, a technological school. While its renowned work in information technology has grabbed the headlines, the school's record in all things 'technological' has been most impressive. It uses all the latest developments in subjects across the curriculum to the benefit of the pupils.

This is Garth Hill's distinctive quality, its main claim to fame. There is certainly something of the 'magnet school' in terms of Garth Hill's accentuation of the technological aspects of the curriculum. What has to be acknowledged, however, is that the emphasis placed on computing *across* the curriculum, and

The Language centre.
Photo courtesy of the *Nottingham Evening Post.*

the policy of *permeation,* have brought rich rewards. There is no corner of the school left untouched by its computer technology. All pupils leave the school, keyboard literate. Ample testimony to this fact is to be found in a comprehensive report produced for the school by its 'head of computer education across the curriculum'. Indeed, remarked one newspaper article, Garth Hill could become to computers what Kettering Grammar School has become to astronomy — the best in its field.

Moreover, as has been argued recently in the *Times Educational Supplement,* 25 September 1987, Garth Hill could well prove to be a forerunner of the city technology colleges being set up by the government:

> No — it is not a city technology college, even if its curriculum does seem to reflect the White Paper, *Better Schools,* and the Technical and Vocational Education Initiative better than most.
>
> But talk to industrialists in the Thames Valley and it will not be long before one of them will say 'Garth Hill Comprehensive *is* a CTC; Kenneth Baker pinched the idea.

Using information technology across the curriculum.
Photo courtesy of the *Nottingham Evening Post*.

The same article ended as follows:

> Garth Hill has won renown for its list of 'firsts' including a computer-based library and a high-tech office for business management training. The question now is how long will it be before the Education Secretary has the bright idea that all schools should employ a business consultant to make better, profit-motivated use of their premises?

Not surprisingly, such comments as these provide the school with some satisfaction and a sense of achievement. Where Garth Hill leads, many other schools are being encouraged to follow. Undoubtedly, the school is in the van of educational change and, whatever the distinctive emphasis chosen for a school, the Garth Hill experience demonstrates how an uncertain future of a school can be quickly transformed into one which holds great promise for both pupils and staff. When looking at a problem a favourite saying of Goodchild's is:

<blockquote>'When one door closes, two more open'.</blockquote>

Stop Press — The next UK first: By the time this book is published another innovation will be well on the way to completion.

Problem: The school needs an all-weather pitch complete with floodlights to serve both the pupils and the local community. Also temporary accommodation for new recruits to the staff of Garth and neighbouring schools.

Solution: A developer has agreed to invest in providing the all-weather pitch with floodlight and changing rooms together with a block of one and two bedroom flats for new recruits to the staff of Garth Hill.

Part II

An Enterprising School

Introduction

In part 2 the aim is to make sense of the Garth Hill Experience. The intention is to offer some theoretical reflections on the story in order to illuminate some of the key issues emerging from the practice. Part 2 is entitled 'An Enterprising School' and we would contend that an enterprising school has in itself (and contributes to in general) an *enterprise culture*. The various aspects of this enterprise culture will be investigated in turn in this section, not forgetting, however, that the power of the various aspects is realized when they are all present and working in combination. An enterprising school, therefore, has the following aspects, all of which are interrelated:

- enterprising and effective *leadership;*
- *a culture* (i.e. shared values and norms) which encompasses and promotes *the enterprise spirit;*
- *an orientation to the management of change* which is enterprising, i.e. innovative and entrepreneurial, and which emphasizes 'continuous improvement';
- an *enterprise curriculum,* the content of which reflects, extends and reinforces the enterprise culture and which is delivered in challenging and interesting ways;
- an enterprising attitude to the *local community* and the world outside its doors and a propensity to feed off and feed into *the enterprise culture.*

The diagram below represents these aspects of the enterprising school:
It is significant that when a report was published recently containing the views of HM Inspectorate, entitled *Education Observed 5. Good Behaviour and Discipline in Schools* (DES, 1987), the message was an unequivocal one. The report focused on the influence of the school as a community on pupils' behaviour and listed the factors which have been emerging from educational research as particularly important in this respect:

- the leadership of the headteacher;
- teachers' expectations of pupils and their work;
- the opportunities for achievement and success which stem from challenging teaching;

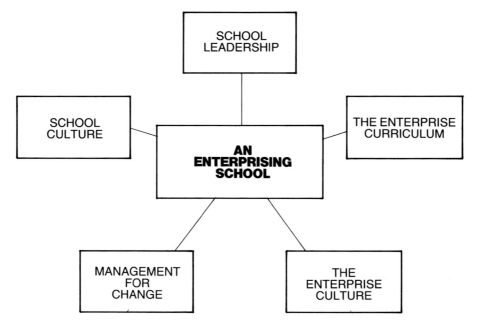

- the active involvement of pupils in their own learning and in the wider life of the school;
- a consensus on essential values and norms consistently applied;
- an awareness of the school as a social institution which influences groups and not merely individual pupils and teachers.

The report goes on to mention the factors 'most often associated with good behaviour', which are:

- good relationships — with mutual respect between teachers and pupils;
- teachers' high expectations of their pupils' academic and social abilities;
- curriculum and teaching methods well matched to pupils' needs;
- the nurturing of pupils' growing maturity and self-esteem.

These lists of factors, we would argue, are significant in three ways:

First, they are contributory factors not only to good behaviour and discipline, but also to the general well-being and 'organizational health' of schools. Conversely, indiscipline could be seen as a symptom of 'unhealthy' schooling. The extension of this same point is that, as Holt (1978) has argued, if the curriculum is 'right' (both in terms of the relevance and interest-rating of its content and the appropriateness of its delivery), then there is less need for elaborate pastoral systems which are designed to pick up the pieces. In short, an enterprising school with an effective and enterprising curriculum is effectively affective.

Second, we are struck by the similarities between our schema (constructed from the experience of Garth Hill) and the findings mentioned by HMI in their report

- the emphasis on the quality of leadership;
- the importance of shared values (culture) in terms of 'moulding' a social institution;
- the levels of expectation and challenge built into the curriculum;
- the relevance and worthwhileness of the curriculum for pupils who will be the adults of the twenty-first century;
- the importance of practical, active and experiential learning opportunities as promoted, for instance, within the Technical and Vocational Education Initiative (TVEI);
- the active involvement of a school in its community.

And, third, as HMI mention in the report, their lists of factors reflect the burgeoning collection of research on 'effective schools' or 'school effectiveness' — particularly as it exists in North America. Moreover, it is striking how much the various elements of this research are in agreement. Austin and Garber (1985) have written about exceptional or exemplary schools and their identification; Purkey and Smith (1985) have provided an excellent overview of the effective schools literature; Fullan (1985) has done likewise; and Clark *et al* (1984) have linked the research literatures on effective schools and school improvement. In the UK, Reynolds (1985) has studied school effectiveness; Reid, Hopkins and Holly (1987) have investigated the processes that are necessary to lead towards the achievement of 'the effective school'; and the ILEA's Junior School Project followed up the Rutter Report (*Fifteen Thousand Hours*) by attempting to identify the factors which foster the success of a school. What is remarkable is the fact that the same factors emerge time and time again in this literature as being the significant ones. The thirteen factors identified most commonly are best summarized by Purkey and Smith (1985) and are as follows:

Nine characteristics (i) which set the context for innovation; and (ii) which can be more quickly implemented.

1 *School-site management and participative decision-making*
— the responsibility and authority to determine the means in order to increase academic performance

2 *Leadership*
— while suspicious of the 'great principal' theory, strong leadership is required to initiate and sustain the implementation process

3 *Staff stability*
— thus allowing for the development of a coherent, consistent school personality (or 'culture')

4 *Curriculum articulation and organization*
— which challenges all the students

5   *Staff development*
    — which is school-wide and which links the expressed concerns of staff to instructional/organizational needs

6   *Parental involvement and support*

7   *School-wide recognition of academic success*
    — and the celebration of these norms

8   *Maximized learning time*
    — active engagement in learning with no disruptions

9   *District (i.e. LEA) support*
    — in recognition of the school's efforts, resources to be made available

Four process/organizational characteristics: (i) which will define the school's culture and the development of its 'climate'; and (ii) which will evolve organically in each school.

10   *Collaborative Planning and Collegial Relationships*
    — by working together, collegiality breaks down barriers; this involves intellectual sharing leading to consensus and the promotion of commonality/mutuality

11   *Sense of community*
    — reduced alienation for teachers and students through inclusion/a sense of belonging

12   *Clear goals and high expectations*
    — channelling energy and effort into a mutually ageed set of purposes ('purposive' leadership)

13   *Order and discipline*
    — an indication of seriousness and purposefulness; rules, once mutually agreed, to be consistently and fairly enforced

This model (or set of 'common properties'), according to Purkey and Smith (1985), provides 'both means and content, process and direction'.

Where the literature is also in agreement is the common assertion that effective schools have effective leaders who promote effective cultures. Deal (1985) has argued that:

> Effective schools are those that over time have built a system of belief, supported by cultural forms that give meaning to the process of education. Just as with businesses, these schools will display shared values and beliefs, well-known and widely celebrated heroes and heroines, well-attended and memorable rituals and ceremonies, positive stories, and a dedicated informal group whose members work diligently to maintain and strengthen the culture.

Moreover, say Deal:

> Although the conceptual match between climate, ethos, or culture has not been specified, it is clear that something intangible about a school — style, tone or social atmosphere — is related somehow to student performance.

Holly (in Reid, Hopkins and Holly, 1987) has investigated the effectiveness of an affective school culture, while also arguing that an effective school develops effectively, i.e. it has the capacity to move forward effectively — by means of developmental processes — in content areas which can be considered 'good', that is, important, worthwhile, and, therefore, justifiable.

It is now time to look in turn at the various aspects of our schema.

Chapter One

School Leadership

> Mature organizations must revitalize one way or another in order to compete in increasingly tough environments. And transforming these institutions requires a special brand of leadership that we are not only advocating but deem necessary if our organizations are to achieve their goals. (Bennis and Nanus, 1985)

Sir Keith Joseph, when Secretary of State for Education and Science, appeared before a Commons Select Committee and said that a good headteacher is the closest thing to a 'magic wand' for any school (quoted in the *Times Educational Supplement,* 11 April 1986). Certainly, the expectation — in both the theory and practice of effective schooling — is that a headteacher will be *the* leader of a school. Headship, therefore, is often equated with leadership. However, Sedgwick (1985 and 1986) has bemoaned the fact that there seems to be a trend in favour of 'greater autocracy' among headteachers, who aim to lead by 'sheer force of personality', consequently 'dragooning teachers into innovatory ways'. He concludes that 'autocratic change is shallow and grudging' and does not become 'rooted'. In his article entitled 'Hammer heads', Sedgwick explained the trend towards 'aggressive management' by arguing that this style 'comes from a perception of industrial models' involving the 'hard-nosed realism of the boardroom and the cut-and-thrust of the market place'. But boardrooms and market places, he says, are concerned with products, not processes; profits, not principles of procedure; and objectives, not creativity. Sedgwick is here speaking for many other commentators who believe that schools should be more democratic and participatory and that headteachers should change their style of leadership accordingly. Indeed, Naisbitt (1984) has argued that:

> The new leader is a facilitator, not an order giver . . . if you can develop the skills of facilitating people's involvement in decision-making processes, you can become a very effective leader . . .
>
> We have no great captains . . . anymore . . . That is because we followers are not creating those kinds of leaders anymore . . . strong leadership is anathema to democracy. The whole idea is that our

democratic system itself, creates a strong, viable society . . . we don't need strong leaders . . . (just) greater bottom-up participation in policy-making.

Sedgwick would undoubtedly agree with these statements. His aggressive, autocratic headteacher is tantamount to being 'Master under God' (*Times Educational Supplement,* 2 May 1986). Yet, as Weindling and Earley found in their research on the first months of headship (and quoted in the *Times Educational Supplement,* 6 September 1985), 'staff say they hope new heads will be like Moses' — teachers wanted the new heads to take on a 'messianic role' — and lead them out of the wilderness. 'The researchers found', it was said, 'that the personal and professional qualities demanded by teachers of a new head were awe-inspiring — ranging from charm to implacability, and from firm leadership to the ability to consult and delegate'. Heads must feel the weight of these expectations — and the weight will be heavier the more the messages are ambiguous and, therefore confusing (if not confused).

Reynolds (1985) has joined this same debate:

> Most important of all, it is highly likely that the key to what makes some schools 'good' is their headteachers, yet this is an area where few British researchers have dared to tread. Fearing local political and union opposition, both the major British studies of school effectiveness have no data whatsoever on the quality of the leadership generated by the head, in marked contrast to the situation in America where 'the effective school principal' has been an obsessional interest for at least a decade . . . the fact that we have no distinct British evidence is a major embarrassment.

Of the work that does exist, that by Lyons, Stenning and McQueeney (1987) identifies the fact that heads are 'still far too autocratic' and, argue the researchers, this damages their credibility; they should discuss problems with their staffs. Overall, say the researchers:

> a picture emerges of heads who are not equipped or trained to deal with the growing number and complexity of staff management problems.

The lack of skill training means, they say, that heads are unable to introduce debates amongst their staffs in order to develop mutual understanding and a *sense of common purpose.*

What is common across the existing research (for example, Weindling and Earley 1986; Lyons, Stenning and McQueeney, 1987) is the variety of the expectations placed upon headteachers by their staff members. Moreover, these expectations may well be contradictory, thus creating a measure of role ambiguity. Some staff, for instance, will argue that a strong head consults his/her staff, others will say that only a weak head goes in for consultation. This confusion certainly adds to the complexity of the role of headteacher — as evidenced within the research of Hall, Mackay and Morgan (1986). This research into 'headteachers at work' recorded the fragmentary nature of the heads' professional lives, with their working days made up of numerous activities, quick-fire interactions and countless instances of 'on the hoof' decision-making. Surprisingly, perhaps, the researchers discovered that the longest sustained activity for the heads is teaching. As the researchers point out, however, the head who teaches can only do so at the expense of other activities. There is an opportunity cost; especially when those other activities are of higher priority, for example, long-term planning for policy or curriculum development. The latter, said Hall, Mackay and Morgan, go largely undone; systematic curriculum review work, for example, is squeezed out of the scenario by more pressing, 'fire-fighting' duties. Crisis management and damage limitation soak up inordinate amounts of time and effort — leaving the headteachers unable to wrest themselves clear of the immediate, the routine and the comparatively trivial. Dealing with this multiplicity of minor problems — is this the way top managers should behave?, ask the researchers (and quoted in the *Times Educational Supplement,* 9 January 1987, under the heading 'complex views from the top'). Most heads in this study are undoubtedly reactive (to people and events) as opposed to pro-active — they are mopping up rather than initiating. What is also clear is that many heads in this sample approach their new role *as teachers*. For instance, the study mentions their reluctance both to institute performance appraisal (which reflects, it is argued, their feelings as former teachers rather than as heads) and to leave the classroom, believing that their teaching commitments not only 'keep their feet on the ground' — thus ensuring that 'they did not forget what life was like for their colleagues at the chalk-face' (quoted in the *Times Educational Supplement*) — but also win credibility in the eyes of the teachers. Teaching is also seen as an enjoyable, therapeutic and most welcome retreat from all their other pressures. No wonder, then, that many of the heads in the study are referred to as 'teacher educators', the other categories being 'leading professionals', 'chief executives' and 'pastoral missionaries'. One overall impression from this British research on the role of headteacher is that of teacher-as-professional, manager-as-amateur.

Three themes, all of which have been touched upon in the dicussion above, are crucial to an understanding of the quality of leadership exercised at Garth Hill:

Theme One: The relevance of industrial and commercial experience for the management and leadership of schools.

Theme Two: The importance of strong, effective leadership.

Theme Three: The current interest in a changing style of leadership.

Given the central importance of these themes, we will now look at each in turn — and in some depth — and, in so doing, attempt to match the practice at Garth Hill with relevant theoretical considerations.

Theme One: *The Business of Leadership*

I run this school very much as a business. (Stanley Goodchild)

Our stance on this issue is based on three related arguments:

1   Schools and the business world have much to learn from each other in what ought to be a two-way process of interactive learning.
2   In the past schools and businesses have enjoyed rich experiences which have served to augment the common pool of 'organizational theory' and, into which, both can now dip for replenishment.
3   Within this learning process, we must move away from stereotypical, somewhat prejudiced views of the strengths and weaknesses of the management of schools on one hand and business management on the other. For example, we need to appreciate that the gun-slinging John Wayne figure of the machismo school of industrial management *is* a stereotype and nothing more.

An issue of the Times Educational Supplement (30 October 1987) contained the headline, 'Most schools could teach industry a thing or two about management'. This article, written by the members of a team from UMIST's Department of Management Sciences, who had been researching management and organization in schools, was strangely out of balance with its purported message. The up-front rhetoric is of schools being a surprisingly fertile source of management advice for industry. Two instances of good practice in schools (the development of an organizational culture and morning briefings) are mentioned, followed by a long list of areas where schools are going wrong and could well learn from industry. The catchy headline is belied by the bulk of the supporting evidence. Indeed, the authors rather nicely sum up their own position:

> Most schools are robust organizations with many good management practices from which anyone in industry and commerce could learn; yet those same schools are likely to miss aspects of elementary motivation of staff and good house-keeping that elsewhere are taken for granted. (Torrington, Weightman and Johns, 1987)

As they say, there are two related, puzzling aspects of life in schools:

- Why do schools pay so little attention to the various needs of adults (i.e. the teachers), especially when the pupils are often so pampered? This point has been made elsewhere by both Sedgwick (1986) and Holly (1985).
- Why are staff-rooms often so squalid — and teachers so tolerant of such working conditions?

Having raised these points, the researchers go on to list other managerial shortcomings of schools:

- Schools often jeopardize their effectiveness by paying scant attention to the adults.

- 'Management' (what it is for, i.e. getting things done, making things happen) is often inadequately understood.
- There is insufficient ownership of ideas which is the 'essential way to get things done'; staff commitment to 'making it work' is vital.
- Members of staff do not value each other sufficiently.
- Staff would welcome appraisal — of the right sort.
- Autonomy is being lost because of a continuing concern about control. It is a question, they say, of having both control and autonomy and getting the right balance between them. Charles Handy (1984) has written on this same issue.
- Schools lose efficiency by neglecting staff facilities.
- Non-teaching staff are under-used and badly treated.
- The common view of resource provision is 'back to front'; it is a rather defeatist view of what we haven't got, as opposed to a more optimistic approach which stresses the resources we have got and what we ought to be doing with them. There is a need to be more positive — in order 'to get the job done'.

Moreover, they argue, people in schools should treat other schools and the community at large as sources of ideas and innovations, not just as the sources of problems and constraints.

Having listed these shortcomings (which, collectively, are something of an indictment), the researchers are still able to round off by saying that:

> Our evidence makes us convinced that most schools are better run than most businesses . . .

Yet all the evidence in their article would tend to point the other way. It is our contention that, in all the areas pinpointed as deficiencies in school management by the researchers, the business world (or at least pockets of it) has begun to make important advances — and from which schools can learn a great deal.

It is the case, however, that the leading edge of current management thinking is as incisive as it is because it has synthesized the lessons from all kinds of organizational experience. Charles Handy in the UK, Peter Drucker and the Tom Peters, Robert Waterman and Nancy Austin connection in North America have all studied the management of schools as organizations in order to be making their practical 'theory'. These are all management theorists with practice in schools — past, present and future — very much in mind. The work of Mintzberg (1973), for instance, is applicable to managerial roles in many different kinds of organization. He identified three role clusters:

- *interpersonal*   figure-head
  leader
  liaison

- *informational*   monitor
  disseminator
  spokes-person

- *decisional*   entrepreneur
                 disturbance healer
                 resource allocator
                 negotiator

This pattern of activities spans both the business and educational worlds.

In addition, in the recent work by Peters and Austin (1985), they are able to include a concluding section on 'excellence in school leadership' and, in so doing, test the ideas in the rest of the book against the good practice in schools and vice versa. And what they come up with is a vision of school leadership (based mainly but not exclusively on industrial experience) which is relevant, new, exciting and far from the stereotypical, 'knee-jerk' reactions of those who want to maintain that schools cannot learn from industry. Of course, at Garth Hill, the emphasis *is* on learning from industry, while, with the advent of a 'business manager', ways are now being sought to put the school and its staff in more of a teaching role, especially in terms of consultancy for computer education. The concept of the 'entrepreneurial school' is of some relevance here.

In their discussion of 'excellence in school leadership', Peters and Austin (1985) acknowledge that many schools have discovered the advantages of having:

- a distinct philosophy which is the 'essence of simplicity' — the 'what' in 'what we are all about here';

- given this intensity of value orientation, opportunities for everyone to 'buy-in' — involving a 'familial approach';

- sensitive, intuitive management which involves '*sensing* where things are O.K.' (or not);

- autonomy to concentrate on the 'how' — in terms of 'how we are going to get there'.

The authors then point out that much recent educational 'theory' (they quote, as an example, Sara Lightfoot's *The Good High School*) is charting similar territory. First, they quote from Lightfoot (1983):

Teachers are typically cast in low positions in the school's hierarchy and not treated with respectful regard. In the worst schools, teachers are demeaned and infantilised by administrators who view them as custodians, guardians, or inspired technicians. In less grotesque settings teachers are left alone with little adult interaction and minimal attention is given to their needs for support, reward, and criticism.

Second, they exclaim: 'how the bells of familiarity ring!' And, like ourselves, they refer not only to the fact that there are traits shared by leaders in schools and businesses, but also that, across the board, these people utilize 'common-sense' thinking in their work but rarely share it — or, indeed, see its importance. Third, Peters and Austin (1985) confirm that school leadership and management are important and that the subject of excellence in education is appropriately high on the national agenda — which is the case, of course, on both sides of the Atlantic.

Given the importance of linking the experience of management and leadership in educational and non-educational settings, Peters and Austin use the framework of ideas contained in their book with which to view the best of practice in schools. They focus on two clusters of major themes:

Cluster One: the importance of *vision-making, the symbolic dimension;* and the *principal/headteacher as sales-person*

Echoing the work of Terry Deal and Allan Kennedy (1982), and indeed Tom Peters' work with Robert Waterman (1982), Peters and Austin stress the importance of both developing the 'character' of the school and providing clarity of vision and purpose. The advice is to:

- promote a 'vivid ideological stance (Lightfoot's phrase) which will imbue the institution with a central, clear philosophy;
- keep it simple if the effort is to be effective and long-lasting;
- live it with intensity; enforce it constantly, consistently, and blatantly; set the tone and foster its permeation of the environment;
- be prepared to protect the vision with fierce determination — showing anger, if needs be, to challenge the 'pretence of complacency' — while delegating responsibility for, and encouraging participation in, the implementation of the vision;
- pay attention to the symbolic importance of such 'niceties' as leaders being available, walking around the school and *not* demanding personal privileges; remember that actions speak louder than words.

As examplar material, Peters and Austin draw attention to one of Lightfoot's case studies in which an inner urban school in Atlanta, in a deteriorating situation, has been 'turned around' by a principal who:

- dominated the school, frequently walking the campus;
- was unwilling to wait, or be held back, in his attempts to improve the situation;
- in the face of apathy, showed the staff who was in charge;
- at the first staff meeting, started with fighting words, along the lines that 'you're either part of the team or you are not';
- stressed the importance of standards of behaviour for the students;
- began with an 'immediate attack via the symbolic — on the shabby physical environment'. Previously, according to Lightfoot, the physical environment had symbolized the deterioration of staff morale. So the principal initiated a highly visible clean-up, with a good coat of paint covering the graffiti — one of the symbols of the former regime. Indeed, the previous situation is best summed up by the principal's own statement: 'I can't believe no-one stood up and screamed about it.'

— 'sold' his school in the local community and further afield. According to Peters and Austin, this same principal now criss-crosses the country with an impressive slide-show, promoting the school's new programmes of work. In so doing, he has earned some criticism from his colleagues for spending so much time promoting the school; yet his promotional work has had its greatest impact not on the outside world, but within the school itself. It has contributed to the generation of pride and self-confidence. Consequently, those in the school feel *worth looking at* when they have to entertain so many visitors and are the subject of so much outside interest.

In some ways there is an uncanny resemblance between the school described in this case study and the details of the recent history of Garth Hill. It could be argued that both headteachers share some of the assets of Lightfoot's good principals: they are showmen, visionaries, masterly users of symbols ('masters of ceremony') and obsessive activists. Another similarity is that, in both schools, it was appreciated that public events should be organized to symbolize the acquisition of a new image. In the George Washington Carver High School in Atlanta, where vocational education has come to mean training for jobs of choice, skill, and status and which rests on a full programe of work study in the community, the symbolic event was a 'free enterprise day'. Garth Hill, of course, has established many similar 'traditions'. It is on such symbolic occasions that the vision is made visible and is extended to the community at large. While the contexts of the schools are so different, their situations are so much the same. Consider this extract from Sara Lawrence Lightfoot's account (in *The Good High School*) of 'Carver':

> Three years ago, Crim (the Superintendent) was getting ready to close Carver High School. It was an ugly reminder of the deterioration, chaos, and unrest that plagues many big-city schools . . . Hogans, an energetic, ambitious young Principal of a nearby elementary school, was chosen to save Carver from total demise. Crim sensed that Hogans was capable of filling the void and thought he might take Carver on as a personal challenge. 'He is a diamond in the rough, a jock who made good . . .' In just a few years, Hogans has transformed Carver. He has used every ounce of his energy and spirit to turn the place around and Crim is proud of his effort. 'He has gotten the kids to listen . . . He has disrupted the inertia'.

For Hogans read Goodchild, for Carver read Garth Hill.

Cluster Two: MBWA; keeping 'close to the customers'; 'tight' and 'loose coupling', etc.

A crucial theme, which is emphasized by Peters and Austin as being equally efficacious in schools and businesses, is their concept of 'Managing By Wandering Around' (MBWA), which in Peters' previous work (*In Search of Excellence* with Robert Waterman, 1982) was only a sub-title within the associated concept, 'A Bias for Action'. When he came to put together his second book, however, Tom Peters was rating MBWA much more highly.

Implicit in MBWA, according to Peters and Austin (1985), are such understandings as keeping in touch, empathy and intensity of involvement. The level of involvement is indicated by such considerations as:

- whether the headteacher hides behind his/her desk;
- the amount of 'pacing the school' that occurs;
- the visibility of the headteacher around the school and in the local community;
- the willingness to find the time for people and their encouragement.

'Wandering around, staying in touch, keeping out of the office', say Peters and Austin, contribute to MBWA; 'it's the mark of the superb factory manager, hospital administrator, division manager, city manager, and also, apparently, school leader'.

MBWA is akin to being 'close to the customers' — the customers being, in the case of schooling, the pupils and their parents. Schools are for maximizing pupil learning. Consequently, say Peters and Austin, teachers have to 'personalize' eduction, heighten expectations and treat all the students as winners — in short, they are exhorted to 'live for the kids'. Moreover, if pupils are teated as adults and with respect (see Hargreaves, 1982), they will respond accordingly. At the same time, however, headteachers need to instil discipline, stability, confidence and a sense of community spirit; what is not required is 'softness'.

Schools, argue Peters and Austin, need to possess loose and tight properties. They should, says Handy (1984), control the what — the clear, shared vision and set of goals — and retain relative autonomy for teachers to pursue the how and give it 'creative expression'. Successful schools, like successful businesses, are mobilized by attention to such concepts as immediacy, creative energy, sensitivity, passion, attention to detail, rhythm and enthusiasm; they need to foster persistence and the 'sheer guts to get on with it'.

Peters and Austin (1985), then, set out to explore the generic skills of leadership — whether exercised in public or private organizations and institutions. Their work is an attempt to up-date Peters' earlier work with Waterman (1982), which identified eight dimensions of organizational effectiveness. Briefly, these were:

A *bias for action*.
Staying *close to the customer*.
Extending *autonomy and entrepreneurship*.
Productivity through people.
An approach which is *hands-on, value driven*.
The need to *stick to the knitting*.
An organization structure which has a *simple form, lean staff*.
Simultaneous loose-tight properties.

As described above, Peters and Austin have further explored these dimensions and re-emphasized certain aspects. Taken together, however, the advice for school leaders is as follows:

- think big; start small;
- combine a high sense of purpose ('lofty ideals') with 'intense pragmatism'; values and *do-ability;*
- *the basic adventure — the pursuit of excellence — is 'not for the faint of heart'; it takes nerve to step out with the purpose of making a difference — and refusing to retreat behind office doors or into committee structures. In short, doing comes before talking;*
- *the journey* is about commitment, persistence, investment; it is 'excellence or bust — you're in for the distance!' It's a question of *sticking with it.* To do so, the leader must have a passion for the adventure and be prepared to provide *meaning* for the participants at both an abstract (i.e. cultural) and an everyday, practical and operational level.

Returning to the beginning of this discussion in Theme One and the quotation from Stanley Goodchild, it could be argued that one meaning of the statement is 'I run this school very much as I would run a business'. What is important is his grasp of the fact that generic skills of strong and effective leadership exist and that our understanding of them is increasing — both in theory and practice.

Theme Two: Strong, Effective Leadership

Never put popularity before conviction.

It (school uniform) doesn't improve educational standards and discipline; that comes from the top.

Involvement is the key to commitment.   (Stanley Goodchild)

It is time to define leadership and answer the all-important question — what makes for effective leadership? Over thirty years ago, Peter Drucker (1955) defined leadership as

. . . the lifting of a man's vision to higher sights, the raising of a man's performance to a higher standard, the building of a man's personality beyond its normal limitations.

Heads are concerned with management, while leadership is one function of management. Heads, therefore, are concerned with management and leadership. While these activities overlap, management is more than leadership and, quite probably, leadership goes beyond the demands of management. Many management activities can be classified as 'administration' — the routine tasks of keeping the show on the road. Leadership, however, is something else.

It is about *change leadership* — commonly referred to as *the management of change,* which may well involve *the management of conflict.* In addition, both management and leadership can be exercised across a range of people and across a range of styles.

In short, then, and according to Buchanan and Huczynski (1985):

- there is no clear separation between management and leadership;
- most managers exercise leadership in some form;
- while to be a manager is a leadership role, leaders are not necessarily managers;
- managers have responsibilities (planning, organizing, supervising, etc.) other than leadership;
- leadership is something more than the discharge of administrative functions; it involves *influencing the actions of others* according to *styles of persuasion. Communication* and *motivation* are important concepts in this context.

Buchanan and Huczynksi list some of the functions of leadership: enabling others to achieve agreed goals; setting/communicating objectives; monitoring performance and giving feedback; establishing basic values; encouraging problem-solving approaches; organizing resources; controlling rewards and sanctions; providing for information, advice, expertise (i.e. consultancy services); providing for psychological and technical support; decision-making, etc. These same authors usefully draw attention to two other aspects of leadership. First, there are the five main bases of *power* possessed by leaders:

reward power: the ability to dispense valuable rewards such as pay, promotion, resources, responsibility, etc;

coercive power: the use of sanctions;

referent power: the propensity to identify with leader characteristics;

legitimate power: the right, bestowed by official, hierarchical status, to instruct;

expert power: conferred by the possession of superior knowledge and expertise.

Second, these dimensions of leader power only come into play when the 'followers' recognize their efficacy and are prepared to follow. Consequently, argue Buchanan and Huczynski, leadership is a property of the relationship between the leader and the followers. While coercion may be involved, so may compliance; the followers have to be willing (or 'impressed' enough) to be influenced. As Southworth (1987) has pointed out, leadership depends on 'followership'; to claim that charismatic leadership is everything, therefore, is, at best, a one-dimensional view, based on the persistent belief in the power of the individual. In fact, Buchanan and Huczynksi decry the 'great man theory' of leadership, which aims to promote the importance of key, powerful, idioscyncratic individuals who can dominate and control the lives of others. Perhaps, however, this line of argument contains one aspect of the truth rather than the complete truth. Key persons may well be important *some times* and *under some conditions.*

Indeed, building on Etzioni (1964), Halpin (1966) and Yukl (1975), we would want to argue that effective leadership has three basic dimensions:

1   Moving beyond *transacting* (administration; i.e. management as coping) to *transforming,* i.e. transcending the hurly-burly of everyday life to determine (whether collaboratively or not) the school's 'sense of mission' and the guiding vision of the organization. Harold Leavitt (1986) has referred to this as transformative leadership.

2   Establishing the *initiating structure* and pressurizing towards productivity and the accomplishment of the organization's vision. This is the so-called *instrumental* dimension.

3   Displaying *consideration* for those charged with implementing the organization's tasks and providing the necessary support services. This is the *expressive* dimension.

Each of these dimensions, of course, is dependent on the other two. Consequently, the effective leader not only creates the vision, but also ensures its implementation; by pressuring and supporting, cajoling and sympathizing, inspiring and healing, forcing and enabling, prodding and sustaining, etc. It is a combination of selling, telling, yelling and gelling (see the diagram below).

Manasse (1985) has referred to these three dimensions — when in an effective, powerful combination — as *purposive leadership.* When working in unison, the three dimensions produce a fourth, the *motivation* of the staff members. Moreover, the whole package is mobilized on a daily basis by means of MBWA as introduced in the previous section

Indeed, this diagram would suggest that there are two — maybe complementary — routes towards motivation. Forceful leadership and the positive effects of a task orientation (for example, clarity of purpose and meaningfulness)

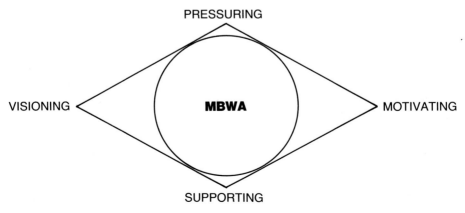

could be said to encourage *extrinsic motivation,* whereas the facilitation of more humane, participatory approaches could engender involvement, commitment and *intrinsic motivation.*

The pressure dimension is task-oriented and the support dimension is people-centred. On the one dimension the leader has to plan, assign tasks, emphasize deadlines, stress productivity, control, coordinate, supervise, criticize, etc.; on the other, he/she has to deal with the needs of individuals and groups, show interest in, and listen to, people, be approachable and friendly, be supportive and allow for participation in operational decision-making. While one dimension is nothing without the other, it may well be the case that, on some occasions, leaders will need to emphasize one at the relative expense of the other. Buchanan and Huczynski, however, argue that the most effective leaders are those who emphasize both dimensions. We would add that the most effective leaders also have a 'feel' as to what adjustments to make in terms of the 'sliding scale' and the continuing relationship between pressure and support. Leadership, then, is also *orchestration.* And, this explains why organizations have to be sailed rather than driven (see Fullan, 1985).

Concerning effective leadership, Manasse (1985) has made what we consider to be a crucial point.

> If it is true that the nature and pace of events often appear to control principals rather than the other way around, how, then, do some principals take charge and assume leadership? . . . What we find, in general, is that effective principals have learned to be *pro-active* within a reactive work environment.

Manasse's Competencies of Average and High-Performing Principals

Cluster	Competencies	
	Basic	High-performing
Purpose and direction	Commitment to school mission	Proactive orientation
		Decisiveness
Cognitive skills		Interpersonal search
		Information search
		Concept formation
		Conceptual flexibility
Consensus management	Concern for image	Managing interaction
	Tactical adaptability	Persuasiveness
Quality enhancement	Developmental orientation	Achievement motivation
		Management control
Organization	Delegation	Organizational ability
Communication	Written communication	Self-presentation

This proactive quality, according to Manasse, involves wresting clear of the administrative mire and finding the time and space to devote to 'purposing'. Decisiveness is also required. And echoing the dimensions described above, Manasse argues that effective principals/heads have a picture of their schools as they want them to be (vision), specific strategies designed to achieve that picture (initiating structure) and the ability to generate commitment to their goals (consideration). Such leaders take the initiative, model appropriate behaviours and communicate high expectations to students, staff members and the community alike. Above all, however:

> effective principals move a school toward a vision of what could be rather than maintaining what is . . . Once they have developed their agendas, effective principals take the initiative to implement them.

Strong leaders, says Manasse, are also resourceful:

- to reflect and support their own agendas, they establish priorities and use time well;
- they marshal human resources by identifying strengths among the staff and finding 'substitute leaders';
- they arrange for coordination and evaluation.

Echoing Peters and Austin above, Manasse argues for the importance of *symbolic leadership* which helps to cement the parts of more loosely structured organizations, thus allowing for centralization concerning the 'what' and decentralization of the 'how'.

Nias (1980) has discussed various combinations of leadership *styles* and *types* and supports *positive leadership* in preference to *passive* and *'Bourbon'*-type leadership. Her positive type shares many of the characteristics mentioned above: commitment (evidenced by high personal and professional standards), accessibility, supportiveness (of teacher development) and the willingness to give a lead in establishing aims for the school. The positive-type leader avoids staff frustration (often engendered by passive leadership) and alienation (caused by Bourbon-type dictatorial leadership).

Leadership 'style' can be construed as a combination of mode/approach and manner/behaviour (see below). This allows for the possibility of type (2) leadership — the directive and involved (committed/enthusiastic) style of leadership detailed in this section.

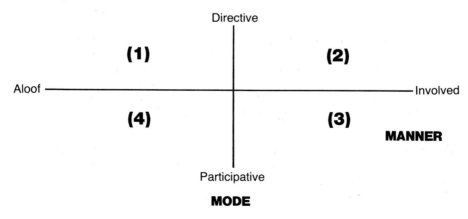

In her research Nias discovered that teachers disliked the kind of leadership style which they saw as 'laissez-faire', indeterminate and 'wishy-washy'. Unfortunately, this style is too often equated with so-called 'democratic' leadership. This diagram, however, allows for another brand of 'democratic' leadership which is a combination of boxes (2) and (3) — as opposed to (4). This style is directive, involved and supportive of staff participation, i.e. strong, participative leadership.

Theme Three: Changing the Style of Leadership

Maybe I was a despot; now I'm a democrat!

Devolving responsibilities — this is now in process.

(Stanley Goodchild)

Over the last five years Garth Hill has experienced a particular style of leadership. Four points are pertinent here:

(i)   it has been Stanley Goodchild's style of leadership;
(ii)   his style has suited both him and the school;
(iii) it has been a style of 'change leadership'. He has been very successful in making changes happen;
(iv)   the style of leadership exercised at Garth Hill is now undergoing some interesting changes.

These points will now be discussed in turn:

(i)   Many headteachers spend their time supervising the routine affairs of their schools. They are extremely busy — often blaming the busy nature of their lives in schools on the increasing complexities of their role. They tend to blame other factors:

> industrial action;
> political meddling and increased demands for accountability;
> work-related stress;
> demographic factors leading to falling rolls,
> amalgamations and closures.

Such heads argue that it pays to keep their heads well below the parapet and that, given the demands placed upon them, leadership gets squeezed out of the scenario. There is no time for transforming; transacting is the shape of their working lives.

Judging by his track record at Garth Hill, none of this seems to be true of Stanley Goodchild. While he is extremely busy, he tries to be busy on the right things. It is a question of priorities; of attending to 'key areas of focus' (see Holly, 1985), while maintaining the routine side of school life. Transacting and transforming are both important to Stanley Goodchild. It is a question of balance. While it is said that, given all the pressures, 'fewer want to become heads' (*Times Educational Supplement,* 17 October 1986) he seems to soak up the pressures and revel in the constant challenges. While some 'beleaguered heads start a helpline' (*Times Educational Supplement,* 17 October 1986) and others quake at the thought of being on a 'discipline tightrope as two are suspended' (*Daily Telegraph,* 29 August 1986), Stanley Goodchild gets on with the job of pushing and pulling Garth Hill into the twenty-first century.

(ii) His style is reflected in box (2) of the diagram above. He is direct and directive; authoritative and somewhat authoritarian. He has undoubted management skills which he utilizes daily and he approaches the job, given his background in educational management, as a *manager* rather than as a (head-)*teacher*. Using the terminology adopted by Hall, Mackay and Morgan (1986) in their research, he is more the 'chief executive' than the 'leading professional', 'teacher-educator' or 'pastoral missionary', although there are elements of all of them in his managerial make-up. While some of his colleagues may not enjoy his style, they can see what he has done for the school — and for them — and are, therefore, more than prepared to back him. Given the fact that he has led the way in terms of turning round the fortunes of the school, it must be in their interests to do so. He is an enthusiast and a winner — a potent combination. His rules are simple ones: support him and he will support you. It is very much the case that his style has become Garth Hill's style. Important descriptors are: forceful; firm; resolved; strong (even brave); purposeful; resourceful; practical; clear-sighted; decisive, etc. He is able to initiate ideas, implement them and sustain them over time.

(iii) In fact, concerning his style of leadership, three points are relevant:

- his style is conducive to the tasks of *change leadership;* he is innovative and entrepreneurial. As well as being an ideas man and a 'missionary', he makes things happen. He's a doer. It is much too easy to dismiss the changes at Garth Hill as a bunch of bright ideas and, therefore, as gimmickry. He is more than prepared to follow through with the ideas, persist with them and support the staff in the delivery of them. Moreover, all the ideas form an integrated package — his original 'vision'. Of course he is pragmatic and opportunistic — that's how he begins to realize the vision over time. And he knows intuitively that, in the change process, it is important to put on the *pressure* in the initial stages and then *support* those responsible for implementation — a case of the *initiating structure* being matched by *consideration.*

- whether his authoritarian approach justifies the use of the term 'despot' is a matter for conjecture, but he is certainly 'benevolent'. 'My approach', he says, 'is relatively aggressive' (which means that he pushes people into meeting deadlines, attaining targets as set and having high standards), but he is also caring, sympathetic and concerned for the welfare of staff and pupils alike. It is almost a question of what has been referred to elsewhere as 'tough love'.

- He is also a fixer. He spends a lot of time on the telephone, mainly 'wheeling and dealing'; on one such occasion, he said:

    You're going to hear me do a bit of bartering now.

He uses the telephone to deal with matters as they arise and before they become problems. It is quick-fire stuff, symbolic of his style which combines rapid decision-making with attention to detail. He 'knows' the importance of MBWA and is a presence around the school. Indeed, Stanley Goodchild's style reflects two of the points already raised in this discussion on leadership.

(a) leadership style is a combination of two sets of factors or dimensions — *mode* and *manner* — and the one can be used to ameliorate the latter. In other words, a stern, strong and relatively authoritarian mode can be 'humanized' by the manner in which the message is put across. It is also a question of sequencing the dimensions. Stanley Goodchild often sets out the parameters for action in no uncertain terms — and then negotiates on the detail;

(b) we argued above that leadership style is also the effective combination of the *initiating structure* and *consideration*. One aspect involves the establishment of expectations; the other involves support in realizing these same expectations.

(iv) In researching this book with Stanley Goodchild over a period of several months, it became clear that, while the school is currently in a new phase of its development, so is his style of leadership. There is much more talk of delegation, the devolution of power, and staff participation. Stanley Goodchild is also withdrawing somewhat from centre stage. It would seem that, in the terminology used by Rensis Likert (1961), he is changing from a 'benevolent authoritative' approach (having previously shown signs of being 'exploitative autocratic') to one which is more consultative, participative and democratic.

It is still, however, a question of emphasis. The ILEA report on effective junior schools (1985) had this to say:

The head is always, in law as well as in fact, responsible for the situations in his or her school. Successful heads have interpreted these considerable powers and duties wisely. They have not been authoritarian, consultative or participative as a matter of principle; they have been all three at different times as the conditions seemed to warrant, though most often participative. Their success has often come from choosing well, from knowing when to take the lead and when to confirm the leadership offered by their colleagues.

Currently, this is the case at Garth Hill, where responsibility is being devolved to experienced 'middle' managers. There is a need, therefore, to release the energies and capacities for leadership of these and other staff members.

Such a change of direction can be further explained by reference to two bodies of theory:

- *Contingency theory:* this stresses the importance and influence of contextual factors. Acknowledging the power of organizational contexts entails recognizing that there can only ever be the leadership style that is best in the circumstances. The ILEA quotation (see above) contains the words, 'as the conditions seemed to warrant . . .' Another facet of leadership, therefore, mut be to diagnose the human and organizational context and to decide what is the best behaviour to 'fit' the situation. Contingency theory, therefore, would suggest that the best leadership style to adopt is contingent on the circumstances in which the school is embedded.

When Stanley Goodchild took over at Garth Hill in 1982, he found himself facing the 'circumstances' of falling rolls, falling reputation and falling morale. He probably realized that things could only get worse:

It is an inescapable fact that some secondary schools will have to close
. . .

As schools get smaller and promotional prospects fade, teachers will see less and less need to do such things as going to faculty meetings or involving themselves in after-school activities.

The forces resisting change will be strengthened. Schools will tend to become smaller and duller as their staffs get older and as promotion and movement become less. An age of technological innovation is not likely to be well served by a teaching force which is resistant to change, but this is likely to happen as teachers get more shut in their own classrooms. Thus we face a situation where schools with rapidly declining numbers may not only find it impossible to teach a full curriculum but where the very mechanism for curriculum development may itself be destroyed . . . staff morale is bound to be under strain as numbers fall . . .

(extracts from Secondary Heads Association document dating from
1978
— quoted by John Sayer, *Times Educational Supplement,* 23 May 1986)

Given this 'environmental turbulence', therefore, Stanley Goodchild was able to take stern measures to begin to remedy the situation. Circumstances demanded that he should do so. Dramatic problems demand dramatic action. He was given a clear mandate; and his directive, assertive style suited the urgency of the occasion. But circumstances change — thus demanding changes of leadership style.

- *Stage theory:* this maintains that organizations and institutions evolve over time and experience stages or phases of growth. Plant (1987) has recently argued this line, basing his work on Blake, Avis and Mouton (1966), Lievegoed (1972), Greiner (1972), and Handy (1984). Lievegoed's path-finding work in this area distinguished between three periods of time, the *pioneer* phase, the phase of *differentiation* and the phase of *integration* (with the phases being separated by periods of crises and turbulence). Greiner listed five phases between which there are various crises (see the diagram below).

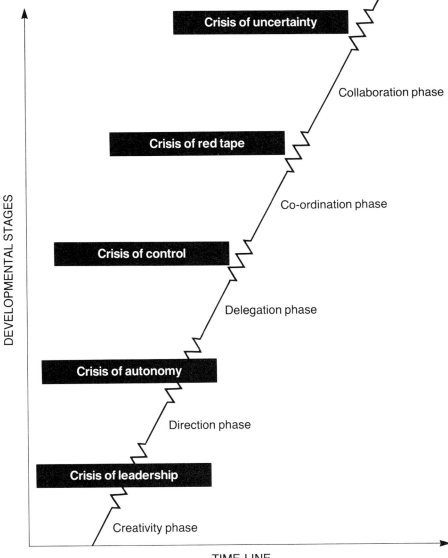

Plant also combines the work of Roger Harrison and Charles Handy in diagramatic form:

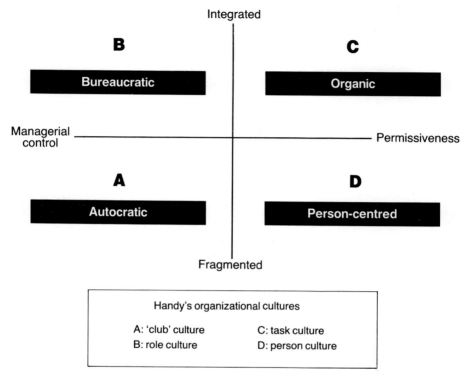

Basing his ideas on those cited above, Plant delineates three main phases:

the autocratic
the bureaucratic
the democratic

According to Plant:

> During the *autocratic phase,* the crucial role of the 'pioneer' or 'founder' is a source of strength — a real driving force. Priorities at this stage include *survival* and what is required is clear leadership and personal, tight control.

> During the *bureaucratic phase,* structures, systems, procedures, roles and job descriptions are established, mainly for purposes of *efficiency* and systematic approaches to management.

> During the *democratic phase,* moves will be made to 'humanize' the inflexible, impersonal structures of the bureaucratic phase.

In terms of these examples of stage theory, Garth Hill, in Lievegoed's terms, is travelling from the pioneer phase to the phase of differentiation; in Greiner's terms, from the *direction* to the *delegation* phase; and, in the terms common to Harrison, Handy and Plant, from the *autocratic* to the *bureaucratic* phase.

As Plant contends:

> Other forms of organization, such as bureaucracy and democracy, are not easily evolved or readily accepted, and are continually threatened by a reversion to autocracy, particularly in times of crises.

It could be argued, of course, that this is what happened at Garth Hill in 1982. In Greiner's terms there was a *crisis of leadership* and a pressing need for single-minded direction and sense of purpose. At this stage, says Plant, strong, charismatic leadership is required. The organization is crying out for a 'prime mover'.

But five years on there are new requirements. Delegation and devolution of responsibility are very much part of the new agenda. And devolving more responsibility to staff members is a reflection of the need to encourage the emergence of 'leadership' at different levels in the organization. Such moves hinge on the understanding that leadership can be exercised effectively by a number and a variety of organizational members. Up till now Stanley Goodchild has been *the* change leader. Most changes were initiated by him and bore his imprint. More recently, however, he has 'sensed' the need to 'cast the net' more widely and to encourage other leaders to replace him at centre stage. But, as he admits, it is difficult — partly because the staff have got used to him being the initiator; they still look to him to take charge. 'Authority dependency' is hard to shake off and the next few months could, in Greiner's terms, be a period of crises prior to the next phase of Garth Hill's institutional development. In *Ten Good Schools: A Secondary School Enquiry* (DES, 1977), HMI, while arguing for the centrality of the headteacher, maintained that what successful schools have in common is:

> Effective leadership and a 'climate' that is conducive to growth . . . Emphasis is laid on consultation, team work and participation, but, without exception, the most important single factor in the success of these schools is the quality of leadership of the head . . . such quality of leadership is crucial for success.

Changes in organizations, then, demand changes in styles of leadership:

> People whose lives are affected by a decision must be part of the process of arriving at that decision; this guiding principle of participatory democracy has seeped into the core of our value system . . . The way institutions are governed influences the quality of life within them . . . (Naisbitt, 1984)

In this extract Naisbitt is making two related points:

- the main argument is a presentation for the case of participatory democracy in organizational life;

- the second point is of concern to Garth Hill at this point in its development. The argument is that the way institutions are led and managed is 'educative' in itself (see Holly, 1986) in that from the leadership style emanates all sorts of messages concerning the ways relationships 'ought' to be constructed. The message is: this is the way to do things. And having received one message over a period of time, the participants can become 'hooked' on it and resistant to any other messages; thus the present 'difficulty'. The staff have grown accustomed to the one way of doing it.

And meanwhile Stanley Goodchild, as the headteacher, is faced with this central dilemma — how to let go and convince others of the rectitude of such a move towards the devolution of power.

'It is difficult', he says; 'the staff are used to the old style — they still look at me to say what they should be doing.'

Changing the style of management and leadership, therefore, is certainly not straightforward. It is a complex business. But if the organization is to develop over time, those in the organization will have to explore this very complexity.

It is acknowledged that the style of leadership and management experienced at Garth Hill since 1982 is in need of a change — maybe even a major overhaul. The style, it is believed, needs to become more delegative, consultative and participatory; more enabling/facilitative, supportive and collaborative; and more 'open' — therefore allowing for more staff involvement and the generation of their commitment and ownership. There also needs to be more *orchestration* of *others doing the leadership*. Staff expertise and strengths need to be identified and harnessed as a major resource; task groups and work-teams need to be 'built'. And all of this taking place within a more open, trusting, confidence-building, yet critical atmosphere. Moreover, given more involvement, the staff will naturally demand more power-sharing.

Reading recent books on 'management theory', it is gratifying to note that many of the themes covered in this section receive substantial endorsement. Based on Peters and Austin (1985), the following diagram emerges. The diagram links the twin emphases, *initiating structure* and *consideration,* and identifies six sub-components/processes:

- leading
- visioning
- initiating
- coaching
- encouraging
- empowering

And all these processes revolve round the core activity, MBWA (Managing By Wandering Around).

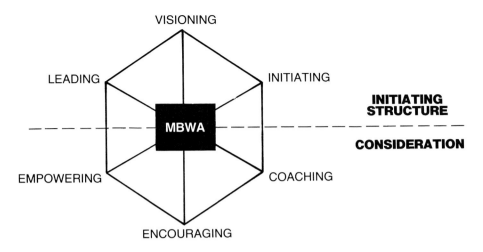

Leading: This is what is done in terms of the role of the figure-head and includes:

> providing high visibility inside and outside the school;
> modelling appropriate behaviour;
> leading by example;
> adding to the image and reputation of the school.

Peters and Austin describe their 'alternative' model of a manager/leader who is 'cheer-leader, enthusiast, nurturer of champions, hero-finder, wanderer, dramatist, coach, facilitator, builder' (as opposed to the former model of 'cop, referee, devil's advocate, dispassionate analyst, professional, decision-maker, nay-sayer, pronouncer'). The mark of the new model is its qualitative dimension — its 'passion', its 'intensity' and its 'drama'.

Visioning: According to Peters and Austin, 'the vision comes first'. Its implementation comes second. Consequently, the leader has to be a cross between a 'true believer', prepared to 'preach the vision' containing 'core values', and the 'chief salesman', i.e. a 'simple and direct communicator'. Above all, however, the leader has to 'dramatize the vision' for his/her organization. 'All business', say the authors, 'is show business . . . That doesn't mean tap-dancing; it means shaping values, symbolizing attention.' Leadership involves combining visioning (and thus cementing the abstract 'culture' of the school) and paying attention to detail. Both levels are symbolic. In addition, the vision has to be realistic — within the grasp of the participants:

> The most effective leaders from all walks of life — the classroom, the battle-field, the corporation — have set down *challenging but achievable visions.*

Initiating: Leaders, to borrow Terry Coleman's apt phrase, are 'movers and shakers'. They are *pro-active* in that they initiate, pressure, show the way and make things happen. They would share Watson's observation in the 'Double Helix':

> If the apple won't fall, let's go shake the tree.

They are the change leaders and the mobilisers of new energies and enthusiasms. Sometimes they have to vent their feelings and voice their displeasure:

> Given commitment to the instructional program, student achieve-ment, and their welfare as their first priority, it may not be surprising that such principals will sometimes knowingly sacrifice short-term feelings of staff.   (Peters and Austin, 1985)

Coaching: This is a vital aspect of MWBA (see below). Coaching, according to Peters and Austin, involves education, sponsoring, counselling and confront-ing:

> To coach is largely to facilitate, which literally means 'to make easy' — not less demanding, less interesting or less intense, but less discouraging, less bound up with excessive controls and complications.

Coaching involves the next two facets of 'consideration', encouraging and empowering.

Encouraging: If the vision (the school's cultural mission) provides the 'tightness' in a school's 'loose-tight properties' (see Fullan, 1985), the 'looseness' comes with the staff being encouraged to go forth and implement the core values in their daily endeavours. Peters and Austin maintain that 'decentralization' is best achieved 'at the point of delivery' — by encouraging staff initiative, entrepreneurship, autonomy, trial and error learning, small-scale experimenta-tion, integrated team efforts (referred to as 'skunkworks') and a climate conducive to risk-taking. Moreover, as Charles Handy (1987) has pointed out, encouragement is crucial — and not just at the initiation stage. It is vital to be built-in over time during the *implementation* stage when colleagues are being exhorted to integrate new ideas into their daily classroom practices. Encouragement (i.e. psychological support) is important over the 'long haul' of the innovation process (see Smith *et al,* 1986). Concerning the goal of 'continuous improvement', one observer said recently, 'Why is it so hard?' Our answer would be: because

- continuous school improvement is a 'never-ending story'; it has to be *done* over time and with *perseverance*. Initiatives have to be sustained;
- it involves 'going against the grain' of past practice;
- long-term support is required;
- participants have to learn how to be supportive and collaborative;
- we have to be prepared to combine 'lofty ideals' with 'intense pragmatism';
- organizations have to be 'sailed rather than driven'. The orchestration

of improvement requires sensitivity and a 'feel' for the tasks in hand. This 'feel' involves a concern for the needs of *people* (i.e. the organization) and their encouragament.

Empowering: This entails the enfranchisement of those charged with 'delivering the goods'. It means *mobilizing* the energies, commitment and the (co-) ownership of staff members generally. They need to feel that it is *their* enterprise. Empowering involves:

- confidence-building and encouraging;
- enhancing (what is already a good performance);
- transforming (an unsatisfactory situation);
- energizing;
- generating loyalty and commitment;
- internalizing resolve;
- doing, i.e. implementing — with support

Empowering, according to Peters and Austin, involves stressing the *do-ability* (of small tasks that can be done by real people) and the *momentum* that comes from building in early successes ('small wins'). Action involves the resolve to move; and this resolve is energized by success and positive reinforcement (see Handy, 1987). Above all, say Peters and Austin, average performers have to be encouraged to find the 'star' in themselves. Block (1987) has argued, in similar terms, for the empowerment of middle managers.

And all of these processes discussed above are activated by means of the common denominator — MBWA. Management By Wandering Around combines such vital ingredients as availability, approachability, understanding, sympathy and immediacy. It enables the leader to pressure and support — routinely. It is where the initiating structure and consideration meet — in action. While the leader is initiating and pushing, he/she is also guiding and helping; MBWA allows the leader:

to make his/her presence felt

to be in charge of instant quality control

to be immediate, purposeful and directive

to provide common goals and to 'sell' the vision

to mandate

to promote positively

to preach constancy

to extol dedication

to talk/teach

to believe

to be decisive

to attend to the overall message

to confront problems

to be accessible/available

to roll up his/her sleeves and do things with/for teachers

to acquire a 'common touch'

to communicate and make it happen by 'modelling' the core values

to extend ownership

to offer positive reinforcement

to be constant

to be dedicated

to listen/learn

to be believable

to be humble

to attend to detail

to help solve these problems

MBWA has a classroom-focus; it enables leaders to 'walk the talk' and to live the vision. Through face-to-face interaction, they are able to pull together staff members and involve them in the life-blood of the school. MBWA is about attention; it is a two-way process. It encapsulates the twin sides of leadership.

One of the latest books from the business world, *Making it Happen* by Harvey-Jones (1988), offers some 'reflections on leadership' which provide further corroborative evidence for themes identified in this section. Harvey-Jones maintains:

> There has never been an instant solution, indeed in some cases there has been no solution at all. What there has been is a steady process of learning that management and business is a pragmatic matter depending entirely on people and how they react. Everything I have learnt teaches me that it is only when you *work with rather than against people that achievement and lasting success is possible* . . . It is an art which is applicable to any enterprise of any size in any area of life's activities. It is applicable to the running of the parish council as it is to the leadership of IBM . . . Management is about people, and manufacturing is about harnessing, motivating and leading people. It always has been, and I hope it always will be.

He points out that there must be commitment to any task on the part of those who have to execute it. Leaders can only make things happen *through* other people.

And these people have to be motivated when the leader is somewhere else:

> 'Plainly', he says, 'in any large enterprise the boss cannot be directly involved in everything, and some means has to be found to transfer his belief and commitment to others.'

The leader's job, he argues, is to create teamwork and commitment, skills and mutual respect and the leadership 'function' changes over time — a major theme both in this theoretical discussion and in current practice at Garth Hill. As leaders of their very different organizations, both Harvey-Jones and Goodchild have so many practices and, indeed, ideas in common. They both share, for instance, a belief in the efficacy of a strong, cohesive organizational culture. Deal (1985) has described the principal's/headteacher's role in promoting the cohesiveness of a school's culture:

> Effective principals are symbolic leaders who pay attention to small, but important, cultural details. Consider a few: Reflecting desired values in everyday speech and behaviour. Anointing heroes and heroines among teachers, students, and parents who exemplify these values. Telling the story of the school's origins or about the person for whom the school was named. Setting aside time in faculty meetings to talk about values and philosophy. Taking the time to introduce a new teacher, student, or parent to the school's culture. Arranging a parents night so that values and heroes or heroines can be celebrated in style.

Preparing a retirement party so that it reinforces values and beliefs embodied in an elder leaving the culture. Telling stories about a student whose reading improved dramatically and giving other storytellers an opportunity to relate such tales in public. Writing a personal note to a student who has done something special. Publicly recognizing a teacher who has gone out of her way to help a student. Organizing a day-long session where students, teachers, parents, and community residents can discuss the values and beliefs of the school.

Little things like these can, over time, transform a school culture. And a strong culture will yield dividends in learning achievement, morale, personal growth, and other indicators of school performance.

Hall *et al* (1986) reinforced this message:

The headteacher symbolises the school both to people inside it and to members of the community. As the highest status person in the school, the head's position has a figurehead function and symbolises the values to be upheld. The ethos set gives important meanings about what the school stands for.

This important point has been underlined by Leavitt (1986). In *Corporate Pathfinders* he argues that organizations need a management mix that blends the motivation of people to get things done (implementation), the logic of problem-solving (strategic planning) and the vision of pathfinding (leadership). Corporate pathfinding, he says, involves the rekindling of the pathfinding spirit and he describes pathfinders as committed believers with strong, clear convictions, thus providing vision, values and determination that add *soul* to the organization. It is the soul of the organization to which we now turn.

Chapter Two

School Culture

But institutionalizing such a pathfinding flavor, building it more or less permanently into the character of the organization, may require truly extraordinary forms of leadership, leadership dedicated to building just such organizations. Culture-building may have to be the pathfinder's central mission.

(Leavitt, 1986)

According to John Harvey-Jones (1988), one of the new demands on those charged with the responsibility of leadership is to create the associated conditions of *vision-creation* and *vision-transference.*

A vision is needed, and the ability to transmit and transfer that vision.

He argues that a leader is responsible for staging the process of deliberation leading to the generation of a collective, shared vision, which has to be translated into 'business objectives', the ownership of which then has to be transferred to the collegial network of staff members. Harvey-Jones emphasizes, quite rightly in our opinion, the benefits of creating opportunities for the 'switching on' of staff (referred to elsewhere as the process of 'buying in'):

In deciding where we should go we have to transfer 'ownership' of the direction by involving everyone in the decision. Making it happen means involving the hearts and minds of those who have to execute and deliver. It cannot be said often enough that these are not the people at the top of the organization, but those at the bottom.

Moreover, he contends,

One reason why you should try to develop the direction in which you think the company should go from both ends of the company at once is that in the process you gain the commitment of those who will have to follow the direction — and 'make it happen' — and in a free society you are unlikely to get the commitment without a high degree of involvement and understanding of both where the ultimate goal is, and the process by which the decisions regarding that goal have been reached.

Six major points emerge from what Harvey-Jones has to say:

(i)   a wider data-base is required which can be used when discussing the shape of the future;

(ii) this process of staff deliberation should combine 'top-down' and 'bottom-up' perspectives (thus synthesizing 'energy and synergy', says Harvey-Jones) and be both wide-ranging and lengthy: it is too important a process to be rushed;

(iii) the process of deliberation centres on such related questions as:

> where are we going?
> where do we want to go?
> where would we like to be?

(iv) the answers to these questions constitute a *vision* of the hoped-for future, a set of aspirations. And these aspirations contain *values,* i.e. statements about what is important, worthwhile and 'good' to be done into the foreseeable future. Some people call these 'mission statements' which taken together constitute a mission for the organization;

(v)   what is being described here is a *collective vision,* i.e. one that is shared by all those concerned and which, therefore, has the built-in commitment of those who will actually make it happen — the 'doers'. A shared, effective and affective vision constitutes a culture for an organization;

(vi) such a culture represents the tightness in 'loose-tight properties' and, as organizations become looser and more autonomous in the ways they operate, it becomes more important, not less.

These fifth and sixth points need some elaboration.

The concept of an organizational or corporate 'culture' has received increasingly wider attention in the 1980s (see Deal and Kennedy, 1983; Kanter, 1982; Peters and Waterman, 1982). What most commentators have failed to do, however, is to distinguish between the related concepts of 'ethos', 'climate' and 'culture'. As Harvey-Jones points out:

> It is only recently, since the publication of books like *In Search of Excellence,* that attention has really been focused on the values and spirit that can be built up in a company. These values are usually traceable to individuals much further back in the history of the company, and, if they are of the right intrinsic worth, they have been preserved, built upon, and transmitted through generations of people.

This 'spirit', which, according to Harvey-Jones, has long been recognized as important in military circles (and also, we would add, in education — see Deal, 1985) provides the power of tradition and continuity. Very often, however, 'traditions' have to be started rather than extended. Nevertheless, traditions, once generated over time, become cherished beliefs which are jealously guarded. These enduring values become *articles of faith* which permeate all levels of organizational life. This is only the case, however, if enough people in the organization come to believe in the values and are prepared to 'cherish' them. And this point leads us to offer an interpretation of the relationship(s) between ethos, climate and culture. We would define them as follows:

> **Ethos** is the intended dimension — as described above. It is the vision and the mission — the leading values. It is the realm of rhetoric; what people *ought* to value.
>
> **Culture** is the vision as enacted. It is the effective, actual, practice-based dimension. It is the realm of reality; what people *do* value. Ethos and culture may or may not correspond; there may well be a 'performance gap' between the intended and the actual, the 'formal doctrine' (see Smith *et al*, 1986) and the informal domain. Indeed, at one extreme, the informal culture may be undisturbed by the official rhetoric.
>
> **Climate** is the school's tone or atmosphere and is the 'felt' or perceived dimension which constitutes the linkage (the performance gap) between ethos and culture. It is a function of the interaction between the two; the wider the lack of correspondence, the more the climate will have a 'separate' existence. Given the elasticity of its functioning, however, the climate will reflect whichever (in terms of the ethos and the culture) is the more dominant, stronger dimension.

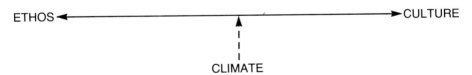

Presumably, given the views put forward by Harvey-Jones (as above) and endorsed by ourselves, the ideal situation is one where the ethos and the culture (and therefore the climate) are 'at one' — where they are identical. The vital question is how they can be brought into closer correspondence. Various relevant suggestions are made by John Harvey-Jones. For instance, the ethos cannot be an unrealistic, unrealizable set of demands — to which those who have to do the work are uncommitted. Commitment and ownership are crucial. To be successful at the cultural, informal level of the 'ethos' needs to be:

- based on a staff-wide dialogue;
- potentially 'stretching', but also 'believable in', identifiable with, realistic, achievable, obtainable and, above all, relevant to the needs, interests and motivations (and, therefore, the likely behaviour) of the staff members. It needs to be both challenging and do-able; tantamount to being a combination of Peters and Austin's lofty ideals and intense pragmatism.

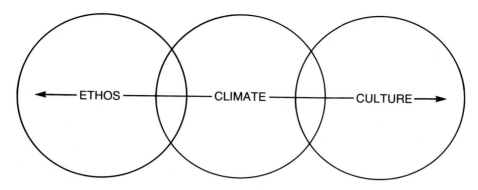

Three dimensions of a school's culture

The argument put forward by Harvey-Jones is that you are more likely to bridge the 'culture gap' if the vision is expressed in both clear and strategic terms. Take the latter first. The elements of the vision when formulated into a 'working agenda' need to offer acceptable, achievable and do-able challenges. This is the stuff of strategic target-setting. And clarity of purpose, he says, is essential for all members to know, understand, internalize and act upon the 'message'. The creation of resolve to do something with the message is crucial; but the *message* will only be successfully accepted and internalized if the *medium* of its construction and transference is a conducive one. In the cultural domain, the medium really is the message. Deal (1985) is at great pains to emphasize this point. Indeed, in his recent writing on the subject of a school's corporate culture, Deal has resuscitated the philosophy of Arnold Gehlen (see Berger and Kellner, 1965). Gehlen saw the concept of culture as central to the process of institution-building. He argued that, due to a biological instability which is characteristic to human beings, there is a need to protect them against themselves. They must be encouraged, therefore, to construct social structures to provide the very stability lacking in their 'nature'. In short, said Gehlen, 'this world, which is culture, must aim at the firm structures which are lacking biologically'.

The major point remains, however, that, whether the gap between 'vision'/ethos and 'culture' is non-existent, small or 'yawning', there is always an organizational culture — of sorts. Whether it is vision-led/ethos-driven or not, a culture exists. One 'culture', for instance, would be for the staff to be accustomed to rampant sub-culturing. Deal (1985) has contended that sub-cultural affiliations can have both positive and negative effects; on the negative side, sub-cultural groupings can:

> Undermine schoolwide values, create sub-cultural battles, or neutralize each other. This is particularly true when sub-cultures, in the absence of schoolwide cultural influences, vie constantly for supremacy and attention. For any school to perform effectively, shaped values must keep various subgroups pulling in roughly the same direction.

Otherwise sub-cultural influences will predominate, and both cohesion and performance will fall victim to a cacophony of diverse voices and special interests.

Moreover, Fullan (1988) has talked about heads/principals being sucked down into the mire of a school's convention-bound, informal culture. Given this potentiality for disruption and disintegration on the one hand and inertia on the other, Deal has argued at some length for the establishment of cohesive, stable cultures in schools (based on shared values and norms). As he emphasizes,

> The concept of school culture introduces another dimension to the effective schools literature. Every school has a culture, although the sense of tradition and shared direction vary significantly from school to school.

In effective schools which have effective and affective cultures, it is the cultural elements which influence the behaviour of administrators, teachers and students and, more generally, a schools 'productivity'. Within the influence of a cultural 'milieu', Deal stresses the power of *symbolism* (the 'spiritual and moral essence of schools', the realm of implicit meanings and hidden purposes) to 'reshape and revitalize the culture of local schools'. Indeed, Deal's key proposition is that 'understanding the symbols and culture of a school is a prerequisite for making the school more effective'. In fact, Deal is intrigued by the linkages between perception, symbols and the sharing of values. He sees rituals and ceremonies as crucial, with their importance deriving from what is 'signalled, expressed, or represented'. 'A succession of ceremonies', he says, 'rekindles faith' with slogans, written philosophies and symbols expressing core values. Indeed, Deal's views are summed up as follows:

> Culture is an expression that tries to capture the informal, implicit — often unconscious — side of business or any human organization. Although there are many definitions of the term, culture in everyday usage is typically described as 'the way we do things around here'. It consists of patterns of thought, behaviour, and artifacts that symbolize and give meaning to the workplace. Meaning derives from the elements of culture: shared values and beliefs, heroes and heroines, ritual and ceremony, stories, and an informal network of cultural players.

Deal (1985) and Deal and Kennedy (1982 and 1983) — along with Peters and Waterman (1982) and Peters and Austin (1985) — maintain that strong performance is dependent on a cohesive culture, consisting of a set of shared values which motivates and shapes the behaviour of organizational members and inspires commitment and loyalty. Indeed, say Deal and Kennedy (1983), 'culture is "what keeps the herd moving roughly west"'. Consequently, they argue:

> The real lesson that schools can learn from business refocuses attention on the culture of the school

Alternatively, of course, Torrington *et al* (1987) have advocated the benefits of an organizational culture (as experienced in education) to the business world.

A school's organizational culture, then, provides Gehlen's 'crust'. It puts the lid on possible conflict. It stabilizes the institution. As a consequence, it both reduces the chances of 'rebel teachers . . . making school impossible to run' (*Daily Telegraph*, 29 September 1987) and alleviates the insecurity and uncertainty accruing from the plurality of 'competing cultures' (Brian Cox in the *Times Educational Supplement*, 24 January 1986). Cox poses the central question:

> Does state education depend on some basic consensus about values and can it survive in our divided, pluralistic society?

According to Cox, the imposition of a particular world view can become accepted as 'common sense', the natural order, by those who are party to it. It becomes *norm-al*. This contribution — i.e. stabilization — is the greatest gift of an organizational culture.

We mentioned above that the terms culture, ethos and climate are often (too often in our opinion) used interchangeably. Rutter's 'ethos' equates with Deal's 'corporate culture' which overlaps with the concept of 'climate' posited by Halpin (1966) and seized upon in the DES/HMI publication entitled *Ten Good Schools* (1977). Miles' notion of organizational health covers much the same ground. It is significant, however, that the characteristics of each climate-type identified by Halpin and Croft (1963) are a set of dimensions (including esprit, engagement, hindrance/autonomy, intimacy, aloofness, consideration, thrust, production emphasis) which are not only 'cultural' indicators but also broadly speaking, constitute the 'felt' atmosphere emanating from and contributive to the school's culture.

Whichever term is used, however, there is certainly increasing interest in the ethos, climate or culture of the school. One recent headline declared that 'governors fired over school's "liberal ethos"' (*Daily Telegraph*, 13 January 1988). Other headlines have included:

'Where learning is a Cardinal virtue'
                              (*Times Educational Supplement*, 23 May 1986)

'The vision: A school where *everyone* works'
                              (*Daily Telegraph*, 20 October 1986)

'A school apart: an all-black independent secondary that actively cultivates "old-fashioned" values'
                              (*Times Educational Supplement*, 22 November 1985)

What values should a school stand for? John Wilson (*Times Educational Supplement*, 8 August 1986) has argued that 'being against elitism, racism and sexism is all very honourable but schools have got to be *for* something as well'.

In another John Wilson article in the *Times Educational Supplement*, entitled 'Dressing the part', he argued that if teachers want respect, they need to project the right image. furthermore, Roger Harris (again in the *Times Educational Supplement*) asked, 'Values: what do schools stand for?' He claimed that, given the era of accelerating change in education, what seems to be needed:

> is a long calm look at the values on which our educational philosophies are based.

Values, standards, virtues, visions and ethos are one and the same. And, for any school to have a cohesive culture, decisions have to be made, agreements reached and practices shared which involve *stances* concerning values, virtues and visions. Value difference passivity (see Holly, 1986) is useful for cultural stability. And cultural stability is highly prized; it is constantly wrought and sought. So much so, in fact, that this very stability brings about the cultural paradox: which is more important — institution-building through the agency of culture or cultural change through the agency of institutions? And are these compatible aspirations? What are being represented here are two propensities: the need to preserve the stability of the status quo and the need to jettison the status quo for the sake of change and innovation. It is a case of having to 'trade in' stability for instability — and the school's culture, designed for one essential task (stability and institution-building), may well prove inadequate when faced with the competing tasks of risking instability for institutional-renewal. This is the central dilemma faced by anyone invoking *cultural change*.

In a changing school (and, in 1982, Garth Hill *had* to change to survive) there is a *cultural* 'Catch 22'. Schools as institutions, according to commentators like Deal and Kennedy, need to build strong, cohesive, stable and affective school cultures. Yet the stronger, more cohesive a school's culture becomes, the less inclined are the participants in that school to introduce innovations — especially if the innovations carry the threat of disturbing and undermining the cultural stability. Innovations, from this cultural perspective, are perceived as potentially de-stabilizing. Accordingly, argues Holly (1986), every innovation has to be filtered within, and screened by, the socio-politico-psychological mix of shared values, norms, attitudes, assumptions and conventions that constitutes the culture of the school. Building on Sarason (1982) and House (1981), Holly (1986 and 1987b) has explored this cultural perspective.

He has discovered, like Sarason (1982),

> the power of the school culture, defined as behavioural regularities and shared assumptions, in successfully resisting and redefining educational innovations.

Holly has referred to this process of filtration as *culturation* and, with Marvin Wideen (1987), has identified three 'forces' within this same process:

> *pro-culturation:* the desire to storm the existing culture and instal an innovation within a school;
> *enculturation:* the desire to resist — or, at least, neutralize — the impact of externally or internally generated innovations;

acculturation: the willingness to learn from, and accommodate, new ideas to enhance the existing culture of the school.

In what Holly has described the 'problem of institutionalization', *changes* are mediated within the *cultures* of *institutions*. And, consequently, one observer sees institutionalization as pro-culturation — the successful installation and embedding of an innovation within school-wide classroom practice — while another sees it as enculturation — the neutralization of the potential radicalism of innovations. Compare these two views as they are reflected in the following passages:

- When Ronald Reagan was returned to power for his second term in office he announced his intention, during the next four years, to 'change America forever . . . from here on in, it's shake, rattle and roll'. Presidential counsellor, Edwin Meese III, nominated by Mr. Reagan to be Attorney General, called on the administration during the second term to 'institutionalize the Reagan revolution so it can't be set aside no matter what happens in future presidential elections'.
- Writing in his recent book, *Making It Happen,* John Harvey-Jones (1988), talking about triggers for change, says that:

  > these three potent forces — people, technology and competition — mean that industry cannot afford to become institutionalized . . . Unless a company is progressing the whole time, it is, in fact, moving backwards. It is quite impossible to maintain the *status quo*, or a steady state position in the international market place.

Institutionalization, then, can represent two sides of the same coin; it can mean success or failure. And this is a central paradox and a central dilemma for all 'innovators': how to achieve stability and security, in Gehlen's terms, without jettisoning the wherewithal to be an 'innovative institution'?

In short, a school's culture can make or break an innovation. No wonder, then, that one headteacher has given a 'warning on threat to "soul of the school"' (*Times Educational Supplement,* 2 February 1986).

Speaking at an annual conference of the Welsh branch of the Secondary Head's Association (SHA), this particular head argued that the recent glut of fashionable innovations in education is devaluing the school and promoting 'a certain theoretical functionalism' which is destroying the soul of the institution. 'I continue to be astonished' he said:

> that the entire emphasis seems to be on change in the curriculum, assessment and pedagogic methodology *at the total expense of the institution in and through which such changes must be implemented.* (our emphasis)

The tension lies in the relationship between institution-building and institution-renewal; both are vital activities and both have to work through the medium of a culture. Moreover, a culture which is developed during institution rebuilding can become the next set of 'barriers' during institution-renewal. Two recent articles from the *Sunday Times* have evidenced, from the experience of the business world, the essentially conservative nature of an embedded 'corporate culture'. The first article points out that people who join organizations constitute 'innovations' and may suffer 'corporate culture shock' when they find that either they do not suit the particular corporate culture that they are joining or it doesn't suit them. The article quotes Peters and Waterman (1982):

> The cultures that have meanings for so many, repel others.

Not everyone is able to share the values and beliefs that make up the culture:

> You might find yourself at odds with the company culture once you become part of it, however admirably you are qualified to do the actual job. That is the story behind many a square peg in a round hole.

In addition:

> Corporate culture is a matter of management style as much as philosophy. In fact, companies have a culture whether they are aware of it or not.

The second article picks up this theme and describes 'how "company culture" can block innovation'. The article, which is based on a survey entitled 'Innovation: The management challenge for the UK', points out that not only is innovation all about the process of successful change, but that it is a different thing from invention. Moreover:

> British industry has been good at invention, but has often fallen down on innovation.

Too often innovations are seen as 'products' and the *process* dimension is ignored. According to the Deloitte team who put together the survey, innovation needs to become an attitude of mind that pervades the organization, committing everyone in it to making things happen and creates the impression that the process is 'a race without a finishing line'. It is maintained in the article, however, that the obstacles to that race are formidable and that there are six chief factors that can hinder innovation — or promote it:

- *staff involvement:* people at all levels need to be involved;
- *market forces:* often used as an excuse for inaction, rather than seeing them as a spur to innovation;
- *resource allocation;*
- *communications,* which need to be informal, speedy and the life-blood pumping through the organization;
- *leadership:* it is the job of the leader to fashion the culture in the light of his/her own vision and then to communicate it;
- *company culture:* which, says the article, is so important, yet so often dismissed as irrelevant.

Consequently, the resolution to the central dilemma — the cultural Catch 22 — is a school culture which embraces innovation and innovativeness. Joyce *et al* (1983) have referred to the 'homeostasis of change', Holly (1985) to the 'development culture' and Harvey-Jones (1988) to 'continuous improvement'. What all these descriptions share is the conception of a stable, cohesive culture which accommodates sufficient openness to countenance the merits of ongoing change and development — and a measure of instability. It's the quality of the concoction that is important. We would argue the following: that

(i)   a continually developing school has a development culture;

(ii) this development culture promotes Joyce's 'homeostasis of school improvement' by means of the learning process of *acculturation,* i.e. an openness to the possibilities generated by change initiatives;

(iii) the development culture more than anything else signifies a *style* of going about the processes involved in introducing and implementing new ideas, practices and people (i.e. innovations) into a school; it constitutes a *capacity* for change;

(iv) a development culture rests on a vision of the future (whether generated by the Head alone or in collaboration with colleagues) which prescribes the 'what' (the goals) but not the 'how' (the means of achieving those goals). Innovations are then possible within the comparatively limited/ limiting parameters of the 'what', but, much more so, within the freedom of autonomy to decide the nature of the 'how'. What is anathema to a development culture is to have a value 'vacuum' — where there is no vision and, therefore, no sense of direction;

(v)   a development culture must have meaning at three levels: the *idiographic* (which entails both the satisfaction of individual needs and the invoking of individual loyalty), the *nomothetic* (the generation of the shared needs of team members and group loyalty) and the *morphological* (the shaping of the organization/an institutional sense of 'form'). The temptation to deny the importance of the idiographic level of meaning must be resisted. Innovations succeed or fail in the classrooms of individual practitioners. As Deal (1985) has observed, there is sometimes an:

> attempt to neutralize or bypass the teacher as an obstacle to educational advancement

Alternatively, however, the nomothetic and morphological levels are equally important and equally powerful — in unifying the staff members in the pursuit of common goals.

(vi) a development culture attends to the messages from 'innovation theory'; that, for example, the innovation process occurs over time and involves various phases — particularly adoption/initiation, implementation and institutionalization (in the more positive interpretation of the term). We would argue that:

(a) most of the time we do not get beyond the initiation stage;

(b) we approach implementation as though we are initiating. This is often part and parcel of the 'pilot mentality' which creates the unfortunate impression that 'it's innovation this term and then it will go away'. Successful innovation does not go away; indeed, it only becomes successful by sticking around and being worked on by the staff over time. It's very much a case, as Louis Smith *et al* (1986) have argued, of the 'long haul' of innovation. The point is that new innovations 'carry' new values — i.e. a new ethos (in the sense that we introduced it earlier in this chapter) — to be implemented amidst the existing conventions of classroom practice. In the early days of initiation, the staff members involved will probably experience the heady excitement and euphoria of being involved in something new. The 'Hawthorne' effect will keep them going. At this point they are on a kind of 'cultural island'; thereafter there is often

> . . . a failure of linkage between systems; the detachment and euphoria which makes time-limited systems so fascinating and productive, help to blind the participants to what they will be up against when they return to ordinary life . . . the decisions reached on the cultural island may be unworkable, inappropriate or very difficult to communicate to those on the mainland.
>
> (Miles, 1964)

Sooner or later, however, participants have to leave the cultural island and re-enter the mainland culture — of daily life in their schools. The new 'ethos' has to encounter the resident culture and be incorporated within it if implementation is to occur. Teachers now have to enact the vision and make it happen — often in spite of their own (previous and existing) cultural dependency. They are working against themselves. This is what implementation is all about; it is when the going can get 'tough' and the excitement turn into resignation and disillusionment. 'Following through', perseverance and support are now the crucial aspects of the process. Making changes tick is only possible if teachers stick with the task of implementation. And this is the essence of the development culture.

Pressman and Wildavsky (1979), in talking about implementation, have this to say:

> Imagination is needed, but so is perseverance

Successful implementation, then, means entering and having a lasting impact within the mainstream culture of the school.

(vii) a development culture is also an enterprise culture — in the sense, as

Peter Drucker has reminded us, that 'entrepreneurs exploit innovations'. Such a culture, therefore, while accommodating enterprising, entrepreneurial attitudes and behaviour, incorporates the view that 'innovations are here to be exploited by schools, as and when they need them' and not vice versa. The concept of the 'relatively autonomous school' (see Reid, Hopkins and Holly, 1987) is relevant here. If a school has the authority to create its own agenda for change — and to prioritise amongst these 'key areas of focus' — then it follows that the pacing, substance and direction of 'innovation' will be determined by the school — through mechanisms which underpin the development culture. Schools with flexible, responsive Institutional Development Plans (IDPs) are currently operationalizing the development culture.

(viii)   the development culture offers an *evolutionary, incremental* way forward — but it is a version of evolution which is not as rational and systematic (i.e. planned) as we would all wish it to be. 'New wave' thinkers like Americans, Karl Weick and James March (who provided some of the background idea for Peters and Waterman when they wrote *In Search of Excellence*) Bert Cunnington and David Limerick in Australia and Andrew Pettigrew in Britain have all stressed the often irrational nature of organizational evolution. Weick, for instance, suggests that organizations learn and adapt *very* slowly. He argues that it is the deep-seated, informal culture, in the form of habituation, that holds back an organization, the members of which pay obsessive attention to customs (what Peters and Waterman refer to as 'habitual internal cues'), long after they have out-lived their usefulness. According to Peters and Waterman, these assumptions are:

> buried deep in the minutiae of management systems and other habitual routines whose origins have long been obscured by time.

Weick argues that this inflexibility stems from the inability of organizational members to wrest clear of the metaphors they use to depict their institutions. Their use of military metaphors, for instance, leads them to overlook the possibility of having different kinds of organization. People *expect* organizations to be run by means of 'line management' and 'a chain of command' with much talk of 'strategy' and 'tactics'. Weick argues, however, that new metaphors have to be found — which support:

improvization rather than forecasting
opportunities rather than constraints
argument not serenity
doubt and contradiction rather than predictability

Cunnington and Limerick (1986) have described this new thinking as the 'Fourth blueprint: an emergent managerial frame of reference'. Their model (D) is alternative to what they refer to as the 'traditional model' (A), the 'human relations model' (B) and the 'systems model' (C) (see the diagram below). They argue that the emerging model contains four new managerial roles; those in senior positions have to be:

1   *a manager of networks*
    Organizations as networks are based on loosely coupled systems of values; their effective management requires the recognition of the differing interests represented and the pursuit of collaborative individualism rather than group consensus.

2   *a manager of self*
    Managers have to operate *above* systems of often conflicting values.

3   *a manager of meaning*
    It is necessary to achieve a higher level of integration through the use of 'transcendental values, values which transcend operational issues' and thus are acceptable to those holding a wide range of interests. Furthermore:

	'Closed' system	'Open' system
'Rational' Actor	**A**	**C**
'Social' Actor	**B**	**D**

(adapted from Peters and Waterman, 1982)

the fourth blueprint recognizes that human motivation can be catalysed through the use of symbolic expressions of such transcendental values . . . An effecive manager is a manager of meaning.

4   *a manager of paradox*
    The effective manager is keenly aware of the paradoxes of organizational life and will seek to resolve the central dilemmas.

This 'fourth epoch' (Peters and Waterman) is characterized by an 'open-system'/ 'social actor'/orientation and 'messiness dominates in both dimensions'. The complex 'social actor' is a 'human being with inbuilt strengths, weaknesses, limitations, contradictions, and irrationalities'. Everything is in flux. Consequently, argue Peters and Waterman (1982), the leading theorists of the new 'paradigm' in organizational thought (like Weick and March) emphasize:

informality
individual entrepreneurship
evolution
and a 'metaphor shift' to counter embedded customs

The same authors conclude, however, that:

> We are confronted with an extraordinary conundrum. Most current theory is neither tight enough nor loose enough. Theory is not tight enough to consider the role of rigidly shared values and culture as the prime source of purpose and stability. It proposes rules and goal-setting to cover these bases. At the same time, most current theory is not loose enough to consider the relative lack of structure and the need for wholly new management logic to ensure continuous adaptation in large enterprises. Indeed, it habitually proposes structural rules and planning exercises — both forms of rigidity — to hurdle this need.

Evolution as adaptation consists of enough 'good tries' to provide, according to the laws of probability, some successes. Consequently, Karl Weick, in arguing the case for 'loosely-coupled systems', recommends two key approaches:

- 'unjustified variation': 'chaotic action is preferable to orderly inaction';
- 'retrospective sense-making': what Charles Handy (1984) calls 'control after the event'.

As Peters and Waterman contend, writers like Weick and March are fascinated by the role that classic evolutionary processes play in the development of organizations. The development culture, incorporating their ideas, becomes the embodiment of this classical view of evolution. It entails persistence, experimentation, trial and error learning, risk-taking and improvization. Incrementalism involves 'small wins', intense pragmatism and a great deal of entrepreneurial small team activity. This is somewhat different to the way that change initiatives in schools are normally viewed. The usual approach is to initiate systematic, planned change which is linear, mechanistic, predictable and rational (the 'model' of innovation practised in the 1960s in the UK). It is tantamount to the 'route march' view of progress. The new management thinkers like Weick and March, however, have discarded this model in favour of one which, according to Peters and Waterman, accepts 'limits of rationality' and cater for such basic human needs as:

- *meaning*
- *a modicum of control*
- *positive reinforcement*
- and a secenario wherein *action and behaviours shape attitudes and beliefs rather than vice versa.*

As has already been mentioned in this chapter, the 'control' comes with the acceptance of the core values — the ethos, the formal culture. Any more control could well lower commitment and depress innovation. The cohesive elements within the operational looseness are cultural ones. The language is also important. Talk of 'temporary structures', 'ad hoc task groups', 'fluid organization', 'action orientation', etc. speaks volumes. We like particularly the baseball metaphor — that movement in developing organizations is opportunistic; there are:

> . . . lots of bunt singles, an occasional double, and a once a decade home run.
>
> (Peters and Waterman, 1982)

Two aspects of this evolutionary approach need to be given particular emphasis:

(a) the development culture as explored above is the blood-stream of *learning organizations* (see Schon, 1971; and Holly in Reid, Hopkins and Holly, 1987). Such organizations are adaptive, continuously sensitive to environmental demands, fleet of foot and capable of 'intentionally seeded evolution' i.e. development. According to Peters and Waterman:

> The organization *acts,* and then learns from what it has done. It experiments, it makes mistakes, it finds unanticipated success — and new strategic direction inexorably emerges. We strongly believe that the major reason big companies stop innovating is their dependence on big factories, smooth production flow, integrated operations, big-bet technology, planning, and rigid strategic direction setting. They forget how to learn, they quit tolerating mistakes. The company forgets what made it successful in the first place, which was usually a culture that encouraged action, experiments, repeated tries.
>
> Indeed, we believe that the truly adaptive organization evolves in a very Darwinian way. The company is trying lots of things, experimenting, making the right sorts of mistakes; that is to say, it is fostering its own mutations. The adaptive corporation has learned quickly to kill off the dumb mutations and invest heavily in the ones that work. One guess is that some of the most creative directions taken by the adaptive organizations are not planned with much precision.

This quotation leads to the second point.

(b) How do organizations remain innovative? How do they stave off 'calcification'? Holly (1984) has posed these questions of schools and Peters and Waterman go some of the way to providing the answers:

- keep experimenting, encourage 'tries', permit 'small failures' and keep things small and incremental through the orchestration of what they call 'chunking';

- be prepared to tolerate 'organized chaos' — 'buzzing, blooming environments' — which is creative but untidy;
- learn from trying and doing things.

The central question broached in this chapter still remains, however; how to institutionalize 'enterprise', i.e. innovation or innovativeness (the innovative spirit). How to structure what flourishes amidst a lack of structure? Certainly the more orderly and 'systematic' things become, the more that continued adaptation will be suppressed. One answer, as discussed earlier, is to differentiate between the processes of invention (i.e. what is done, according to Peters and Waterman, by 'small bands of zealots operating outside the mainstream' of formal structures) and innovation — the long haul towards immanence. The art is to achieve a balance where organizations have structures and are still able to retain their inventive spirit and innovative capability.

Several general points emerge from this discussion of some pertinence to Garth Hill School and its development:

- First, it is not just a case of 'structures' (procedures, committees, hierarchies, compartmentalization, etc.) inhibiting innovation; just as repressive, if not more so, is *the 'old' culture* which binds the participants within its (shared) conventions, assumptions, customs and expectations. The 'old' symbols have done their symbolizing — the participants may well be addicted to them and forced into making plastic responses. A curious culture malaise will have set in (often referred to as inertia), with an in-built cultural level of intolerance. At best, low risk change strategies will be tolerated and 'change' will be as slow as possible. Any innovative organization can get like this. It is the so-called 'dark side of institutionalization' — endemic enculturation, to which the only response is proculturation, i.e. a new ethos/vision and a new set of challenges with which to inspire staff members.
- Second, given this dependency on 'history', it makes no sense to wait for 'pre-conditions' to appear before initiating changes. 'Climate-setting' often comes during the change process, not before.
- Third, the new business manager at Garth Hill (Alan Watts), on 'secondment' to the school from his company, Hewlett-Packard, recently told us that H.P. was mentioned in Peters and Waterman (*In Search of Excellence*) as one of the most successful companies in the USA because it had 'institutionalized' its employees, i.e. succesfully socialized them so that they share certain core values. We now have three interpretations of 'institutionalization':

(i)   successful installation and incorporation (pro-culturation);
(ii) successful rejection, neutralization or cultural domestication (enculturation);
(iii) successful internalization of a value commitment; cultural inclusion (inculturation).

There must be an important relationship between the first and third definitions. It could be argued, therefore, that what Stanley Goodchild had to do — back in 1982 — was the following:

(a)   achieve proculturation by introducing a new ethos (core set of values) and institutionalize it, i.e. gain its acceptance among and across his staff;
(b)   achieve inculturation by starting early, being dramatic and symbolic; use plenty of ritual and ceremony;
(c)   co-opt the support of the local 'environment' and be responsive and sympathetic, i.e. 'close to the customers';
(d)   look to promotional work to 'market' the new image of the school and thus enhance its previously flagging reputation.

Alternatively, however, conventional management thinking would have told Stanley Goodchild to wait, have a good look around, initiate procedures and structures and then introduce some 'safe' changes. Fortunately, he chose both to ignore conventional wisdom and to 'stand' it on its head — and, in so doing, did many wrong things right. Undoubtedly, he would have agreed with Karl Weick's statement that 'they (schools) are managed with the wrong model in mind'. Loosely-coupled organizations are best unified through cultural affiliations. Stanley Goodchild sensed the importance of the cultural and symbol importance of creating new 'traditions'. He needed to revamp a rather tired ethos. And then along came the issue of school uniform.

We would want to argue for the symbolic importance of school uniform and the symbolic importance of its reintroduction at Garth Hill in 1982.

Along with the new emphasis on the importance of school assemblies, prize-givings and sports activities, school uniform provided what Deal would refer to as the symbolic and cultural dimension of school life. More than anything else, Stanley Goodchild, largely instinctively, has attended to the central task of unifying the school around ritual and ceremony, heroes and heroines, and symbolic activities generally. School uniform is redolent of cultural values. It sets an ethos. It creates an image. It adds to the 'authority' of education, says John Wilson in the *Times Educational Supplement*.

> Recently, teachers have stressed the latter (humanity and fallibility) at the expense of the former (professional authority): fearful of their own authority, they have very rapidly dismantled the whole apparatus of uniform, hierarchy, tradition and ritual that used to display and prop up their professionalism.
>
> In some form or other — by some kind of dressing, window-dressing, or setting the stage — that apparatus has to be revived . . .
> being professionals, we owe it to our clientele to appear as such.

In the case of Garth Hill, the reintroduction of school uniform was heralded as a 'quiet revolution' and a 'return to traditional values'. Simultaneously the media announced that the pupils were 'only too happy to dress like Mum and Dad did' and were eagerly returning to 'competitive sport frowned upon by the previous head'. The panoply of ritual may well be traditional in its image, but that is because, traditionally, educationalists had a keen sense of the importance of cultural symbolism. And institutions, it is now acknowledged, need these essential cultural underpinnings — thus the deluge of media coverage given to the decline in school sport.

Most of these articles stress that, with extra-curricular sports activities, competitive sport and the provision of a full physical education programe all seriously at risk, much has to be done to turn the tide. As Anne Sofer maintained (in 'Sporting chances' *Times Educational Supplement*), because 'team spirit' evokes the public schools and the glories of empire, it has suffered guilt by association.

> 'In fact', says Sofer, 'many of its most parodied features are worth reflecting on — for instance the idea that individual glory can worthily be sacrificed for the benefit of the team, or that 'sportingness' — that is, a stringent code of conduct coexisting with keen competitiveness — is an important way of keeping the whole activity civilized.'

When some educationalists renounced the 'trappings of elitism' (i.e. school uniform and competitive sport), they were also renouncing the trappings of institutional character and culture. In so doing, they left a cultural vacuum — to be filled by other influences. Schools as institutions suffered. As one headteacher remarked to us recently, it is best to move forward from a position of strength; create institutional stability (through the agency of school uniform, sporting activities, etc.) and then innovate like mad in the curriculum arena'. And it is largely the head's task to create the ethos — the cultural ground-rules.

Southworth (1987) has written interestingly about the appointment of a headteacher and the implicit understanding that his/her task is to determine the school's ethos along the lines of his/her underlying philosophy. Consequently, says Southworth, as a result of this 'succession issue', there is an invitation to make a cultural break with the past:

> If heads are autonomous, able to set the ethos for the school and 'unify' the staff within a framework of values compatible with the head's beliefs, then one would expect that there would be discontinuity . . . when a change of heads occurs what could be happening is a change in the school's value system

Given this likelihood of cultural discontinuity, new heads are supported in launching rapidly into change initiatives by two factors:

- staff expectations of impending changes;
- the fact that the incoming head is able to view his/her school with a freshness and a detachment that could well soon be lost. Ironically the 'wait and have a good look' approach can mean that the objective, dispassionate and 'un-encultured' edge will soon be lost. If heads act in support of the prevailing norms from the beginning (in order to feel comfortable and accepted), they could well become prisoners within their own schools. Heads can either dominate — and act as

gate-keepers for — the 'culture club' or fall foul of its machinations (see the diagram below). Heads determine an ethos-driven culture or find themselves at the mercy of a culture-driven ethos.

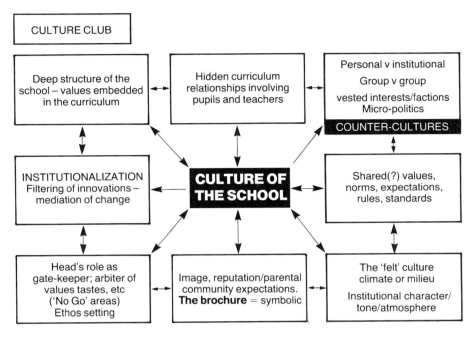

A diagramatic representation of the 'culture club' phenomenon (reprinted from **School Organization**, 1986)

This chapter has charted some of the inter-linked aspects of this diagram. The intention has been to stress the importance of the 'structure' of a *development culture* which is

- directly linked to the ethos (and vision) established for the school; and
- capable of entertaining and furthering an innovative, enterprising spirit.

To end this chapter, and to link some of the themes emerging from our discussion of both *school leadership* and *school culture*, we would make the following observations:

(i) the meaning of 'institutionalization', will be interpreted according to the way we define 'institution' — the way we see and carry around a picture of an 'institution' in our heads. According to Meyer and Scott (1983), this picture is *normally* one which bespeaks conformity, standardization, uniformity, control, regulation, supervision, procedures, rules, standards, etc. We expect institutions to promote these things. And such expectations, they argue, are tantamount to an ideology. Institutions, as we are led to perceive them, are devices for control.

(ii) these expectations and perceptions are carried around with us as deep-seated assumptions concerning the way things will be. We carry conventions and norms and use them to judge the world around us: they also dominate our practice. It is difficult to wrest clear of such pre-conceptions. Thus, and this is a most relevant example, Sergiovanni and Corbally (1986) talk about the professor who lectures most persuasively on the new theories of James March and Karl Weick and then goes off to a staff meeting and argues for clear goals and the articulation of them in a set of standardized procedures linked to rational decision-making structures. As Sergiovanni and Corbally reflect, ideas are so ingrained that even scholars who disclaim the ideas intellectually, espouse them in their everyday practice. Thus, like this professor in the example, we expect institutions to be formal structures; that, to be considered legitimate, they must be rationally structured, logically operated, the efforts of staff members coordinated and controlled in some systematic form, and the 'outputs' standardized.

(iii) Manifestly, there are implications here for the process of learning. If something is different from, and does not conform to, what we are expecting, do we recognize it? Do we reject it out of hand? Do we classify it as unconventional? Consider this quotation from a record sleeve:

> In fact, (Cannonball) Adderley is partly responsible for institutionalizing (Charlie) Parker, by playing Parker — like lines that are easier for listeners to follow.

There is a need, it seems, for bridges across the dissonance gap (see Holly, 1987b). Any new message has to be within the grasp of the recipients (according to their conventional 'taste') to gain acceptance; and the recipients have to be 'open' enough to stretch out and receive it (see Gadamer, 1975). And it is the same with a new ethos for a school as it is for new theories about how schools should be organized — the messages must be within the grasp of the participants and they must be willing to listen. Suggested changes must be 'relevant' and the participants must see the need for the changes.

(iv) One headteacher, talking about the process of making improvements in her school, said recently:

> Get it first, formalize it second.

She went on to say that it is important to remain *optimistic,* to see the *opportunities* in every situation, to *stimulate interest* ('it's infectious', she said), and to create *'elbow'* room' — entailing, she said, creating more 'open structures in which others can come to the fore'. And herein lies the major message of the last two chapters. As Charles Handy (1984) maintained, it is a case of combining a lived philosophy ('hands-on, value driven') with a 'bias for action'. Handy, after Peters and Waterman, talks about effective organizations (both schools and businesses) having 'control after the event' (i.e. trying it and we'll see if it works) and fostering leaders and innovation throughout the staff membership. Handy said:

> The atmosphere, Peters and Waterman write, is not 'that of a large corporation but rather a loose network of laboratories and cubby-holes populated by feverish inventors and dauntless entrepreneurs who let their imaginations fly in all directions'.

Handy also talks about transforming (Leavitt's transformative) leadership 'lifting' the *spirits* of the staff into supporting common institutional purposes (the key values — the 'what'), while the organizational *energy* is galvanized within small, autonomous teams/task groups whose responsibility is the delivery of the 'how'. The aim, says Handy, is freedom of action — by controlling the 'what' but not the 'how'. Furthermore, he argues:

> Too many schools find it too tempting to control the 'how' centrally and delegate the 'what'. That becomes tightly-coupled anarchy — not excellence.

Handy and several other commentators — on both sides of the Atlantic — argue that schools as loosely coupled organizations should play to their strength — that they are loosely coupled. One of our colleagues recently defined institutions as 'organizations with values'; perhaps an alternative definition, based on the emerging theory, is that they are 'values without so much organization'. In other words, institutions like schools need to be stronger in values and somewhat weaker on organization.

Cunnington and Limerick (1986) have endorsed this combination which they refer to as:

- *metastrategic vision* (the value orientation), plus
- organizations as *networks of loosely coupled systems of action*.

They argue that schools as organizations have to cater for:

- collaborative individualism
- proactivity and entrepreneurialism
- value difference
- the emotional, non-rational dimension

Their concept of 'metastrategic vision' is an interesting one. They see it as embracing not just 'culture', but also 'strategy' and 'structure'. It constitutes, therefore, both ethos (in our definition) and some ideas about its implementation; it is, in their words, the 'mission definition', involving both the 'driving values' and a 'map' of how these values can be achieved.

The other side of their organizational equation — 'networks of loosely coupled systems of action' — accentuates collaborative individualism (it's more like having a team of cricketers than footballers, they argue), and the capacity to keep the organization fluid and responsive enough for members to move through different systems of action and initiate and exploit a range of opportunities. It is a question, then, of decentralization and differentiated networks within an integrated, corporate culture. According to Cunningham and Limerick, it is the corporate culture that is used to:

> release and catalyse human energy.

And, in ways that begin to link the themes of this chapter with those of the next, Cunnington and Limmerick stress that the management of change is the 'number one issue today' and

> whereas slow incremental change can be based on the patterns of the past, the challenge facing today's organizations is dynamic quantum change in which the patterns of the past become a hindrance rather than a help.

While accepting this statement *to some extent* and acknowledging a similar point made by Charles Handy (1987) — that *discontinuity* is essential (eventually) in the change process — we would not want to discard the concept of *incrementalism*. We see this as akin to Peters and Austin's 'chunking' and their 'intense pragmatism'; chunks of change and small advances which are activated in a piecemeal, pragmatic and opportunistic fashion and which, cumulatively, zig zag towards the accomplishment of the school's vision. The paths forward may well look much more ordered after the event — it really is a case of retrospective sense-making.

Cunnington and Limerick's conception of a metastrategic vision is akin to the tripartite arrangement put forward by Harold Leavitt (1986) — involving pathfinding, problem-solving and implementation. It could be argued (as in the diagrams below) that pathfinding is all about *ethos*-making, that

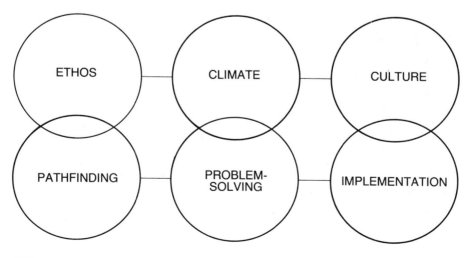

involvement in problem-solving can create a *climate* of collaboration, which, in turn, leads to committed implementation amidst the informal *culture* of the classroom.

What we would contend is that Leavitt's balanced approach provides the vital linkage between the discovery of a leading vision or ethos (path-finding), collaborative inquiry (problem-solving) and the renewal of everyday classroom practice (implementation). This linkage mobilizes the change process.

Indeed, Leavitt (1986) points up some of the same dilemmas charted in this chapter. He maintains that path-finding tends to be an individualistic, enterprising pre-occupation, while implementation (and, to some extent, problem-solving) has to be more participative. His suggested resolution to this particular dilemma is to build an organizational culture that accommodates both styles:

> One route to an effective plural and parallel union between pathfinding and participation is to build an organizational culture that welcomes both styles: a culture that puts high positive value on *both* pathfinding individualism and cooperative implementing.

The second dilemma explored by Leavitt (and ourselves in this chapter) is the power of an organization's culture to resist change initiatives — and, indeed, to resist being changed itself.

In this lengthy extract from *Corporate Pathfinders*, Leavitt gets to the nub of the question:

> Culture is an umbrella word. It refers to a whole package of implicit, frequently unconscious, widely shared beliefs, traditions, values, morals, expectations and habits that characterize a particular group of people. Culture is to the organization what 'personality' and 'character' are to the individual. Like our personalities, our organizational cultures are usually more clearly visible to others than to ourselves. They're too much a part of us for us to see them very clearly. Like the character of individuals, the moral and ethical qualities of our organizational cultures are so deeply built in that we hardly notice they are there.
>
> Cultures, organizational and otherwise, serve important functions for us. They are comforting, they are controlling; and they limit and direct our vision.
>
> They comfort us with their familiarity because it's just the way things are, and perhaps also the way things have always been, we find it hard to see beyond our cultures, to other ways of thinking, feeling, or acting . . . We value our cultures. Our cultures' ways become the right ways . . . Cultures can thus become highly resistant to change. Indeed, the stronger the culture, the more widely shared and deeply held are its beliefs and practices and the harder it is to change.
>
> So cultures, organizational and otherwise, are (i) real; (ii) mostly taken for granted; (iii) extremely controlling and directing of our behaviour; and (iv) very hard to change.

Cultures, then, provide the security of the 'known' and the reassurance of inclusion — a sense of belonging. Once the ropes have been learnt, the signals picked up and the special language acquired, full membership rights can be conferred — in exchange for an implicit ageement to abide by the rules. This is the cultural contract. Thereafter, as Leavitt maintains,

> culture shapes the eye of the beholder

Through the members affirming the legitimacy of cultural controls, cultures determine whether change will happen. A culture, according to Leavitt, is a powerful tool to discipline the organization — thus the central dilemma explored in this chapter: institution-building through the agency of a school's culture at the expense of institution-renewal. And Leavitt's resolution to this dilemma mirrors our own: make the organizational culture work for the school and its change process (the development culture). The advice is to use its power positively and use it to unite the school behind the chosen vision; in so doing, says Leavitt, unifying the 'total human side of the enterprise' and creating a human community. Rather the school as an organization be determinedly turned into the wind — in order to make headway — than it be continually buffeted and at the mercy of the cultural elements.

Another dilemma arises when the culture of the organization differs sharply from that of the surrounding 'society'. Moreover as Leavitt points out, even in cases where organizations are able to create cohesive (internal) cultures, sub-cultures and counter-cultures exist within the 'parent' culture. Leavitt describes this phenomenon in graphic terms:

> . . . if an organization tries to build a culture, trouble is a certainty. The parent society will perceive the offending organization as an illegitimate enemy, and either imprison it with restrictive legislation and social pressures, or deport it, or kill it altogether. Moreover, recruits from that society will need serious remodelling to live in the new and different organizational culture.

Leavitt's solution concerns the need for a school to work in and with its 'society' to shape a common culture, i.e. one which embraces and accommodates the values of the school and its community. The concept of 'ecological niche' is of some relevance here.

Bennis and Nanus (1985) refer to *positioning* — the search for a viable niche in the community. They point out that this process is more proactive than reactive (schools can, in their words, 'develop effective forecasting procedures to anticipate change') and involves not only changes in the internal environment, but also the creation of receptivity in the external environment. Schools, they say, have to act upon the environment to make it more congenial. Above all, however, Bennis and Nanus argue that schools as organizations have to establish a new linkage between their internal and external environments in terms of negotiation and mutual accommodation — thus echoing the solution suggested by Harold Levitt.

A school's culture, then, provides some of the answers to the three dilemmas posited by Leavitt and outlined above:

Dilemma One: The individualistic orientation of pathfinding versus the participative nature of implementation

- **resolution:** a school culture which encompasses and supports both dimensions

Dilemma Two: Cultural stability and control versus the possibility of change and renewal

- **resolution:** a school culture which consists of a robust *development culture*

Dilemma Three: A culture class between the school's (internal) values and those of its external community

- **resolution:** being reactive and proactive in the search for common ground and supportive ecological niche.

'Passing the Baton'

Warren Bennis and Burt Nanus (1985) have charted similar territory to ourselves and Harold Leavitt. They advocate the efficacy of *attention through vision* (the creation of a compelling focus, a clear and attractive agenda), the importance of extending this vision to others in terms of *meaning through communication* (the creation of a shared vision and the aligning of people behind it) and the centrality of the establishment of the appropriate *social architecture* (or culture) to give shape to the common enterprise.

> 'Leadership', say Bennis and Nanus, 'by communicating meaning, creates a commonwealth of learning and that, in turn, is what effective organizations are'.

Transformative leadership, then, creates a unity of purpose and the *linkage/bridging* necessary to instil in others commitment to, and enthusiasm for, this vision. Those in the organization must be mobilised to accept and support the new vision — to make it happen. It is a case of management for change.

Chapter Three

Management for Change

. . . the role of the leader is much like that of the conductor of an orchestra. The real work of the organization is done by the people in it, just as the music is produced only by the members of the orchestra. The leader, however, serves the crucial role of seeing that the right work gets done at the right time, that it flows together harmoniously, and that the overall performance has the proper pacing, coordination and desired impact on the outside world. The great leader, like the great orchestra conductor, calls forth the best that is in the organization. Each performance is a learning experience which enables the next undertaking to be that much more effective — more 'right' for the time, place and instruments at hand. And if in the long run the organization succeeds, it doesn't at all detract from the quality of everyone else's work to suggest that it was the leader who made it possible for the organization to learn how to perfect its contribution.

(Bennis and Nanus, 1985)

This chapter builds on the power of proactive leadership and the cohesion of a cultural vision and introduces the central questions:

How to get there?
How to effect successful change?
How to manage the process of implementation?
How to realize the vision?
How to pass the baton?

Charles Handy (1987) supports our view (expressed towards the end of the previous chapter) that the change process is one of *discontinuous incrementalism.* He points out that:

Change is not what it used to be . . . Thirty years ago change meant more of the same; it was incremental change, continuous change. More of the same only better . . . We know better now. Change is often discontinuous, different, not more. But old habits die hard and we do not yet comprehend or feel comfortable with lines that do not run straight. Discontinuous change means . . . that what used to work does not work so well any more. It means a range of new uncertainties.

In these new change scenarios, says Handy, the past will not provide the answers. Neither, we could argue, will existing theories concerning the management of change provide any answers. What is required is a new theory to guide new practice. Handy finds all this disconcerting (discontinuity can turn established truths on their heads) and yet exciting:

It opens up new possibilities. The old order has to change. Old conditions no longer seem to count for much. What used to be insurmountable road blocks are now only obstacles, to be removed or got round.

Given that the future is full of uncertainty, Handy has four important points to make:

- First, it is very much a case of learning (as opposed to teaching) the way into the future.

- Second, this learning (as both Fullan, 1985, and Lieberman, 1986, have said) is best done *with* other people.

  Handy concludes:

  Discontinuous change . . . requires that you learn to behave like a scientist, asking questions, seeking possible answers, testing possibilities. It helps if you are always asking why, if you can get others to help you, if you are happy to keep making mistakes until you find something that works, if you think of life as a bundle of opportunities waiting to be developed and if you have the self-confidence to think that you can do some of that developing . . . Of course you need some basic skills, competences and knowledge to start with, but it is an attitude of mind as much as anything, a way of approaching life, *an implicit learning theory if you like.*

- Third, in such a dynamic, learning situation, while we cannot be 'bound by our own precendents . . . it is habits that are harder to change'. The risk-taking that is demanded will entail taking risks with our attitudinal 'security blankets'.

- Fourth, it is very much a case, says Handy, of exploring the 'inverted doughnut'; or what he calls 'doughnut thinking'. The doughnut is 'inverted' in the sense that the hole in the middle is the solid part and the outside is all space. The core, he argues, represents all those central values and tasks, while the outside space represents uncertainty — in the forms of risk and ambiguity:

> The implications of the doughnut go further. In conditions of continuity organizations and societies seek to maintain stability by giving people roles or doughnuts which are almost all core. That way things are more predictable. Indeed many jobs deliberately eliminate any room for discretion; they cut out the outer space of the doughnut . . . I am suggesting, however, that under conditions of discontinuity we all will have to learn to live with bigger doughnuts, with more space. It is that sort of learning with which I am concerned, because, ironically, under the pressure of uncertainty most people and institutions instinctively do the opposite, they creep back to the core.

Given the challenges, however, people must be exhorted to move into the spaces and become more

- experimental;
- tolerant of failure;
- ambitious;
- self-confident;
- resourceful;
- flexible;
- creative;
- cooperative;
- supportive and mutually reinforcing;
- encouraging of each other.

Indeed, says Handy, *change* (i.e. discontinuity) and *learning* are linked by *encouragement*. If the previous chapters have concentrated on the core concerns — the *initiating structure* — this chapter has as its central theme the *consideration* and the support mechanisms necessary to empower organizational members to operate at the edges and boundaries of their experience without retreating headlong into the dictates of habit.

The management of this kind of change will form part of a 'complex, dilemma-ridden, technical, sociopolitical process' (Fullan, 1985). Given that the style of change will be less linear, less sequential and less continuously incremental, much of current thinking concerning innovation theory may have to be jettisoned and reconstituted on the strength of new practice. And this will take time. At present we must satisfy ourselves with pointers into the future of the

'Starship Enterprise'.

Undoubtedly, some popular beliefs concerning innovation and the management of change will prove to be redundant and misconceived:

(i) The view of innovations being merely materials and resource-packs will be finally laid to rest.

(ii)   The conception of the process of innovation as being composed of various phases — adoption/initiation, implementation and institutionalization — will have to be re-examined.

(iii)   Continuous improvement will be considered as a vital part of the enterprise culture — as an alternative to a 'dependency culture', i.e. dependency on a tired, constraining, reactionary culture. *Proculturation,* involving the transformation of the existing culture, will involve the initiation of an enterprise ethos and its exploration in practice. While mutual adaptation (involving the gelling of the old and the new) will lose some of its currency, the 'best of the old' will provide the launch-pad for the exploration of the spaces.

(iv)   Currently, commentators advise schools to beware of the dangers of *innovation overload* and to order priorities for development.

This makes good sense and we would not want to advise otherwise. Indeed one of us has written about 'the developing school' (Holly, 1985) having, as one of its hallmarks, the process of 'prioritization'. There is some evidence, however, that in a situation where there are 'multiple initiatives', if there is clustering (i.e. the various initiatives have a common denominator such as the emphasis within current curriculum innovations on new approaches to learning and more varied teaching styles), then there is a chance of achieving a 'critical mass'. At this 'tipping-point' the overlapping demands achieve such a volume of intensity that the central imperatives become more impactful. It is difficult to ignore a cacophony of demands which are all making the same noises. A multitude of 'bright ideas' may well share some central concerns and 'force through' the core ideas. Pressman and Wildavsky (1979) have written persuasively on this theme.

(v)   The conventional approach to persuading teachers to change their classroom practice is to aim to change their attitudes and values first (through 'conversion') and then, so the theory goes, their practice will change accordingly - in line with their newly acquired convictions. Again, some new evidence would suggest otherwise. Both Fullan (1985) and Guskey (1986) have argued that *trying* new classroom practices can lead to successes which, in turn, strengthen the resolve to continue, followed by more successes and more positive attitudes to the changes. In other words, as Fullan has argued, understanding, knowledge and *belief* (including the internalization of the value of these changes) can arise later rather than earlier; using and doing come before believing.

> changes in attitudes, beliefs, and understanding tend to follow rather than precede changes in behaviour. (Fullan, 1985)

The other five points are stated briefly here but will be elaborated upon in the rest of this chapter.

(vi)   Much time and effort have been spent on initiating changes; as Fullan (1982) has stressed, however, *implementation* is now the key concern.

(vii)   To be able to support implementation much more has to be learnt about how *to do support effectively* (the basis of *consideration*).

(viii)   As a consequence of the 'chunking' approach to implementation, schools as organizations will have to indulge in much more 'retrospective sense-making' and, in Handy's terms, 'control after the event'

(ix)   In terms of the emphasis on *collaborative individualism,* staff members will have to learn how to balance collaboration with the individual pursuit of excellence, the 'enterprise' with the 'enterprise spirit'.

(x)   The management of change (i.e. the deliberate planning of change) will lose its currency; much more crucial will be *management for change* — in three ways:

- management enabling and sustaining staff members in their implementation efforts;
- management establishing the climate for change;
- management empowering those who are charged with accomplishing changes in their everyday practice.

Of relevance to these points is the model of the innovation process suggested by Peters and Austin (1985):

It would be easy to dismiss all this as idle 'star-gazing' — and anyway, we can hear our British readers saying, 'they would do those things in America and in business wouldn't they — this is education we're talking about; business and industrial models are totally irrelevant'. Except that:

- commentators like Peters and Austin are talking about educational as well as business organizations;
- if terms like reflective and innovative practitioners and task/working groups are substituted for 'skunks' and 'skunkworks', perhaps it all then sounds more palatable, more possible and more like what, in many cases, *is being done already.* Whatever the future holds is probably in existence — somewhere and in some form.

Of all those writing and talking about change management in education, Michael Fullan seems to have the surest grasp of where we are, where we are going and, of course, how we get there. In his seminal publication entitled *The Meaning of Educational Change* (1982) and in a string of articles thereafter, he has explored the nature of the change process. Fullan (1987) has noted, for example, the fact that the initiation/adoption stage of the innovation process has received much of the attention — for various reasons:

- the temptation to have 'innovation without change' and to keep things 'bolt-on' rather than 'built-in';

Figure 8: **Innovation Process**

A model of the Innovation Process

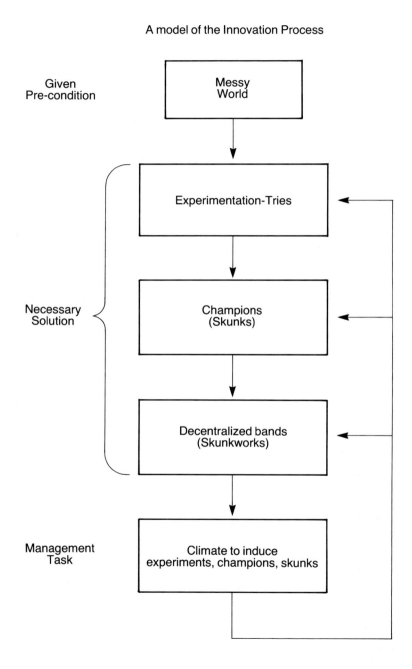

- the naive optimism of many 'hero innovators', whose missionary zeal has proved so off-putting to the very people they should be 'converting' (see Sarason, 1982);
- the fact that people expend all their energy on developing and initiating innovations and have got nothing left for the crucial tasks of 'follow through';
- the fact that initiating projects is more glamorous, visible and less time-consuming than the rigours of *front-line work;*
- plus the fact that we have only recently begun to understand the importance and some of the characteristics of *implementation.*

Indeed, Fullan's greatest contribution has been to focus on the *implementation stage* in particular and to stress, like ourselves, that *implementation* is about

- what really matters in the change process;
- *doing, trying* and *following through;* it's about *sustained effort* over time. It's essence, therefore, is an 'action orientation' (Fullan, 1987);
- mobilization; about galvanizing teachers to change their classroom practice in significant ways;
- rolling programmes of work which are fluid and dynamic;
- and, above all, *making change stick.*

It is significant how the language used to describe implementation is different; terms like *sustaining* (the effort over the *long haul*), *doing, making, achieving, changing, mobilizing* and, above all, *persevering.*

In the popular vernacular, it's a new ball game.

Therefore, we have to play it differently. The rapidity of change is the constant factor which has to be taken into consideration. Change will not go away or be compartmentalized into 'what we do after half-term in the summer term'. As Harvey-Jones (1988) says, the organization which is standing still is actually going backwards. In terms of coping with the welter of changes, Fullan (1987) has listed various 'implications for action'. His insights include the following twelve points:

(i)   effective entrepreneurs exploit innovations;
(ii) 'if only' statements should be avoided;
(iii) given the new reality of multiple innovations, try to prioritize and 'do two well and the others as well as possible';
(iv) on the one hand, the fetish of (elaborate) planning should be avoided; planning can become a substitute for *action;*
(v)   on the other, it should be remembered that the action or implementation plan has to be implemented, i.e. amended in the light of events as they unravel;
(vi) 'start small but think big'; there should be 'modest plans and ambitious effort';
(vii) all those involved should beware of the 'implementation dip' when those doing the innovative work feel insecure, deskilled and under stress;

(viii) it should be remembered that 'innovation' involves new content and new processes — and attending to both is vital;

(ix) innovation, to be successful, requires both pressure and support;

(x) while the 'brute sanity' of some reformers is to be avoided at all costs, mandation (i.e. pressure) may well be important in the early stages, whereas participant ownership is crucial thereafter. As Harvey-Jones (1988) maintains, nothing much will happen unless the participants are committed to 'making it happen' ('it' being implementation). Fullan has referred to this combination as 'high initiative' plus 'gradual empowerment'. Similarly, leadership for change is crucial, especially during the early stages, when, according to Fullan, there is a need for a *strong change advocate.*

(xi) building on the work of Joyce and Showers (1980), Fullan argues for the importance of continuing, effective in-service training (INSET) which helps teachers to consolidate new skills and apply them in the classroom situation. Holly, James and Young (1987) have called this 'Applied INSET', i.e. in-service training opportunities which are practical, relevant, classroom-focused and targeted on the current needs of the participants;

(xii) Building on the work of Little (1981) and Lieberman (1986), Fullan (1987) argues that through intense interaction in small teams there should be a sharing of the 'considerable burden of development required by long-term improvement'. The membership of these *task groups* will provide the *critical mass* required for successful change efforts. Indeed, in terms very reminiscent of Peters and Waterman/Peters and Austin, Fullan contends that within this small-scale, interactive team-work, the members have to:

- beware of being over-committed, too enthusiastic;
- tolerate the ambiguities and uncertainties involved in there being no fixed (once and for all) solutions;
- beware being too 'unmanageable', too 'off the wall';
- avoid the pitfalls of 'talking' and not 'doing'. Their responsibility is to be activists for change.

Moreover, as Fullan (1985) has remarked,

> When successful improvements are accomplished, they involve individuals working in small groups and other collective ways, attaining technical mastery, a sense of success, and new meanings.

Such groups, he says, work on the basis of *interactive professionalism.* They act as scouting parties for their colleagues, reconnoitering the opportunities for educational advance. The members of such teams establish 'footholds' for their colleagues and achieve 'leverage' for change. More than anyone else (and returning to Fullan's earlier point), they are the ones who are outward-looking on behalf of their school — and who are the entrepreneurs always poised to exploit innovations.

Michael Fullan's work is important not only for its relevance and wisdom, but also because it spans both educational theory and practice and those of the business world. His point concerning the exploitation of innovation first appeared, for instance, in Peter Drucker's book, *Innovation and Entrepreneurship*.

> Innovation is the specific tool of entrepreneurs, the means by which they exploit change as an *opportunity* for a different business or a different service. (Drucker, 1985)

In short, says Drucker, entrepreneurs act as change agents, seeing

> change as the norm and as healthy. Usually, they do not bring about the change themselves. But — and this defines entrepreneurs and entrepreneurship — *the entrepreneur always searches for change, responds to it, and explores it as an opportunity.*

In so doing, they fulfil four conditions:

(i) to succeed they need to build on strengths and to ask — which of these opportunities 'fits the bill'?;

(ii) they need to remember that innovations demand, at root, changes in behaviour;

(iii) while they are prepared to take risks, they also minimize them. They are not so much risk-focused as *opportunity-focused;*

(iv) above all, however, they need to see that innovation is *hard, focused, purposeful work*. It makes great demands on their diligence, persistence and commitment; ingenuity is no good on its own.

Innovators, says Drucker, do not defend yesterday — they *make* tomorrow.

This emphasis on making change happen and purposeful innovation has been echoed recently by two other commentators, Matthew Miles (in education) and Roger Plant (from a business standpoint).

Miles (1987) has most usefully provided some 'Practical guidelines for school administrators: How to get there'. He contends that all change initiatives need to satisfy certain conditions — from the 'user's' point of view. There is a basic need for:

- *clarity:* teachers must understand clearly what is expected of them;
- *relevance:* teachers must feel that the changes being promulgated are meaningful, practical, applicable and connected with their everyday concerns;
- *action images:* teachers must be able to visualize what is expected of them — what the changes look like in practice;
- *will:* this is the dimension of motivation, interest and involvement; teachers must acquire the *internalized resolve* (see Holly, 1987) to do something with their newly-acquired knowledge;
- *skill:* given the action orientation, teachers must acquire the necessary *skills* to be able to *do* the action as envisaged. *Skill acquisition* connects *knowledge* and *successful action*.

In the same article Miles produces a 'causal map', comprising the complex network of factors leading to successful implementation. Elements in his map include such 'preconditions' as a principal/head teacher with *leadership* and management skills (1); some *school autonomy* (2) (involving, says Miles, loose-coupling and an active non-regulatory style); staff *cohesiveness* and trust (3); and a good *fit* between the change programme and the local context (4); the aspects which pertain to the process of implementation itself. These include: *power-sharing* (5) — critical, says Miles, in creating *staff willingness* and initiative during implementation (10) and making the change initiative 'person-independent'; i.e. *institutionalization* (15); *rewards for staff* participation (6), including *control over resources (9); the need for a shared vision* (7) plus the creation of a purposive climate which allows for the long-term accomplishment of this vision, i.e. *programme evolution* (13), leading to *organizational change* (16); and *control over staffing* (8), *external networks* (11), *coping strategies* (12) which are all part of *'good implementation'* (14). These elements can then be assembled with the necessary conditions into matrix form:

Selected Findings re Key Factors	Clarity	Points of Relevance	Action Images	Issues of Will	Necessary Skills
(Preconditions)					
(1) Leadership					
(2) School Autonomy					
(3) Staff cohesiveness					
(4) Good programme/fit					
(5) Power-sharing; initiative-taking and empowerment for staff					
(6) Rewards for staff					
(7) 'Vision' sharing					
(8) Control over staffing					
(9) Control over resources					
(10) Staff willingness/ commitment					
(11) External networks					
(12) Coping; problem solving					
(13) Evolutionary programme development					
(14) 'Good implementation'					
(15) Institutionalization					
(16) Organization Change					

from Miles (1987)

Furthermore, Miles makes a vital point concerning the management of change in schools (see also Holly and Hopkins, 1988). He points out that the bulk of innovation theory (and, indeed, much innovation practice) assumes that change initiatives are specific innovations, generated externally and probably imposed on schools. The enterprising school, however, has enough freedom to make its own agenda for action, i.e. to generate changes from within. Consequently, says Miles,

> Some prior research has emphasized 'fidelity' pressures as important to successful implementation. However, many of these studies have been of programs, for example, quite concrete, self-contained activities that have relatively minimal impact on the basic structure of the school or its objective. In this study we are dealing with something very different, something approaching a *reform*. An adaptive, evolving approach seems more useful . . . Letting go of technocratic planning models helps convert what looks like 'sloppiness' to coherent development.

Plant (1987) has produced a comprehensive introduction to the themes of *Managing Change and Making it Stick*. Like Holly (1985), Plant suggests a five-stage process of bringing about change:

(*What do we need to look at?*)
1   recognizing the need to change
2   mobilizing commitment of the critical mass
(*Where do we want to get to?*)
3   building a shared vision for change
(*Where are we now?*)
4   diagnosing current reality
(*How do we get there?*)
5   the implementation of change
(*How are we doing?*)

Plant points out, however, that such a 'logical path doesn't often work'. In this context, Plant makes four points of central importance:

- First, he asks, can change be managed? Can changes be directed, planned for, controlled, shaped and influenced (i.e. managed) or is it a case of simply surviving and being buffeted by them? And how much can the implementation of change be organized (in terms of instituting mechanisms, procedures and structures) and prove *enabling* without them being *disabling?* This tension between the promotion of change initiatives (including the freedom to maximize the potential of such changes) and any attempts to structure the process is a recurring theme throughout this chapter. It is particularly important given the current message: that *loose coupling* is vital when it comes to the 'how' of the change process.
- Second, 'making change stick' occurs by getting the 'how' right. And,

as Harvey-Jones (1988) argues, success or failure hinges on the level of staff interest, commitment and involvement. What is crucial, argues Plant, is how people feel they are treated during the implementation process. Successful change occurs through people, not in spite of them.

- Third, mechanisms for staff involvement have the potential to release staff energies, transfer ownership to the participants and

> help to begin the process of moving and set the climate for implementation.

- Fourth, says Plant, the principle of 'parallel implementation' has to be safeguarded; i.e. that staff deliberation (for example, diagnosis) is not allowed to preclude staff action. Both are important and should happen simultaneously — and feed into each other.

Getting started on change involves:

- vision-building: establishing a clear vision towards which to move purposefully;
- recognizing the need for change and mobilizing commitment to change; sifting through the 'cultural clutter' by means of situational or climate analysis. In the GRIDS project (see MacMahon *et al*, 1984) this stage was called the *initial review;*
- reviewing in terms of *where are we now?* and *what do we need to look at?*

Plant (1987) argues that it is important to analyze the present condition — in evolutionary terms — of the organization. As mentioned earlier the work of Blake, Avis and Mouton (1966), Lievegoed (1972) and Greiner (1972) is of some relevance here. Plant builds on these writers and talks, for example, about the *autocratic phase* of a 'born-again organization', characterized by the dominance of the pioneer/founder; the urgent need for survival; (possible) rapid growth, etc. During this early stage, other important tasks are:

- becoming clear what needs to be retained;
- communicating the need for change;
- organizing visits to other schools or organizing 'visits' by participating staff to their own school.

Holly (in Reid, Hopkins and Holly, 1987) has maintained that a cycle of school development can be activated through the application of various kinds of internal evaluation:

- needs analysis;
- classroom observation;
- target-setting;
- strategic evaluation;
- and monitoring.

The style of development of central concern in this chapter is what Holly calls 'strategic evaluation' — or how do we get there? Plant (1987) makes five pertinent observations:

(i)   It would be a mistake to ignore the 'submerged organization':

> Whether the organization goes through any real or lasting change, however, depends entirely upon how much energy is injected into influencing the submerged, murky, and often uncharted depths . . .

(ii)   It is important to launch into *development* in an *evolutionary* and *incremental* way.
(iii)   Understand the likely resistance (to be able to do something about it) and build in supports.
(iv)   While it is important to avoid 'analysis paralysis', Plant argues for the inclusion of data collection and analysis as part of the development process. The 'capacity to learn', he says,

> is a key to managing change.

Lieberman (1986) calls this process 'collaborative inquiry'.

(v)   Where Plant and Harvey-Jones are in complete agreement is when they argue that if the staff members have been 'switched on', for 'high stickability' of the changes, the 'how' of what is to be achieved is a matter for delegation and the provision of operational space — what Harvey-Jones refers to as 'headroom'.

One central argument seems to be whether 'structures' motivate or demotivate, enable or disable, enhance or impede change initiatives. A second, related argument is that growth and development conducted the OD (Organization Development) may not lead to major, radical change. Holly (in Reid, Hopkins and Holly, 1987) has argued for development as opposed to innovation — for gradualist, incremental (in the continuous sense), 'evolutionary' approaches which build on present strengths and grow out of what the school and the staff already have to offer. The contention made by Holly, and indeed Roger Plant, is that this ordered approach to change is more likely to have a lasting impact. This approach rests on the dictionary definition of 'development' which includes the bringing out of potential, the exploitation of natural resources, a bringing to a more advanced, highly organized state and an advance through successive stages — a spiral. This helical view of change entails a much more integrated, holistic and organic approach. But, as Stanley Goodchild believes, it might not be appropriate for 'high risk, rapid innovation'. Presumably low risk innovation is more acceptable and, with the increasing emphasis on teacher-initiated reform, it could be argued that, inevitably, the 'risk' elements in change initiatives will be lost during the process of innovation. Alternatively, however, by structuring the developmental process around different approaches to evaluation — in procedural (action) steps — in a somewhat mechanistic manner (see the diagram below), staff members are in receipt of the

Figure 9: **Procedural (Action) Steps** *Source: Reid, Hopkins and Holly (1987)*

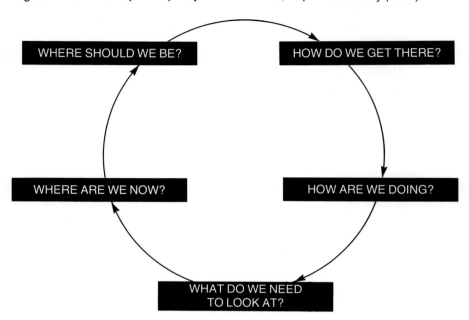

transfer of ownership — it is *their* programme of action for development — and as the GRIDS Project team always insisted, the procedures suggested within such a scheme do not have to be followed slavishly. In the end a great deal depends on the school, its stage of development and its context. One school may well need and thrive on a structured, ordered and 'managed' OD style approach, while another may prosper on the more entrepreneurial, unfettered, 'under-managed' approaches suggested by Peters and Austin.

The OD approach of GRIDS aims to offer a school an organic, coherent programme of internal development which involves strategic planning, cyclical and systematic approaches to change and development and small-within-large-scale collaboration (i.e. interest groups — 'specific review teams' — are formed to report back to the rest of the staff). Initiating, implementing and monitoring the internally-generated change process is built into the design. Above all, like Joyce *et al* (1983), the scheme aims to provide the 'structure of school improvement'.

The innovative, operating-at-the-edges approach promoted by Peters and Austin, organizationally-speaking, is obviously much more fragmented and is composed of lots of 'small tries', 'small wins', etc. The term 'building-block' is used by both approaches. On the one hand, the OD approach (see Holly, 1985) describes what is to be integrated (for example, school-focused in-service training experiences) as a 'building-block' for school development; on the other, Karl Weick refers to the small team and its work as a 'building-block', which, he argues, is much more difficult to unravel and *which can be arranged in various kinds of configurations*.

Maybe the difference between the two approaches is not as great as first appears. The one approach attempts to 'make sense' of the work prospectively, the other operates retrospectively. Sooner or later, however, both approaches are faced with the same dilemma — how to fuse individual and small team enthusiasm to the mainstream of school development?

Holly and Martin (1987) have built on the ideas of Fenstermacher and Berliner (1985) and Dadds (1986) to produce a 'profile of development' which can be used for both planning and evaluation; i.e. 'plotting' the school's development:

Profile of development

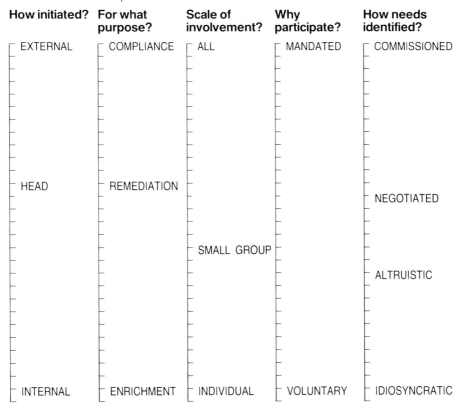

(Adapted from Fenstermacher and Berliner, 1985)

This profile can be used to plot the nature of the change process, the balance between externally/internally-generated initiatives, and the levels of staff involvement and representation. While the question of equilibrium (in terms of a school's contextual relationships and its stage of development) is an important one, what is also crucial is finding ways of 'structuring' procedurally the 'passing of the baton'. From the point of view of linking the vision-builders — the pathfinders — to the implementers, i.e. the staff-at-large, Bennis and Nanus (1985) maintain that the way to overcome the 'change problem' is not the simple exercise of power and control, but the achievement of voluntary commitment to shared values. The aim, they argue, is to integrate what must be done with those who must act. Ways have to be found, then, of carrying the vision across the school in order to not only mobilize the energies and commitment of staff members, but also convince them that it is worth changing their classroom practice. This was the main dilemma faced by the GRIDS Project (see Holly, 1984) — how to enthuse the whole staff enough to suffuse their (individual) classroom practice. While we would readily acknowledge that individual enterprise can be stifled by too much 'organiza-tion' — too much of a procedural straitjacket — we are not convinced that Karl Weick's recipe is organized enough. It could be seen as almost too enterprising, too individualistic, too hit and miss and too reliant on the 'hidden hand' of individual altruism.

Harold Leavitt (1986) has offered, in our opinion, a more balanced view of the change process. He suggests that the connecting rod between pathfinding and implementation is problem-solving — which he sees as embodying the more logical and rational approach to organizational life. 'Problem-solving', organizationally-speaking, entails a capacity for the internal generation and filtration of change initiatives. This capacity, say Bennis and Nanus (1985), should consist of an institutionalized, formal planning mechanism through which the organization identifies and evaluates new issues, designs and considers alternative policies, generates a consensus about appropriate actions, and provides major changes in direction. Such advice would be too mechanistic for some commentators. As usual, however, Harold Leavitt's advice seems eminently sensible. Organizations such as schools, he argues, should find areas ripe for creative problem-solving (for example, climate analysis) and begin to make small steps towards larger changes. He advises organizations to rediscover their youth by establishing non-specialized (i.e. interdisciplinary), non-hierarchical, non-formalized and non-bureaucratic groupings, thus injecting entrepreneurial, improvisational and informal elements into organizational change scenarios. Problem-solving, then, is synonymous with team-based collaborative enquiry and, according to Leavitt, it provides the linkage between path-finding and implementation.

Staff involvement in problem-solving activities can:

- harness the enterprising spirit of individuals and small groups on behalf of *the* enterprise — the school;
- build the bridge from vision-making to classroom practice;
- provide some procedural structure for this process of linkage;
- generate staff commitment and energize the transfer of ownership;
- capitalize on the benefits of collaborative team approaches;
- through the agency of these learning groups, enable the school as an organization to learn its way forward.

Warren Bennis and Burt Nanus (1985), like Charles Handy (1987), link the transformations involved in constant change with the learning process:

> Organizational learning is the process by which an organization obtains and uses new knowledge, tools, behaviours, and values. It happens at all levels in the organization — among individuals and groups as well as systemwide . . . Groups learn as their members cooperate to accomplish common goals. The entire system learns as it obtains feedback from the environment and anticipates further changes. At all levels, newly learned knowledge is translated into new goals, procedures, expectations, role structures, and measures of success.

These same authors usefully differentiate between *maintenance learning* (the acquisition of routines and the maintenance of the existing system) and *innovative learning*. The latter consists of:

- the anticipation of emerging issues and the analysis of trends;
- experimentation and adaptation;
- learning from other organizations;
- applied training;
- some concomitant 'unlearning';
- an openness and a receptivity to new learning;
- a search for new challenges;
- respect for innovation and risk-taking
- an effective planning process, which, according to Donald Michael, is 'the mode by which a complex social organism can learn what it seeks to become, perceive how to attempt to do so, test whether progress has been made, and re-evaluate along the way whether the original goal is still desirable'.

With staff teams that experience and promote innovative learning and creative problem-solving, certain process outcomes will accrue. Over time, the teams tend to become more open, more supportive and more trusting. While trust has to be earned, say Bennis and Nanus, it is also the lubrication that makes the organization work. Trust comes with predictability, reliability, integrity and consistency; 'choosing a direction and staying with it' (i.e. persistence) is vital. As these same authors maintain, trust is allied to confidence, self-esteem and empowerment; it can result in 'courageous patience'.

> Innovation — any new idea — by definition will not be accepted at first, no matter how sensational the idea may be. If everyone embraced the innovation, it would be difficult to take it seriously — as an innovation. Innovation causes resistance to stiffen, defense to set in, opposition, to form. And any new idea looks either foolish or impractical or unfeasible at first. It takes repeated attempts, endless demonstrations, monotonous rehearsals before innovation can be accepted and internalized by any organization. This requires staying power and, yes, 'courageous patience'.
>
> (Bennis and Nanus, 1985)

What is required, then, is the informality and flexibility of group-work on behalf of organizational development and a mix of individual, small team and joint enterprise on the one-hand and informal and more formal endeavour on the other. The small task-group would seem to be the fulcrum of such activity. It links the individual practice and enterprise of staff members to the corporate enterprise and it embodies the spirit of chunking in two ways: it allows the members to concentrate on one area of focus (content) and it incorporates the benefits of the team approach (process).

Figure 10: **Tensions of School-Based Development**

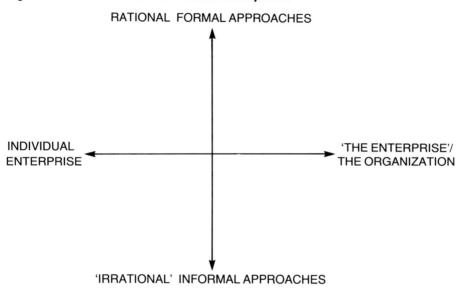

To conclude this chapter, and to restate some themes touched on in previous chapters, we make five basic points concerning the management of change or, as we prefer to say, *management for change:*

First, proactive yet responsive change leadership is vital.

Clark *et al* (1984) have emphasized four aspects of change leadership: the capacity to be

- directive and set high expectations;
- persuasive, communicative and *'influential'*;
- facilitative;
- supportive.

Support, both technical and emotional, is crucial. It is the embodiment of consideration and provides the means, the encouragement, and, therefore, the empowerment to move forward into the 'black box of implementation' (as Fullan describes it).

Harvey-Jones stresses that the role of management is to identify the direction of change and bring about conditions in which it can occur. These 'conditions' include the following:

- the initiation of the continuous effort to 'break the cultural mould'; thus avoiding

  the tendency for organizations to silt up (which) seems to be a law of corporate nature: operatives finding the easiest but not necessarily the best method; middle management sticking to a comfortable level of stability; empire-building by conflicting senior management interests; or simply the ultimately, fatal resort of relying on what worked well in the past.

- the appreciation that staff members have a favourite hobby — watching the reactions and behaviour of the Head and that it is important to lead by example and for the 'leader' to be seen to be experiencing change personally.
- the realization that climate-setting is all-important. What is needed is a climate conducive for making changes;
- the understanding that the change leader has a responsibility for overseeing the rate and pacing of change. While 'staying put is not an option' (Harvey-Jones) and there must be continuous improvement, there has also to be established a realistic balance between waiting too long and going too fast and too much against the grain:

  Wait too long and you have lost control, move too soon and you will lack the commitment which is vital to success. (Harvey-Jones, 1988)

And while change leaders are important, Harvey-Jones concludes:

I do not believe in the myth of the great leader who can suddenly engender in his people a vision and lead them to an entirely new world. I believe that the reality is more traumatic and more demanding.

Certainly it is more demanding for those having to make change happen, i.e. those responsible for *doing implementation*.

Above all, however, the leader has to create the understanding that change is a way of life. Harvey-Jones (1988) admits to two obsessions: *change* and *people*.

Without change, nothing is possible . . . remember the dinosaurs!
Whether change is comfortable or not, it is inevitable.

Given the discomfiture arising from being involved in change initiatives, Harvey-Jones always comes back to the *people* in the organization. They are the key to success; they will make it happen.

In short, then, without the right kind of leadership change will not happen; and change will not happen unless those who are led are prepared to make it happen.

Second, the orientation to a 'steady state' of continuous improvement is not gimmickry, far from it. It is not 'innovation for innovation's sake'; because (a) as in the case of Garth Hill, it is very often a question of survival; and (b) the clustering of innovations mentioned earlier creates an intensity of impact, a critical mass, which is essential for change to occur. As Pressman and Wildavsky (1979) have argued, during implementation, innovations get changed, lost along the way, unintentionally thwarted, distorted; it needs strength in numbers for the core understandings of these innovations — the central thrust — to be accepted as 'common practice'. We would argue that both these points go some way to explaining the success of the recent change efforts at Garth Hill.

Third, and building on Harvey-Jones above, successful change also requires *altruism* for *action*. While remembering Jerome Bruner's words — that 'you more likely act yourself into feeling than feel yourself into action' — the point to emphasize is that the burden of *action* is eased by sharing it — by being supported by the *altruism* of others. Peters and Austin (1985) stress that:

> The best bosses — in school, hospital, factory — are neither exclusively tough nor exclusively tender. They are both tough on the values, tender in support of people who would dare to take a risk and try something new in support of those values.

Given the fundamental importance of the leading vision, Peters and Austin argue that in terms of its implementation there are two sides to the equation — the 'toughness' in terms of an almost unmerciful attention to detail and the 'softness' provided by the spirited, emotion-filled passion and trust involved in the shared, supportive nature of the quest.

Altruism for action is all about the *people* dimension; it is the embodiment of the *consideration* that supports the *initiating structure*. And this consideration involves *supportiveness* which, in turn, entails understanding, attention, sensitivity and the mobilization of support which is both technical and psychological (see Fullan, 1985). In-service activities and staff development schemes can provide for both the 'applied' technical training and the emotional support that comes from team-work - see Joyce and Showers (1980) and the DELTA report on TRIST (Holly, James and Young, 1987). Above all, argue Peters and Austin, 'soft is hard' — a crucial point in our opinion.

Fourth, change is facilitated within learning organizations (as argued by Handy and Bennis and Nanus). Many organizations, according to Peters and Austin (1985), forget how to learn — or become incapable of learning because they forget the benefits of staying small, responsive, flexible and adaptable:

> Through chunking, a corportion encourages a high volume of rapid action. The organization acts, and then learns from what it has done. It experiments, it makes mistakes, it finds unanticipated success — and new strategic direction inexorably emerges.

The learning organization is also the adaptive organization. It cherishes smallness and looks for what Weick calls 'small wins' by utilizing small team effort. Indeed, 'the small group', argue Peters and Austin, 'is, simply, crucial to innovation'. Learning organizations, in the views expressed by Drucker and Peters and Austin, also cherish and celebrate entrepreneurship. Small bands of innovators (skunks/skunkworks — terms coined by the Lockheed corporation in World War Two to describe its *unconventional* approach) work at the edges of decentralized organization. They have plenty of 'headroom' and are encouraged to be self-managing, self-motivated, self-directed and capable of expressing themselves within 'collaborative individualism'. Such teams are encouraged to be energetic, fast-moving and innovative. Ownership is the key to their success. Acording to Harvey-Jones (1988), it is no longer a case of coordination and control of the implementation process at the centre of the wheel; given clarity of purpose,

> it is perfectly possible for all those at the rim of the wheel to self-optimize, and to align themselves.

Learning organizations know, through experience, that

> innovation . . . just doesn't occur the way it is supposed to.

Innovations are often mundane, incremental, and constitute small gains which accumulate over time. Improvization is the key concept. While, argue Peters and Austin (1985), people like to explain and to be tidy (it is agreeable to think of our achievements as the outcomes of a flawless chain of brilliant decisions and deliberate planning') and would like to deny that most innovation occurs as a 'result of desperate groping and frequent backtracking'. Pragmatism, during implementation, reigns supreme: it is, say Peters and Austin (1985), the 'Wee Willie Keeler' approach. Keeler, apparently, was a baseball player in the 1890s and early 1900s, who reached the sport's Hall of Fame by hitting only thirty-four 'home runs' in a career which lasted over twenty years. He liked to score many, many 'singles'; he was the 'consummate opportunist'. According to this view, most innovations do not arise from substantial planning exercises, vast research projects, lengthy reflection, big teams, or even big breakthroughs. Life in innovative organizations, say Peters and Austin (1985) is essentially unplanned, even 'messy':

> Unfortunately, most innovation management practice appears to be predicated on the implicit assumption that we can beat the sloppiness out of the process if only we can make the plans tidier and the teams better organized.

Organization, they say, should take advantage of this seeming sloppiness, and should not attempt to fight it.

Fifth, and this, say Peters and Austin 'is the $64,000 issue; if the messy-world-experiment-champion-skunkwork paradigm makes sense, then we need to create a climate that induces all the above to occur — a climate that nurtures and makes heroes of experimenters and champions'.

Innovative organizations 'smell' of innovation.

In short, as a whole culture, they innovate.   (Harvey-Jones, 1988)

They provide a thorough-going, conducive context for innovation — an entrepreneurial environment. Moreover, it is most significant that Peters and Austin (1985) refer to the innovative properties of such companies as IBM, Hewlett-Packard, 3M and Apple. Such companies are either situated within a stone's throw of Garth Hill or have supported the school (or both):

> Innovating is the priority at Hewlett-Packard (as it is at 3M) . . . the parallels between Hewlett-Packard and 3M are striking, especially in their language.
> (Peters and Austin, 1985)

And, of course, this statement can be extended to include Garth Hill. The motto of all three organizations could be 'don't wait — do it'.

The emphasis on 'getting on with it' is substantiated, according to Peters and Austin, by constantly talking about getting on with it:

> If you want innovation, you have got to talk — incessantly — about innovation.

In addition, such talk is stimulated within external networks such as those existing within Silicon Valley in the USA and its British equivalent in the Thames Valley. This milieu for innovation is crucial.

Two related questions remain:

- What happens within these small innovative teams (which Tom Peters delights in calling 'skunkworks')?
- What has to happen to these teams and their 'products' for them to count towards organizational development?

One answer to the first question is that the team members do *collaborative enquiry,* often referred to as action research or action learning. Peters and Austin would condone the emphasis on this kind of activity. They call it 'analysis' but it is analysis through immersion in the practice of the 'real world' (i.e. data collection) and then applying it, rather than 'keeping it bottled up forever in the pristine, sterile, temperature controlled, dust free lab or test kitchen'. 'We are adamant', they assert,

> about labeling this pragmatic immersion process 'analysis', because in many quarters today only the abstract stuff is viewed as 'analysis' . . .
> Get hard data. Get it quickly. That's the key.

This kind of 'applied' or action research has got an impressive pedigree in both educational and business circles and on both sides of the Atlantic (and, indeed, in the 'quality circles' of Japanese and German industrial concerns).

Indeed, collaborative enquiry has occurred within both small team improvement efforts and whole school initiatives, for example the GRIDS

Figure 11: **The Cycle of School-Based Improvement Through Self-Evaluation**

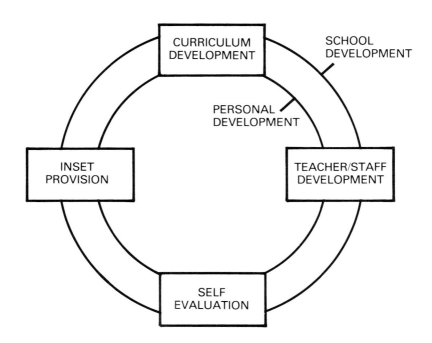

project. Indeed, self-evaluation in schools has tended to occur within one of these two formats (see Holly in Southworth, 1987). Holly (1984), however, has pointed to a central dilemma, which he refers to as the 'problem of institutionalization'. In his research it became apparent that, on the one hand, whole school initiatives became 'institutionalized' early on, i.e. they lost their creative impulse by being too 'organized'. On the other hand, the small team work was denied access to the institutional mainstream and, after much initial enthusiasm (on the part of the individuals concerned), the effort was quickly dissipated. There are at least four reasons for the failure of these small teams to have an institutional impact:

(i)   When the interest group is entrusted with the task of 'diagnosis', says Plant (1987), the work becomes so seductive — and ownership so rife — that the task of managing the interface with the rest of the organization (which also moves on) gets forgotten. In one sense, the team members get 'too full of themselves' and their work.

(ii) If the condition of *critical mass* is not attained and 'a certain volume of experiments, champions and skunkworks' remains un-accomplished, sa ? Peters and Austin, then the 'possibility of continuing innovation collapses'.

(iii)   The members of the small teams are often their own worst enemies. Consider the implications of this question from Peters and Austin:

> In the halcyon days of organizational development in the 1960s and 1970s, cooperation and conflict-smoothing were considered the most desirable traits for any human being working in a sizeable enterprise. Our champions, however, are usually not the souls of sweetness and light.

While Peters and Austin see this as a strength, other observers might well see it as a weakness.

(iv)   Continuing the previous point, Plant (1987) uses 'open systems theory' to argue that organizations are often conservative, not willing to move too far from the *status quo*:

> So any attempt to change direction by influencing one small part of that system will come under great pressure from *status quo* 'antibodies'.

It is a question of 'sub-systems' being keen, thrusting and innovative, but then, says Plant, 'bumping up against "invisible" barriers' and pressures. In other words, changes in one part of the organization begin to affect what goes on in the other parts — and so they (these other parts) react accordingly. Thus when task groups are formed, attitudes outside can harden and resistances accumulate.

Presumably, however, the work of small teams can be championed by those charged with the leadership of the organization. Leader negativity or even neutrality could lead to the isolation and repudiation of the members of a small team and all they stand for. But the positive championing of a team by the senior staff and the official promotion of their work within the organization could have dramatic effects. The question remains, however, as to how the senior management of a school can extend the ownership rights (galvanized within the task group) to the wider staff group. Given these points, therefore, it has to be said that there is at least a question mark hanging over Tom Peters' total confidence in the efficacy of the small group. Perhaps one approach — either that of the semi-autonomous task group or that of Organization Development (OD) — is more appropriate for a school depending on its present stage of development. If this is the case, what does this mean for Garth Hill?

It does seem that Stanley Goodchild has been performing the 'pioneer' role and doing the work of another 'founder'. Certainly his work at Garth Hill could be given the title of 'starting again'. Returning to the possible relevance of stage theory, Plant has argued that what comes after the collaborative (i.e. democratic) stage and the 'crisis of uncertainty' is a reversion to a more authoritarian regime:

> My own experience suggests that what happens at the end of the collaboration stage is that there is an increasing confusion about the

core mission of the organization which requires some form of return to strong, clear leadership. Whether the leadership can be of the same single-minded, power-oriented type as existed initially seems very unlikely, but there is certainly a need for either an individual or — more likely — a small, powerful team to lead the organization strongly and to provide a clear, strong sense of purpose and mission. It is quite possible that the mission will involve breaking up the organization into smaller sub-units which have autonomy within a clear overall framework and culture.

(Plant, 1987)

One thought that occurs to us is that Stanley Goodchild has been for Garth Hill a one-man 'skunk', whose single-handed activities could be described as 'skunkworks'. He introduced the entrepreneurial spirit into Garth Hill and received legitimation for this unconventional move by obtaining the support of the local community and local industry. His 'enterprise' permeated the culture of the school.

Stanley Goodchild, then, has been Garth Hill's innovator and entrepreneur, the arch initiator. His own disposition, his preferred 'model' of management and also his wide experience of management have all come together in his directive style. This combination of a *directive initiator* has been deemed to be effective in the school improvement literature (see Hall *et al*, 1984). the DESSI reports (see Crandall *et al*, 1983) stressed that forceful leadership plus support create the impetus — the triggering — and the wherewithal for changes to occur. Indeed, in the effective schools literature, there is much talk about the importance of *instructional leadership*, but, as Fullan and Newton (1986) have pointed out, while much is known about the implementation of mandated change at elementary school level,

> very little is known about change processes, particularly pertaining to *internally-initiated innovation, in secondary schools.*

The research by Weindling and Earley (1986) confirms both the central importance of proactive, change-orientated leaders and the fact that many change initiatives are generated from within schools (albeit often in response to external pressures) where there is *much more interest in change* on the part of administrators and teachers than is normally considered to be the case.

> (In sum) effective principals are able to define priorities focused on the central mission of the school; and gain support for these priorities from all stakeholders.

(Fullan and Newton, 1986)

As was mentioned in the previous chapter, we strongly suspect that much of the literature on innovation in education is talking about the *management of the initiation of change*. This is particularly the case if early implementation is categorized as initiation. While this is a crucial stage in the innovation process (and the head's role is clearly vital in triggering change), our interest here is in implementation proper. Fullan and Newton argue that the challenge is to move from a theory of change, which has established the centrality of the head's role, to develop a *theory of changing* where the emphasis is on the dynamics of managing change. What, they ask, are the strategies used to interest and involve staff — and keep them interested and involved? The case material presented here will have gone part of the way to answering their question. Staff need to be made aware that implementation is the top priority; change leaders, therefore, need to be both *forceful* (by exerting strong, continuous pressure; they 'have to go to centre stage and stay there', say Fullan and Newton 1986); and *resourceful*. We have argued that the support function — the consideration — should take precedence at this stage — but not at the expense of maintaining pressure. This should remain constant. The problem is, as Weindling and Earley (1986) have testified, that once 'initiation' is activated and implementation is underway, the innovations are 'mentally ticked off' and heads as change leaders turn to the next task, the next innovation. These researchers concluded that, while heads are major initiators of change and thus play a major part in innovation, they often delegate day-to-day responsibility (for implementation) and retain a watching brief. This, of course, might not be a problem if the 'baton' is handed over successfully. And it is this passing of the baton to the next line of 'innovators' that is all important and is currently taxing Stanley Goodchild at Garth Hill. The task seems to be one of getting the entire cast at centre stage — and keeping them there.

In terms of the management of *implementing* change, therefore, sophisticated leadership is required which not only maintains the pressure and provides much of the linkage for the support (including external consultancy), but also:

- puts MBWA into action by getting amongst the action. The medium really is the message and — in classroom support — the 'jacket-off sleeves-rolled-up' approach is essential to maintain the morale of teachers facing the stresses and strains of daily implementation. There is a Dutch proverb ('de boer voelt het door zijn klompen heen') which roughly translated means 'the farmer's foot is the best fertilizer'. In terms of the cultivation and nurturing of new classroom practices, the head's supportive, enthusing presence is indispensable.
- exploits opportunities for innovation. At Garth Hill, for instance, Stanley Goodchild was able to exploit the concern for the school's future and introduce various changes which, in turn, guaranteed that the school has a prosperous future.

As one door closes, two other doors open.

We had to change to survive . . .   (Stanley Goodchild)

- attends to such 'pre-conditions' as climate-setting and team-building
- orchestrates the progress of the 'Learning School' by facilitating and then making organizational sense of all the individual, small team and whole staff activities. Fusion is what is required here. What is also

required, as Fullan (1986) points out, is the encouragement to see implementation as a learning process — which can be enhanced within the intense collaboration of a small team.

- maintains procedures and processes which allow change initiatives to come to the fore. Fullan and Newton (1986) have drawn attention to one of the rights and responsibilities of the 'relatively autonomous school' — self-initiated, internally generated innovation. Naisbitt (1984) has argued persuasively that, for this to happen, the internal processes have to be in place and fully functioning:

> Change that bubbles up from the grassroots has staying power.

> For best results, the people in the institution must have *ownership* in the new vision . . . decisions will be made from the bottom-up in a participatory fashion rather than top-down.

> Rethinking: a constant, long-term process . . . The word *process* should be emphasized . . . (It) is not a product you get or bring in from the outside. It is something that occurs inside an institution (but well instructed by what is going on outside) . . . And it must be a shared vision, a strategic vision.

It is the quality of these internal processes which is then reflected in the quality of the 'products' — the innovations. High quality process and content — both are essential for school improvement. It's further proof of the adage that 'it's not (only) what you do, it's the way that you do it'.

In his latest book *Thriving On Chaos,* Tom Peters (1987) has addressed this very issue. He argues that *the* goal is *quality* and that those organizations that continually achieve this goal have twelve characteristics in common.

(i) management is obsessed with quality
There is an emotional attachment to its pursuit and it is at the top of every agenda. Peters quotes an Apple executive who said:

> I don't think you should ever manage anything that you don't care passionately about.

And this passionate obsession needs to be on-going. 'Commitment', he stresses, 'means persistence. A serious quality commitment is forever'.
Moreover, he says,

> Quality programme leaders report that programmes stall around the 12-to-18-month mark. Award programmes become stale. Team leaders are worn out. The easy-to-find problems have been solved. Moreover, there are doldrums every couple of years thereafter — forever. Commitment means gritting your teeth and dreaming up as many new wrinkles as you can to pump life back into the programme.

(ii)   there is a guiding system, or ideology.
This is our 'ethos' or Cunnington and Limerick's 'metastrategic vision'. According to Peters,

> most quality programmes fail for one of two reasons: they have system without passion, or passion without system.

(iii)   quality should be measured
This is best done by the participants, by the 'natural work group, team or department itself':

> It must not be done 'to' such groups by an accounting department or by an audit or inspector brigade, or there is a high risk that the process will become bureaucratic.

His other points, in brief, are that

(iv)   everyone needs to be trained in how to assess quality

(v)   quality should be rewarded

(vi)   problem-solving activities should cross department boundaries

(vii)   small *is* very beautiful

(viii)   constant stimulation is vital — to 'ward off the doldrums'

(ix)   'everyone plays' as 'partners for profit'

(x)   a 'shadow' structure (a task group) should be formed and given the responsibility of promoting quality improvement

(xi)   as quality goes up, 'costs' go down

(xii)   and, just as we have stressed, *it's a never ending journey*

A 'quality' education rests on the quality of the effective curriculum, i.e. what goes on in classrooms. Innovations do not guarantee quality. Teachers adopt and implement innovations and, in changing their classroom practice, improve on the quality of what goes on already. As Peters says, it's a case of getting better all the time. Innovation, then, hinges on three processes:

- the process of innovaton in terms of adoption/initiation, implementation, etc;
- the process of 'institutionalizing' (i.e. embedding) the new practices within and across a school;
- the practices themselves — the classroom process. There has been much talk in the 1980s of the importance of more varied teaching and learning styles and the refurbishment of the *inner or internal curriculum*. This is central to the conception of *an enterprise curriculum*, as described in the next chapter.

Chapter Four

The Enterprise Curriculum

> The children in the first year really are getting a very advantaged schooling.
>
> (Garth Hill student)

A veritable deluge of curriculum change has occurred at Garth Hill since 1982, but perhaps not in the way it is supposed to happen — nor in the way theorists would have us believe it happens. Much of the work has been internally generated and often resource-led. Stanley Goodchild's *resourceful* approach — there cannot be a better equipped school in the country — has meant that the staff have been constantly challenged to adapt the curriculum to the possibilities arising from the resources. Indeed, John Naisbitt (1984) has argued that there are three stages in innovation:

- during the first stage, it is important to 'take the path of least resistance' and not to 'threaten people . . . (thus) reducing the chance of abrupt rejection' and to ensure the 'avoidance of dissonance';
- the second stage consists of using new ideas 'to improve previous innovations . . . what we already have';
- and the third stage involves 'new directions . . . unimagined now . . . but created by the innovation itself'.

But innovation, concludes Naisbitt,

> doesn't travel in a straight line; it weaves and bobs and lurches and sputters . . . (we) accommodate it, respond to it, and shape it. This interplay proceeds as part of a lurching dynamic of complicated patterns and processes.

Of some significance for Garth Hill and its technological orientation is the fact that Naisbitt's comments relate to the introduction of the computer. It could be argued, however, that the unevenness of the process of innovation in this important area has been ameliorated somewhat by the introduction of more effective in-service training. Bruce Joyce and Beverley Showers (1980) have argued that impactful, effective INSET has five major components:

- presentation of theory or a description of the skill or strategy to be utilized;
- modelling or demonstration of the skills or new teaching/learning approaches;
- practice in simulated and classroom settings;
- structured and open-ended feedback/performance appraisal;
- coaching for application (hands-on, in-classroom assistance over time).

Significantly, their work was specifically related to the introduction of computing in schools. At Garth Hill staff training has been instituted alongside the introduction of various innovations in the computer field to enable the teachers to begin to change their classroom practice. Indeed, Michael Durham in the *Daily Telegraph* (25 January 1988) has argued recently that such training has been, if anything, all too successful.

> School computers are beginning to have a profound effect on the very content of the curriculum and those who believed that the only changes resulting from their introduction would be to the mechanism by which traditional subjects are taught are in for a rude surprise.

Durham's is a critical analysis of the impact of computers in schools; he warns of the dangers of the erosion of subject boundaries; a decline in the teaching of factual information; and a denial of the importance of reading and books. On the credit side, however, Durham has to admit to the motivational effects of computers on pupils' learning. They are more involved and more engaged in the learning process and, therefore, more stimulated to learn in the first place. In terms of independent learning, pupils are much more able to discover things for themselves. Yet Durham is still able to head his article, 'thought machine threatens pupils'; and he concludes (rather disapprovingly) by claiming that schools are becoming 'technological fun-palaces stuffed with microcomputer gadgetry of every kind'. From a more academic viewpoint, Ronald Ragsdale (1987) has voiced similar misgivings. He has written about the 'computer cornucopia', the urgent need for more discernment and the blind faith in the 'futuristic ideology' of high technology which is tantamount to 'idolatry'. He is concerned that there are dangers of elevating (computers as) 'means' above (educational) 'ends', displacement of the regular curriculum and trial and error learning bordering on 'superstitious behaviour'. He, too, mentions the (possible) beneficial effects on pupil learning — the state of 'mindfulness' and the emphasis on interactive and participative learning (see Papert, 1980) — and concludes that curriculum development in this area should be monitored by staff members themselves acting as teachers-as-researchers. This merger of research and development (teachers' research running concurrently with their implementation efforts) would enable those closest to the action to match actual with intended outcomes and to check for positive and/or negative side effects. Given the large scale commitment to computer technology at Garth Hill, such teacher-centred research and development (self-evaluation) work might well prove to be an important next step. Lawrence Stenhouse (1975) wrote persuasively about the role of teacher-as-researcher and the central task of analyzing the 'performance gap' between curricular intentions and the reality of the learning process:

> We appear to be confronted by two different views of the curriculum. On the one hand the curriculum is seen as an intention, plan or prescription, an idea of what one would like to happen in schools. On the other, it is seen as the existing state of affairs in schools, what does in fact happen . . . The central problem of curriculum study is the gap between our ideas and aspirations and our attempts to operationalize them . . . The gap can be closed only by adopting a research and development approach to one's own teaching, whether alone or in a group of cooperating teachers.

The task, then, is one of 'empirical evaluation' (see McCormick and James, 1983) in terms of investigating both the received, effective curriculum (what is actually going on; the classroom everyday reality; and the extent and quality of pupil learning) and the nature of the performance gap between the actual and the intended.

In their seminal paper entitled 'On the risk of appraising non-events in programme evaluation', Charter and Jones (1973) argued that the task of investigating the success (or failure) of innovations-as-intended has to be conducted on four levels:

Level 1: Institutional commitment
Included in this category are statements of intentions (akin to Smith and Keith's 'formal doctrine'), and public announcements which set direction and goals; legitimize the (re)allocation of resources and elicit enthusiasm and support. They are declarations of 'binding commitment'.

Level 2: Structural context
'Structural' alterations are 'those changes in formal arrangements and physical conditions that form the context within which staff members carry out an educational programme'. They are, say Charters and Jones,

> usually of the sort that can be effectuated by managerial directives or acts and include such things as . . ., changing job titles, forming and appointing committees, assigning responsibilities, purchasing instructional materials, making equipment available, knocking out classroom walls, scheduling classes, and so on.

Level 3: Role performance (staff perspective)
Charters and Jones refer to this dimension as the degree of actual implementation, i.e. a teacher's actual use of an innovation. As they point out, changes in teacher behaviour are far from automatic.

Level 4: Learning activities (student perspective)
Charters and Jones maintain that:

> The manifest purpose of the teacher's role performance is to produce learning in students, but this cannot happen directly. The best the teacher can do is to induce students to engage in activities deemed instrumental in the covert psychological processes he hopes to affect . . . opportunities for slippage are enormous.

Any investigative work, therefore, has to explore the quality of learning outcomes and the links in the causal chain between the four levels. With this in mind, Charters and Jones conclude:

> The study of the school's organization and management, often regarded as dealing with matters peripheral to the core issues of instruction and learning, can be viewed as a partner helping to forge the chain.

In using this scheme with which to view the innovative practices of Garth Hill, there is ample evidence to suggest that both levels 1 and 2 have been more than adequately covered. Proactive leadership, mission statements and the influx of resource provision has fostered the change efforts. Whether the impact of this undoubted institutional commitment and structuring of the context for innovation has been maximized in terms of the teachers' role behaviour and the students' learning outcomes needs to be the subject of further investigation. The range of classroom dimensions provided by Goodlad and Klein (1970) — and drawn attention to by Charters and Jones — is likely to be most useful in such an exploration. They listed twelve focus areas in their 'framework for classroom observation':

(i) *Classroom Milieu*

This is the climate of the classroom, the atmosphere and the environment for learning. It's the 'feel' of the place — does this classroom 'feel' conducive for learning? It's also the look of the place — is there recent work from the pupils on display? Above all, is it the kind of room where pupils want to come and learn? 'Is it', say Goodlad and Klein, 'colorful and bright or drab and barren?'. In this category, what cannot be ignored is the teacher and his/her 'feel':

> Is she warm and supportive or negative and punitive?

(ii) *Instructional Activities*

This is the question of teaching and learning styles which is currently receiving so much attention. For instance, ask Goodlad and Klein, is the classroom and the learning therein teacher-centred or student-centred?

> How does the teacher bring pupils into the subject matter? Is she the source of knowledge, telling the children then questioning them on what they have been told? Perhaps, on the other hand, the children pose relevant questions and spend much of their time seeking information and preparing reports. Do they work primarily as individuals, a total class group, clusters or sub-groups? Do they appear to rush through their work or is the pacing relaxed and leisurely?

(iii) *Subject Matter*

This is the focus of what actually is being studied and its impact on the pupils. How are they reciving it and does it appear to 'grip' them?

(iv) *Materials and Equipment*

This category includes resources, books, worksheets, materials, art supplies, science equipment, hardware and software, audio-visual aids, etc. It's the collection of 'mechanisms' for learning.

(v) *Involvement*

Are both the *teacher* and the *pupils* interested in, engaged with, and motivated by what is occurring in the classroom? Is there obvious enthusiasm for the task in hand?

(vi) *Interaction*

What is the nature of the interaction in the classroom and what is its quality? What is the role of the learners? Are they active or passive in the situation?

Is the interaction pattern predominantly teacher to child, child back to teacher, child to child? Do children merely respond to teacher-posed stimuli or do they take the initiative? Are they exchanging ideas with each other?

(vii) *Enquiry*

Is the classroom process open-ended and explanatory or (fore)closed? Is the process of learning, ask Goodlad and Klein, one of seeking out or being given conclusions?

Building on the work of Stephen Kemmis, we would argue that there are five levels of learning and that exploratory *enquiry learning* is the highest level (see below)

Level	Task Orientation	Style of Learning
A	Recognition	Template matching
B	Recall	Recitation
C	Reconstructive understanding/comprehension	Paraphrasing
D	Intuitive understanding	Experiential learning
E	Constructive understanding	Enquiry learning

viii) *Independence*

The nature of the learning situation in terms of freedom and control. What is the framework of rules?

Do children move quietly about the room attending to their needs? Do they ask permission to leave their seats? etc.

(ix) *Curriculum Balance*

What is the range of experiences being offered the pupils? Is it a subject-based or interdisciplinary approach being used? Are the HMI/DES areas of experience (the aesthetic and creative; the ethical; the linguistic; the mathematical; the physical; the scientific; the social and political; and the spiritual) being catered for — whether in one lesson or across lessons — and are the various aspects of achievement being acknowledged? Hargreaves (1983) lists these aspects as:

- the acquisition of propositional knowledge for examinations;
- the capacity to apply knowledge in practical situations;
- personal and social skills;
- pupil motivation.

Are these different areas of achievement being emphasized so that all pupils have opportunities to succeed?

(x) *Curricular Adaptation*
To what extent have curriculum 'packages' and resource materials been amended for the classroom situation? Does the teacher modify these materials in the light of his/her knowledge of the particular group?

(xi) *Ceilings and Floors of Expectancy*
What kinds of pupil performance and attainment levels are reflected in the classroom activities and processes? Are the pupils being challenged sufficiently? Is their work and progress being assessed adequately?

(xii) *Staff Utilization*
Does the teacher seem isolated from his/her colleagues within some 'cellular' arrangement (see Joyce *et al,* 1983) or is he/she being well supported within a more collegial framework? Is there collaborative planning and evaluation going on? Is there any team teaching?

This comprehensive list of categories provides a useful framework for beginning to observe the quality of the learning process in classrooms. It is increasingly the case that classroom observation is seen as one of teachers' professional responsibilities within their own continuing education (see Holly, 1987a). This trend reflects the new interest in pupil learning, in learning styles and in what teachers have to do to facilitate and enhance learning. Certainly, within all the recent innovations in the secondary field — GCSE, CPVE, TVEI, B/TEC courses, the national Lower Attaining Pupils' Programme (LAPP) and records of personal achievement/profiling, etc — the rhetoric concentrates on teaching styles and new approaches to learning. And, in terms of teaching/learning approaches, variety is seen as all important. The influential paragraph 243 from the Cockcroft Report sums up this view:

Teaching at all levels should include opportunities for
- exposition by the teacher;
- discussion between teacher and pupils and between pupils themselves;
- appropriate practical work;
- consolidation and practice of fundamental skills and routines;

- problem solving, including the application of the material to everyday situations;
- investigational work.

With 'mathematics' deleted, this list makes good sense right across the curriculum. Listed below are some of the emphases within new approaches to learning:

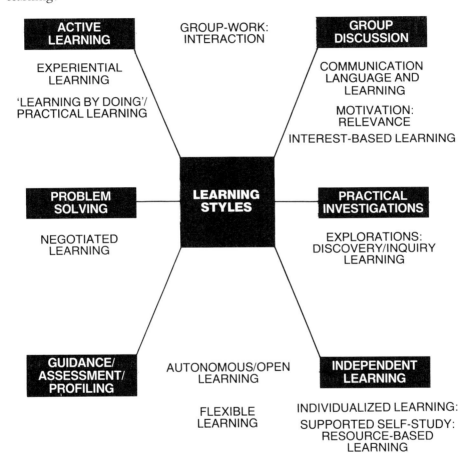

Above all, however, this current interest in the facets of pupil learning arises from:

> the underlying purpose . . . (which) is to improve the teaching and learning process *in the school*.
>
> (GRIDS Handbooks)

This statement reflects the aspiration to improve schools at two levels: at the level of what happens in individual classrooms and at the organizational level.

We like to refer to these levels as:

- the external curriculum
  This is a combination of the levels 1 and 2 of Charters and Jones; it is the institutional and organizational dimension. It is what happens outside classrooms (but may well have an impact in the classroom);
- the internal curriculum
  This is what happens *inside* classrooms, thus spanning all the categories suggested by Goodlad and Klein and Charters and Jones levels 3 and 4.

As Charters and Jones maintain, what we have chosen to call the internal curriculum has a direct bearing on learning outcomes, while the external curriculum has a more indirect influence. But there is an influence — and that is important. In *What Works: Research About Teaching and Learning* published by the US Department of Education (1987) the effective schools literature is summarized and the following argument emerges:

Research Finding The most important characteristics of effective schools are strong instructional leadership, a safe and orderly climate, school-wide emphasis on basic skills, high teacher expectations for student achievement and continuous assessment of pupil progress.

Schools with high student achievement and morale show certain characteristics:

- vigorous instructional leadership;
- a principal who makes clear, consistent, and final decisions;
- an emphasis on discipline and a safe and orderly environment;
- instructional practices that focus on basic skills and academic achievement;
- collegiality among teachers in support of student achievement;
- teachers with high expectations that all their students can and will learn, and
- frequent review of student progress

Effective schools are places where principals, teachers, students, and parents agree on the goals, methods, and content of schooling. They are united in recognising the importance of a coherent curriculum, public recognition for students who succeed, promoting a sense of school pride, and protecting school time for learning.

The message is an unequivocal one: not only are the external and internal curricula linked, but get the former right and you are well on the way to bringing about general improvement in the latter. We would want to argue that there is a definite connection between the two spheres but that the linkage is rather more complex than the impression given in this summary. In the case of Garth Hill, the *external curriculum* is exceptionally strong. There is institutional commitment to the changes in abundance; and the structure, especially the resourcing, of the curriculum could not be surpassed. In terms of the *external curriculum*, therefore, it could be argued that the pupils of Garth Hill are, indeed, very privileged. In terms of the *internal curriculum* (i.e. what happens in classrooms), there have been major changes — especially where teachers have been able to rise to the challenges set by the high levels of resource provision. But the implementation of innovations (for that is what the internal curriculum is all about) takes time to be galvanized. As reflected in previous chapters, the school is growing and, with this growth, certain emphases are changing. It could be argued that the 'weight' (of attention and effort) is swinging from the left to the right of the diagram (see below) and that while the aspects listed on the left hand side will continue to be important, the aspects on the right hand side are now *more* important — thus Stanley Goodchild's intuitive understanding that it is now time to devolve more power to the staff generally. Eventually, of course, there will be a real need to evaluate the quality of the school's provision in both the external curriculum and the internal curriculum and, indeed, the former's effectiveness and impact on the latter. Self-evaluation would not only add to the teachers' feelings of ownership, but also enable them to investigate beyond the rhetorical 'facade' and to study the classroom processes and the actual student outcomes. The central question to pose is that, given the strength of the external curriculum (achieved by the sheer quality of the school's facilities and resource provision);

The External Curriculum	The Internal Curriculum
The quality of the school as an organization	The quality of the internal processes of classrooms
The formal dimension	The informal dimension
Leadership in the school	Leadership in the classroom
The initiating structure	Consideration
Establishing an ethos	Practising an ethos
The head as innovator	Staff members as innovators
Pressure	Support
Initiation of change	Implementation for change
Management of change	Management for change
'Handing over the baton' (extending opportunities for commitment and ownership)	'Accepting the baton' (accepting the responsibilities of ownership)
(Self) Evaluation of whole school issues	(Self) Evaluation of learning outcomes

is the quality of the classroom learning process keeping pace? In other words, is the internal curriculum successfully matching, and building on, the external curriculum?

If enough evidence is found to answer this question positively, then it could be argued with some confidence that a pupil at Garth Hill is advantaged in both spheres — in terms of high quality resources and in terms of high quality learning experiences. Taken together, that would indeed be an 'enterprising curriculum'.

The TVEI philosophy is incorporated in our whole approach.

(Stanley Goodchild)

So far in this chapter we have tended to concentrate on the *delivery* of the curriculum — how teaching and learning are best facilitated. But what about the *content* of the curriculum? The *Enterprise Curriculum* is essentially about both delivery and content. Clemson and Craft (1981), when discussing the 'good' or the 'effective' teacher, used the following table:

Teacher-types based on content and method		
	Suitable Content	Unsuitable Content
Effective method	The 'good' teacher	The 'dangerous' teacher
Ineffective method	The 'poor' teacher	The 'non-teacher'

The argument is a persuasively simple one; that the successful teacher has effective method (effective, that is, in maximizing opportunities for learning) and good content. It is the good content to which we now need to turn our attention.

The quotation included above was Stanley Goodchild's reaction when asked during an interview about the impact of the Technical and Vocational Education Initiative (TVEI) on Garth Hill. He suggested that the impact was not as great as perhaps was experienced elsewhere because the kind of work suggested within TVEI was already being implemented at Garth Hill. TVEI offered nothing new; it merely set the seal on developments already under way in the school. It follows, therefore, that if Garth Hill is like TVEI, TVEI is like Garth Hill; so talking about TVEI in general is much like talking about Garth Hill in particular.

Hopkins (1986), in a very useful survey of recent developments in secondary education, has noted the importance of the emergence of the Manpower Services Commission (MSC) in the education field and the supporting influence of the Further Education Unit (FEU), especially its publication *A Basis for Choice* — the so-called 'Mansell Report' (1979). Hopkins also notes the high profile of many of the recent curriculum innovations (often MSC-inspired) and their cumulative potential for radically transforming the nature of secondary education. He points out that these innovations fall into three categories:

(i) *curriculum initiatives*
     included here are the Technical and Vocational Education Initiative (TVEI); the Certificate of Pre-vocational Education (CPVE); the Youth Training Scheme (YTS) and the Lower Attaining Pupils' Progamme (LAPP).
(ii) *new examinations and assessment schemes*
     included here are the General Certificate of Secondary Education (GCSE); and the examinations offered by the Business and Technician Education Council (B/TEC), the City and Guilds of London Institute (CGLI) and the Royal Society of Arts (RSA). Profiling/recording of achievement also falls within this category.
(iii) *supporting initiatives* included here are TVEI-related In-service Training (TRIST) and Grant-related In-service Training (GRIST); self-evalution schemes and School-based Review (SBR); management training; and Local Financial Management (LFM).

Hopkins then singles out TVEI for closer attention. He gives some background details (that it was first announced in November 1982; it is administered and financed by the MSC; it was originally composed of fourteen pilot projects; and it was set up ostensibly for the development of a technical and vocational curriculum for the 14-18 age range) and then quotes from the introductory letter by David (now Lord) Young, as Chairman of the MSC to chief education officers (dated January 1983):

> Each project would be capable of providing a four year course, commencing at 14 years, of full-time general, technical and vocational education, including work experience. Courses would be for young people across a wide range of ability and would lead to nationally recognised qualifications. Within this framework, young people would be encouraged to develop broadly based occupational skills and competencies. The purpose of each project and of the pilot scheme as a whole is to explore and test methods of organising, delivering, managing and resourcing readily replicable programmes of education of this nature and the kind of programme, curriculum and learning methods required for success.

David Young also added that 'our general objective is to widen and enrich the curriculum in a way that will help young people prepare for the world of work and to help students learn to learn'.

Hopkins (1986) goes on to argue that a number of criteria for pilot projects were laid down, among which were the following:

1 Equal opportunities should be available to young people of both sexes and they should normally be educated together on courses within each project. Care should be taken to avoid sex stereotyping.

2 They should provide four year curricula, with progression from year

to year, designed to prepare the student for particular aspects of employment and for adult life in a society liable to rapid change.

3   They should have clear and specific objectives including the objectives of encouraging initiative, problem solving abilities and other aspects of personal development.

4   The balance between the general, technical and vocational elements of programmes should vary according to students' individual needs and the scope of the course: but throughout the programme, there should be both a general and a technical/vocational element.

5   The technical and vocational elements should be broadly related to potential employment opportunities within and outside the geographical area for the young people concerned.

6   There should be appropriate planned work experience as an integral part of the programmes, from the age of 15 onwards . . .

7   Courses offered should be capable of being linked effectively with subsequent training/educational opportunities.

8   Arrangements should be made for regular assessment and for students and tutors to discuss students' performance/progress. Each student and his/her parents, should also receive a periodic written assessment and have an opportunity to discuss this assessment with the relevant project teachers. Good careers and educational counselling will be essential.

Hopkins (1986), in his overview of developments in secondary schools, looks at the characteristics shared by TVEI and the other related curriculum initiatives. He finds the following features:

(i)   the emphasis on the *14-18 age range* which, in time, is likely to have two important effects:
(a)   the possible erosion of the 16+ 'barrier'; and
(b)   the possible 'wash back' effect on the curriculum, 11-13;

(ii)   the emphasis on *vocationalism,* linking education with training, the 'world of work' and work experience and stretching across the ability range. This feature of TVEI gave rise to early reservations often voiced in forcible terms. Bernard Barker (*Times Educational Supplement,* 23 March 1984) wrote about the 'slow TVEI poison' and Maurice Holt (1983) claimed that vocationalism would be 'the new threat to universal education'. Holt's article invited a rejoinder from C J Lea, Birmingham's TVEI Project Director, who endorsed the 'Vocational Focus', claiming that:

What we are striving to develop within TVEI is a loosening of the subject-bound curricular strait-jacket; a moderation of the harsh distinction between education and training and an approach to the presentation of the curriculum that more readily generates the motivation and builds the confidence of many young people from the age of fourteen to eighteen. By removing the quite artificial division separating pre- and post-sixteen education and training we see ourselves as the liberators, because we are providing a strong bridge between school and work, and between learning from theory and learning by practice, which is far more substantial than the structures provided by a career education programme on its own.

(iii)   the aspiration to provide *equal opportunities* and to institute affirmative action, thus moving beyond availability;

(iv)   the introduction of *skills-based approaches* within *modular courses*. Hopkins sees the 'package' of a core curriculum plus objectives-based modules and criterion — referenced assessment as the new 'norm', supported by much talk of a 'skills-based curriculum'. Holly (1987a) has tried to disentangle the skills rhetoric and discovered the following threads:

   (a)   basic skills: literacy, oracy, numeracy and, increasingly, 'computeracy';
   (b)   core skills — to be learnt and developed within the core curriculum;
   (c)   specific skills — often tackled within the modular structure, for example, approaches to safety first;
   (d)   practical skills, for example, problem-solving;
   (e)   study skills and information handling/retrieval;
   (f)   personal and social skills/'life skills'/self-assessment,
   (g)   skills related to areas of the curriculum, for example, learning science by doing science (see Hilton, 1983);

(v)   the exhortation of school-based curriculum development — for teachers, within the framework of criteria as set, to develop new curricular approaches. TVEI, is what the teachers make of it; and thus the widespread emphasis on monitoring and evaluation to keep track of this 'dispersal' model.

   Hopkins makes the point, however, that, given the overloading of tasks on the participating teachers, there was a strong temptation to look for ready-made examination courses;

(vi)   the emphasis on *new approaches to assessment* and *profiling*, with the latter providing a broader view of an individual pupil and a more balanced view of pupil achievement;

(vii)   the linkage of *personal and social education, career work* and *guidance* with the (pre)vocational thrust;

(viii)   as mentioned earlier in the chapter, the universal interest in more
active, experiential *approaches to learning* and non-didactic, less authoritarian *teaching styles*.

In terms of the impact of TVEI at Garth Hill and elsewhere, a rather more
in-depth discussion is required. Holmes and Jamieson (1983), writing prior to
the introduction of TVEI, talked about the emerging need for 'the new
vocationalization' which would countenance the curricular importance of
preparation for adult life and the ramifications of youth unemployment.
Despite economic, social and political pressure for change, they argued, the
educational system seemed unable to respond; consequently:

> Most pupils are being taught the same material, by the same methods
> and are being examined in the same way as they were ten years ago.

Looking back over that period, Holmes and Jamieson saw the division between
education and training being maintained, very little occupationally specific
work being transacted in schools and what was occurring (woodwork,
metalwork, office practice, etc) was of comparatively low status. Furthermore,

> neither the content, pedagogy nor assessment system was much in tune
> with industrial needs.

Some signs of new life were appearing, however, with the introduction of Craft,
Design and Technology (CDT), Modular Technology and the 'entrepreneurial'
work of the Royal Society of Arts (RSA) and the City and Guilds London
Institute (CGLI).

Given the social and economic background which had resulted in youth
unemployment, Holmes and Jamieson could see five different kinds of
educational response:

(i)   further concentration on the traditional curriculum to make pupils more
        competitive in the tighter job market;
(ii)   tighter relationships being formed with local employers, often through
        the agency of careers work, including work experience;
iii)   leisure pursuit courses being introduced, tantamount to 'education for
        unemployment';
(iv)   courses being introduced which focus on preparation for self-employment
        — a thrust being encouraged by the Department of Trade and Industry
        (DTI) —, entrepreneurship and 'mini-enterprise' schemes;
(v)   a new concentration on a wider view of vocationalism involving work
        experience, social/life skills courses and assessment through profiling.

At the end of their paper, Holmes and Jamieson are able to announce the
introduction of 'the government's TVEI programme',

> an initiative that brings direct state intervention in the secondary
> school curriculum, (which) has been born out of sheer frustration with
> the pace of change.

Watts, in an article entitled 'redundant approaches to the world of work' (*Times Educational Supplement,* 25 November 1983), charted similar territory by arguing that youth unemployment challenged many of the basic assumptions built into the structure of the educational system. While, he contended, the educational establishment still saw vocational matters as being improper educational concerns, the young and their parents were expecting schools to help them enter worthwhile jobs; moreover, society was expecting schools to develop in young people the knowledge, attitudes and skills which will enable them to contribute to the economy. Furthermore, he argued, it is no paradox when, in situations of high unemployment, the bonds between education and the world of work become tighter; when employment is scarce, people are much more likely to judge educational provision by vocational criteria. Employability becomes the key issue and there is greater investment into securing employment for youngsters. While this has certainly been the case at Garth Hill — and the school is justifiably proud of its fine record in finding jobs for the pupils — the emphasis on 'the new vocationalism' is composed of wider concerns. In the terms used by Watts, vocationalism is not so much about *selection* and *socialization,* it is more about *orientation* and *preparation:*

> *Orientation* consists of deliberate curricular interventions to help students to understand the world of employment and to prepare them for choices and transitions on entering it.
>
> *Preparation* is the development of specific skills and knowledge which students will be able to apply in a direct way once they are in jobs.

Pring agrees. In his paper entitled 'In defence of TVEI' (1985), Pring maintains that education needs to provide specific vocational skills alongside a more general education; moreover, he argues, there is a need to adopt a more balanced approach to the world of work and the technological base of industry (involving the jettisoning of the traditional 'contempt for the practical and for the productive part of the economy'). He says:

> To sum up; there are significant social and economic changes that affect both the personal well-being of individuals and the social and economic demands upon the educational system. Postponed entry into employment, prospects of unemployment, shifting unemployment patterns, the increasing technological base of industry and of information exchange and communication, the undermining of traditional values and ways of life, the unpredictability of what the future holds in store — all these should enter into that continuing educational debate about aims and values. Many teachers have for a long time thought so, and have questioned the validity of an educational experience that does not seem to relate to these matters.
>
> In defence of TVEI, therefore, I see it as a catalyst that, within a system which for too long has been captivated by a narrowing and inadequate notion of 'liberal education', has stimulated a vigorous and

(in my local experience) imaginative reappraisal of the curriculum and of the educational purposes which it should serve. As one senior teacher, for whom I have a very profound respect, explained, it had legitimated that which for many years she and her colleagues had been trying to do, but which they felt went against the normal expectations of the school. For her and for many, there are contradictions between curriculum reality, educational theory, and learning aspirations (so admirably identified by Mr. Lea in Forum), which went unacknowledged at the official level but which teachers are only too aware of. TVEI would serve a useful purpose if it did nothing else than make these contradictions explicit and stimulate us to rethink our educational aims along the lines that are already demonstrated in some of the best TVEI practice.

TVEI, Pring maintains, is three things:

(i)   it is a *proposal* (based on the criteria), which is both broad and flexible and which incorporates personal development, technical knowledge and a vocational orientation;

(ii) it is *curriculum practice*, 'shaped and given substance . . . by groups of teachers', involving new teaching styles, an emphasis on the 'pastoral curriculum' (involving counselling and guidance) and curriculum development concerning the new technologies;

(iii) it is an *aspect of social policy*, which, depending on how successful it becomes, is either echoing the differentiation of educational opportunity or is laying the ghost of the 'fossilized liberal education' once and for all.

Above all, Pring emphasizes the importance of TVEI in its attack on four 'false dichotomies'.

(i)   'Liberal' versus vocational
(ii) Education versus training
(iii) Practical versus theoretical
(iv) Process versus product.

He concludes:

> The kind of radical challenge embodied in TVEI might be summarised as follows: schools need, in the light of wider personal and social developments, to re-examine the educational aims embodied in their curriculum organisation, teaching styles, and subject content. This re-examination must necessarily look at the very way in which we conceptualise 'education' and the transactions that are conducted under its title. Such concepts incorporate distinctions (and thus divisions between people) that are less and less defensible — such concepts and distinctions, for example, as 'vocational/liberal', 'training/education', 'practical/theoretical', and 'process'product'. TVEI, whatever the social function it might eventually serve, has forced us to reconceptualise

processes through which we educate young people. In doing that it has in many schemes affected teaching styles, found a place for the practical and experiential, reassessed the role of assessment, made us more conscious of equal opportunities, questioned the autonomy of (and lack of coordination between) schools and colleges, and given prominence to technology especially as a tool of communication and of enquiry.

Despite Pring's optimistic analysis of the work of TVEI, Leach was able to announce that 'TVEI will fail' (*Times Educational Supplement,* 31 October 1986). His argument is an important one: TVEI

cannot succeed within the present structure of secondary education . . . (especially) because it is precisely those elements which motivate students and engender the enthusiasm for education for its own sake which are least able to fit into the structure of education as it exists today.

In other words, TVEI is in danger of being too successful. The emphasis on developing initiative, motivation and enterprise has become constrained within the 'content-laden curriculum' and the stranglehold of the examination system.

Yet Leach's pessimism was not matched by the ebullient enthusiasm of Newman. His article ('The TVEI money that bought success') in the *Times Educational Supplement* described the radical changes introduced in his school in terms of both modularization, new modes of delivery and team-teaching. Like Newman, we would argue that, *in practice,* Leach's pessimism has proved unfounded. Structural change — under the influence of TVEI — has begun to occur. We would argue that important changes have occurred in five areas (three at least of which are 'structural' in the meaning of the term used by Charters and Jones):

(i)   the structure of the curriculum and curriculum content;
(ii)   resource provision;
(iii)   approaches to learning;
(iv)   timetabling; and
(v)   assessment, including examinations.

In terms of the structure and content of the curriculum there has been a remarkable turn around. TVEI has added to the legitimation of such (formerly low status) activities as CDT, science and technology, business education and courses in food and nutrition. On the one hand, high technology, including control and modular technology, electronics, microprocessor-control, robotics and information technology (IT), has entered schools with some gusto. On the other, the performing arts, art and design, graphics, etc. have been given a fresh impetus. Vocational work has tended to concentrate on preparation for work in community care, the food industries, transport services, retail and distribution, and administrative, clerical and office studies. And while the TVEI curriculum has occupied 30 per cent of the timetable, its influence has also been felt in the other 70 per cent. Economic and industrial awareness courses, for example, are often seen as a justifiable part of the 'core' curriculum (see below); so the 'hi -tech curriculum' has arrived with TVEI.

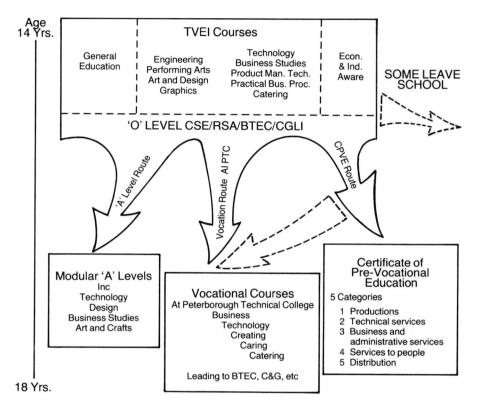

Resource provision, from the schools' perspective, has been one of the strengths of TVEI. TVEI has accelerated the computerization of the curriculum, i.e. has enabled computers to spread across the curriculum. But resource provision has not consisted of equipment alone. While microcomputers, microprosessors, word processors and workshop equipment have been made more widely available, so have additional teachers, ancillary/support staff and the necessary INSET for staff training. As the DELTA report (by Holly, James and Young, 1987) evidenced, TRIST (TVEI-related In-service Training) proved to be a powerful and supportive set of training experiences.

'Learning by doing' is one of the hallmarks of TVEI (see below). Students have been encouraged to enter learning situations where they *experience:*

- real tasks to perform;
- real problems to solve;
- working life;
- community service;
- outdoor and residential activities.

There has also been much more emphasis on *negotiated learning* made possible by the flexible use of modules.

The implications of modularization have had a knock-on effect on school timetables — the bastion of the structural dimension. Modules demand blocked time and this has had interesting effects on the rest of the timetable. The drive towards curriculum integration and interdisciplinary enquiry has had similar repercussions.

Last, but certainly not least, TVEI has begun to make inroads in assessment and the examination system.

There has been cumulative pressure on the examination structure:

Push to offer vocational courses at 'O' and 'A' levels.
(*Times Educational Supplement*, 21 February 1988)

Old-style exams must go to meet jobs challenge.
(*Times Educational Supplement*, 10 January 1986)

Breaking up is not so hard to do!
(*Times Educational Supplement*, 13 December 1985)

ILEA chief sees onward march of the modules.
(*Times Educational Supplement*, 9 January 1987)

John Tomlinson, in the second of these articles, was quoted as follows:

. . . Our society must radically alter its views of the worth of all its people — and open far more opportunities for them to grow in wisdom as well as to seize hold of opportunities for enterprise.

The pressure is on not only the structure of examining, but also the ways that achievement and competence are conceived of and assessed. The RSA's 'Education for Capability' programme (with its emphasis on the 4 Cs — competence, creativity, cooperation and the ability to cope) and the introduction of profiling schemes (compulsory in TVEI) have contributed to this particular trend.

In many ways, however, the work has only just begun. Despite the announcement of the 'Ten year programme to extend TVEI' (*Times Educational Supplement*, 4 July 1986), the accompanying White Paper, *Working Together — Education and Training,* and the setting up of the National Council for Vocational Qualifications (NCVQ), these points need to be kept in mind:

- Before these announcements, TVEI had grown considerably from the original 14 pilot projects. Even so, however, the cohort mentality meant that only a small percentage of the school population has been TVEI-ed. Alternatively, *permeation* across the curriculum has occurred in some schools — like Garth Hill.
- Articles are being written saying that there are only 'Five years to save the economy'. (*Times Eucational Supplement*, 31 October 1986)

The education and training system, it is argued, does not occur in schools alone. Competitiveness, inventiveness, enterprise and the necessary follow-up skills need to be fostered throughout the system for the *Enterprise Culture* to have any meaning. There has been *some* TVEI-led reform of the secondary curriculum, but there is a need for many such key growth points in all sectors of education and, indeed, in society at large. What is required is cultural change.

One version of the enterprise culture in education is the emphasis on the recognition of the importance of student success, involving a wide conception of achievement (which is competency-based). Self-esteem, confidence and motivation are seen as vital ingredients in the student's learning process. When TVEI was first introduced, however, Richard Lindley was able to write in *The Listener* (3 March 1983).

> In effect, the longest period of compulsory education in Europe has proved an extended and very effective training in failure for (many) children . . . why go to school simply to be told you are no good.

The enterprise culture in education, then, is about personal development, skill acquisition and the maximization of learning opportunities. It is also about jobs and the world of work. David (now Lord) Young's experience with the charitable organization ORT (Organization for Rehabilitation through Training) and its avowed intention of providing pupils with marketable skills — thus making them attractive to employers — is evidence of this orientation. It could be argued, of course, that given these two emphases within the enterprise culture — personal development and employability — the pupil gains on both sides of the equation. Lindley, for instance, maintained that although ORT

> is working with young people who have often been rejected by the state system, it insists that it manages to get a considerable number of them back into the higher stream of technical education. And the prospect of acquiring a marketable skill seems to motivate the less able; they learn to read, write and count because they need it for their work.

Lord Young, in his work at the MSC and the DTI, is an undoubted champion of the value of the enterprise culture in education. In the 'School to Work' section of the *Times Educational Supplement* (19 December 1986), under the headline 'Enterprise pilot will urge young to boldly go', an article described the MSC's pilot project arising from the Youth Training Scheme (YTS) which contains 'enterprise training'. At its launch, Lord Young acknowledged the twin aspects of the project:

(i) He saw its main aim as encouraging the development of an enterprise economy. 'Young people', he said, 'who act in a self-reliant and entrepreneurial manner will be the workforce of tomorrow'. He claimed, moreover, that *enterprise had been squeezed out of the classroom* and that for twenty-five years schools had not given attention to the concept of self-employment or acknowledged the existence of the world of work. In fact he was arguing for the acceptance of the economic facts of life.

(ii) In addition, however, he claimed that 'enterprise' is wider than 'entrepreneurialism' or business interests. It is very much a case, he said, of youngsters not only needing to be enterprising in a wide variety of situations in and out of work but also — to be able to be enterprising — by developing the personal skills involved in problem-solving, initiative-taking, decision-making, and resource management.

This article concluded by pointing out two things. First, that this MSC pilot programme was being prepared by 'Entrain' — a consortium of Young Enterprise (the agency which promotes mini-companies in schools) and Shell, the oil company; and, second, that the project aimed to encourage the same kind of approaches being promoted in TVEI schemes, i.e. the acquisition of *personal skills* and the *changing of attitudes*. Two years on, in his new initiative at the DTI ('The Department for Enterprise'), Lord Young is playing the same tune.

Under this kind of influence, then, within the educational version of the enterprise culture, two things have emerged:

(i) There is the emphasis on mini-enterprise schemes in schools, preparation for self-employment and the management of small businesses, i.e. developing a business sense, running a mini-enterprise project, under-standing the structure of companies and the mechanics of wealth creation, etc.

(ii) There is also the emphasis on skills for enterprise, relating to *capability, confidence* and the *capacity* to make things happen. According to Johnson *et al (1988),* these skills include:

self-awareness	leadership
self-confidence	risk-judging
creativity	problem-solving

They are embodied within *active learning* approaches, contribute to *personal development* and can be developed within or apart from a business context.

In a recent, stimulating article by Ian Jamieson and Tony Watts (*Times Educational Supplement,* 18 December 1987), they point out that 'squeezing out enterprise' can no longer be blamed on schools but on the projected National Curriculum. They argue that there are two powerful educational 'lobbies' — the one is concerned with the development of an enterprise culture, the preparation of young people for adult and working life and with the production of a skills-based curriculum focused on *doing* rather than simply on *knowing* and the other is preoccupied with maintaining 'academic standards' and the traditional subject-based curriculum — and that the second pressure group seems to have gained the ascendancy in the 'battle for high ground of policy'. The authors provide six reasons for their stance:

(i) The rhetoric of the consultative document on the national curriculum does pay lip service to the 'enterprise lobby' — it mentions the 'challenges of employment in tomorrow's world', equipping pupils 'with the knowledge, skills and understanding that they need for adult life and employment', and the benefits of 'an enterprising approach' with a reliance on solving 'practical real-world problems' — but these comments are 'empty words' and constitute 'mere posturing'.

(ii) The massive 'core' curriculum composed of traditional school subjects, which represent 'the educational culture in which most parents, industrialists and teachers were themselves reared'. But, they argue, 'real-world problems' are best tackled within interdisciplinary approaches — as, they say, the business world is rapidly coming to understand.

(iii) The prescribed curriculum leaves little room for manoeuvre and negotiation — thus negating many of the recent moves towards student-centred learning, active learning, curriculum negotiation, etc. Moreover, by retreating within subject boundaries, 'it makes it difficult for local industry and adults other than teachers to make a full contribution to the work of the school'.

(iv) Experiential learning — such a powerful force in school-industry links — may be another casualty. Work experience, work shadowing, residential courses, outdoor pursuits and community-based activities are all much more difficult to build into an inflexible subject-based curriculum.

(v) The tension (built into the document) between the recording of achievement — so vital to enterprise experiences — and the national system of testing and assessment.

(vi) The relegation of TVEI (it is mentioned approvingly, but only in passing), which, according to Jamieson and Watts:

has been the major force for promoting cross-curricular initiatives, active learning, new forms of assessment and other features of enterprise-oriented learning in schools.

Whether the enterprise curriculum, as manifested in TVEI, is constrained (as Jamieson and Watts would have us believe) or liberated by the National Curriculum remains to be seen.

Chapter Five

The Enterprise Culture

The empowered principal working collaboratively is far more responsible than the dependent principal. Dependency is closer to helplessness than it is to responsiveness. The message . . . is that individual principals, with or without help, must transcend the problem of dependency if it is to be resolved, and hence, if principals are to be effective.

(Fullan, 1988)

Everyone can do what we've done . . . but how far they get along the continuum depends on various factors . . . it's a question of getting the mix right.

I'm Managing Director, Press Office, 'Marketing and Sales' — all rolled into one.

Schools are more competitive — they have to sell their wares.

Parents need to be given something positive to do.

It's a question of investing in the school; companies come back to us when they get something out of it.

The Government's proposals — they're catching up with Garth!

These quotations, arising from interviews with Stanley Goodchild, provide the terms of reference for this chapter. The accompanying diagram establishes the central themes of the chapter.

Marketing the School

Garth Hill's success story began with the arrival of Stanley Goodchild and his awareness of *public relations*. Indeed, Weindling and Earley (1986) found that the new headteachers in their research sample were very aware that one of their first tasks had to be the promotion of the school's image. This was, said the researchers,

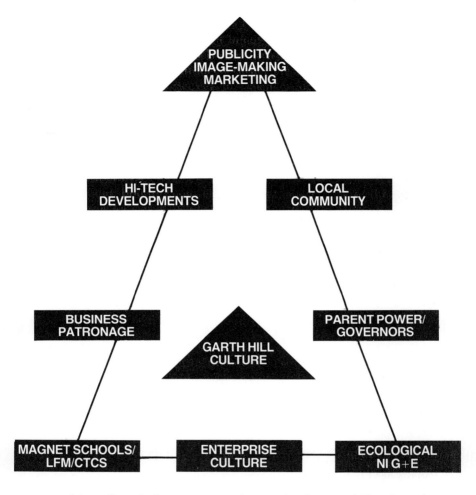

PUBLICITY
IMAGE-MAKING
MARKETING

HI-TECH
DEVELOPMENTS

LOCAL
COMMUNITY

BUSINESS
PATRONAGE

GARTH HILL
CULTURE

PARENT POWER/
GOVERNORS

MAGNET SCHOOLS/
LFM/CTCS

ENTERPRISE
CULTURE

ECOLOGICAL
NI G+E

something of particular concern to the new heads, especially where the community had a low opinion of the school or in areas where the roll was falling . . . changes in this category included building improvements, the introduction of school uniform, improved liaison with the feeder primary schools, new school reports and a newsletter for pupils and parents . . . Most of the new heads were aware of the need for good 'public relations' and publicity, and had established links with local newspapers and community groups.

According to John Greenall (*Times Educational Supplement*, 15 January 1988), it should not take the arrival of a new head or a crisis invoked by falling rolls and the machinations of parental choice to do something about the school's reputation. He argues in an article entitled 'How to improve your image' that every school should have a coherent public relations policy. Given recent government legislation, he contends that schools are becoming more overtly competitive with each other and for external funds; they need, he says to 'nurture their reputations' by instituting good public relations practices. He argues, however, that such practice is:

- for bringing long-term benefits rather than solving short-term problems;
- not just window-dressing or a matter of receiving favourable press coverage;
- about planned and sustained attempts to establish and maintain goodwill and mutual understanding between a school and it various 'publics'.

He sees a school introducing a public relations policy in two stages:

1   Using systematic, but informal research methods, the staff members should ascertain the present reputation of the school. This trawl will introduce *strengths* to build on, *weaknesses* to work on and *communication breakdowns* . . . Early 'remedial' action can be taken immediately.

2   A publicity group should then be formed to promote the school by means of:
    (a)   speech days, sports days, and annual meetings; those valuable 'public' occasions when the school can present itself;
    (b)   attractive, welcoming literature, for example, the school brochure;
    (c)   the local press and, increasingly, local radio stations. These local media can cover student activities and achievements, school building programmes, public events, charity activities, sports results, staff changes, etc.;
    (d)   posters advertising exhibitions, displays, open days, sports events, etc. and newsletters for parents.

Smith and Keith (1971) see this public relations work as an extension of the school's 'formal doctrine' (or ethos, as we have referred to it). They see the formal doctrine as the codified vision or ideology and then see three aspects of this:

- *Mandate:* the formal directive by the 'legitimate authority' (inside or outside the school) to implement the formal doctrine;
- *Institutional Plan:* the school's particular conception of the doctrine and the 'means' of its execution; and
- *Facade:* the formal doctrine as presented to the multiple publics of the school — parents, 'patrons', local residents, lay and professional audiences, etc.

It is the facade or projected ethos/image which is crucial in public relations terms. Extending Greenall's point, if the formal ethos is projected as the school's image, the danger is that the informal culture — if different from the ethos — will be reflected in terms of the school's 'popular' reputation. As Greenall says, every member of the school helps (or hinders) in terms of public relations. The school could get 'caught out' — if the informal reality belies the formal rhetoric. If a school can develop over time an effective, affective (i.e. cohesive) ethos-in-action, then it will be in a strong position to 'sell' itself. Presumably, the more successfully cohesive the culture (in terms of the ethos-in-action), the more likely the school will feel secure enough to be pro-active and galvanize community support for itself.

This has been Garth Hill's greatest strength. Its formal doctrine or ethos has been matched enough in practice for the school to be able to 'market' itself with confidence and some panache. The high-tech image has also been the indisputable reality; scores of visitors from home and abroad can vouch for this. In publicity terms, Garth Hill has achieved unparalleled coverage in both the local and national press and on regional and national television. The school has been featured several times on regional TV news programmes (BBC's *South Today* and TVS's *Coast to Coast*), Breakfast TV, John Craven's *Newsround,* the national TV news and a Thames Television special. The following events have received TV coverage:

The reintroduction of the school uniform (1982)
Girls in basketball final (1983)
Berkshire's computer bus (1983)
Prestel/Computer Centre/Micronet (1983)
Launch of the Times Network Systems (TTNS) (1984)
Japanese TV coverage (1985)
Hi-tech Office (1985)
Business Centre (1985)
Computer link for Parents (1985)
Micro-live (1985)
Preparations for GCSE (1985)
Breakfast Bar/Restaurant (1987)
Hi-tech Library/Drama Studio (1987)
Young Enterprise Scheme (1987)
Appointment of a Business Manager (1987)

Garth Hill School has also been featured on two promotional films:

Making It Happen. British Industry Year. (Central Office of Information).
Getting The Message. The Information Industry. (DTI).

This television coverage of Garth Hill's 'string of firsts' has been matched by an unprecedented amount of press coverage which has kept the school in the public eye. The more this has happened — in an upward spiral — the more the school has been able to attract financial support. The morale of the school has soared. As the subject of so much attention, the members of the school must feel worthy of attention. Successful public relations, therefore, works for the school — inside and out. As with the staff and students of George Washington Carver High School in Atlanta, given the external interest, the school 'grows' accordingly. Marketing a school may be an alien activity for many educationalists, but Garth Hill has much to show for it.

In its own way, the television coverage has substantiated the hi-tech image of Garth Hill. Across the programmes, the school has been described as follows:

'a technology showcase'
'the school is very much the exception . . . no other school has resources quite like it'.
'an Aladdin's Cave'
'information technology is here to stay'
'unparalleled resources'
'its pioneering, hi-tech image'
'the school is tapping into world-wide information resources'

It may sound larger than life, but all these statements can be substantiated. That has been one of the secrets of Garth Hill's success. Part of this same secret is to 'persuade' the parents that what they want is what the school wants to deliver. This 'partnership' has to be created. Someone has to meet with the parents to convince them; and it cannot all be one way. The partnership has to be 'founded on mutual support' (*Times Educational Supplement,* Editorial, 19 February 1988). Interestingly this same article touches on the discussion above:

In reality, schools have to take society as they find it, and that means accepting that the values which parents bequeath to their pupils — and absorb, with their pupils, from the media and the consumer society — are part of the raw material of education. They generate a hidden curriculum far more powerful, far more intrusive, than the formal teaching of the school, no matter how carefully supervised.

Each school, however, creates its own ethos. By the standards of manners and personal relationships it sets, it creates expectations and bench-marks. How teachers treat their pupils affects the way pupils treat each other. Some schools demand and achieve formal courtesies which may or may not translate into more general self-discipline. Others tolerate informality which may or may not degenerate into a breakdown in the teacher's authority.

The 'secret' is not to aim for an ethos which will be unachievable in action. Having said that, however, the good school with effective leadership will be pro-active and sell itself in the market-place. It will realize that the support of the community has to be won — and earned.

Three central points arise from this discussion:

- first, as Southworth (1987) has maintained, the head is the gatekeeper and boundary figure between the school (as a community) and the local community. He/she can either be pro-active and take the school into the community or be reactive and respond to the whims of the community. Proactive heads, according to Manasse (1985),

  achieve a balance between community involvement and maintaining control over outside influences. Principals shape community and parent expectations, channel parent participation into acceptable, non-disruptive avenues of service, and disarm volatile critics.

Consequently, at Garth Hill, the decision regarding the uniform issue was

made on their (the pupils') behalf, not by the school, but by their parents. (TV News)

- second, the reactive stance allows cultural confusion into the school:

  outside the school are the values and traditions of parents and the local community. In many communities different values are championed by different interest groups or subcultures. External values affect the culture of the school, shaping what goes on inside . . . For a number of reasons, many public schools today have become pockets of mediocrity and places of despair and disinterest rather than of hope and enthusiasm. In most cases forces outside the schools have stimulated the erosion. (Deal, 1985)

  This has meant the 'weakening of identities', 'tarnished images' and 'cultural fragmentation' — all of which can pull schools apart. As Hutchinson (1986) has shown, it can also reduce a school's capacity to be innovative.

- and, third, Deal (1985) concludes that 'a strong organizational culture can provide justification for the continued faith and support of both participants and outside constituencies . . . By projecting an image of what the school stands for, culture affects the perceptions and confidence of parents in the community'.

Are *parents,* however, partners, clients/customers, consumers or custodians? John Goodlad (1987) has maintained that there are three change scenarios in education:

scenario (a), which he calls *reform,* involves changes from within the internal system of schooling — without changing it (innovation without change).

scenario (b), involves dismantling the system by invoking changes which are 'client-driven' rather than 'system-driven'. He mentions a parents' voucher scheme as an example of this approach to change.

scenario (c), involves generating alternative approaches within a 'more healthy eco-system' which spans the boundary between the school and its local community.

'The central thrust must be', he says, 'not to eliminate the system but to eliminate the pathological aberrations causing the system to be dysfunctional.'

Goodlad's scenario (c) is his preferred approach: it has, he says, six advantages:

(i)   it creates a *local partnership* and does not pit the local community against the school or vice versa;

(ii)   within such a partnership (a 'healthy ecology') a *healthy school culture* can be fostered; which becomes the *heartbeat* of the school;

(iii)   such a culture *must* also be a development culture — the vehicle for the improvement journey. Goodlad supports our own view expressed in chapter two of this section that a school's culture can be either those 'pathological aberrations' which impede change or the vehicle for removing them. Consequently, schools with a *development culture* are successful in 'welcoming change, anticipating imperfections'. They have Naisbitt's process of 'rethinking' as a 'cultural regularity'; and this process — leading to continuous improvement and self-renewal — is one of continuing inquiry involving *dialogue decision* and *action*.

(iv)   such a school with such a culture does not passively accept every expectation thrust upon it but shows discernment (by ordering priorities) and agrees on a 'hard-rock agenda' after a dialogue with general — not special — interests;

(v)   this dialogue creates opportunities for empowerment, involvement and 'buying into' the agenda;

the dialogue also creates the *partnership* based on a balance of interests. Within the dialogue the school becomes attuned to the social context — both locally and more broadly — and to wider educational debates:

> The dynamic, renewing school is more self-consciously connected to society's expectations and convictions regarding sound educational practice.

Within Goodlad's view of an ecological approach to school renewal, then, he sees a need for the 'outside' to be challenging and supporting while the brokerage of change is conducted internally — within a spirit of enquiry.

Richard Andrews (in Goodlad, 1987) takes a similar view; that what is required is increased bonding and a breaking down of the boundary between school and community, the mobilization of community resources, and *boundary spanning* which includes 'routine purposive information acquisition'. What a school needs, he argues, is a 'niche' in the community. But within such a close relationship, he asks, whose values will dominate? The danger is that faced with conflicting agendas, the school's staff will retreat behind the 'barricades'.

Smith *et al* (1981) have introduced a 'longitudinal nested systems model' which contains the view that, over time, a school is the object of varying social and economic forces which contribute to the reshaping of a school's practices and, indeed, its character.

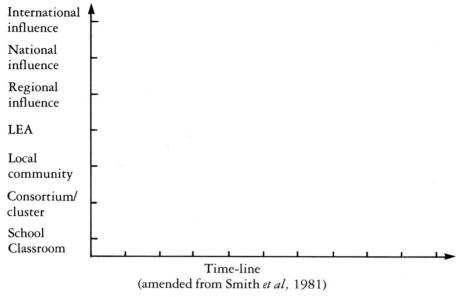

Time-line
(amended from Smith *et al*, 1981)

One way of looking at the changes at Garth Hill is to combine some of the points raised above into the following diagram (again, amending Smith *et al*, 1981):

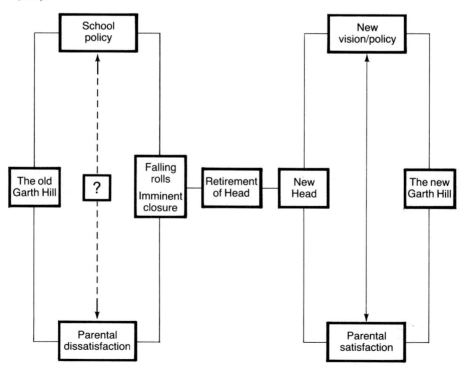

The view expressed by Smith and his colleagues is one of schools, in the 'long haul', having to adjust to the currents of the external social and economic forces, represented by the parents but which are influential at all levels of the 'system'. Their view would be that the old Garth Hill fell out of step with such forces and that the new Garth Hill has redressed the balance — to be 'successful'. Given Goodlad's views, how much autonomy a school can manage to retain in such a situation is another matter.

Certainly, with the 'power to parents' movement gathering momentum, such questions will become increasingly important. Judging by sections of the media and their use of opinion polls, parents are far from happy with their children's schools:

'Parents support exams shake-up in state schools'
Daily Telegraph/Gallup (September 1987)

'Schools given lower marks'
Daily Telegraph/Gallup (22 December 1986)

'Poll confirms poor public opinion of secondaries'
MORI/(*Times Educational Supplement,* 18 July 1986)

'Hearts and minds still to be won'
Gallup/Channel 4 20/20 Vision/*Times Educational Supplement* Editorial

The Secretary of State for Education and Science, Kenneth Baker, when speaking to the 1986 Conservative Party conference (and reported under the headline 'Baker's course to put governors at the helm', *Times Educational Supplement,* 10 October 1986), commented as follows:

While socialists see education as a means of social engineering, we see education as a springboard for individualism, opportunity and liberty. By creating opportunities for the child it confers freedom of choice and action for the young adult. For us, education must fulfil the individual's potential, not stifle it in the name of egalitarianism.

Education can no longer be led by the producers — by the academic theorists, the administrators or even the teachers' unions. Education must be shaped by the users — by what is good for the individual child and what hopes are held by their parents . . .

. . . Our Education Bill radically changes the composition of school governing bodies. It gives these bodies new powers and responsibilities. We will end the dominance of the local authority and its political appointees. It will no longer be possible for local authorities to foist a headteacher on a school against the wishes of the governors . . .

There will be more parent governors elected by all the parents. But now it's up to people all over the country and to you, your friends and neighbours to respond by coming forward as governors to assume greater responsibility . . .

If there is a good headmaster or a good headmistress then the school will be good. That is why I want to see more power given to the headteachers. I want to see them together with their governing bodies controlling more of the money spent in their schools.

I want to see headteachers win back the standing and place they had in society fifty years ago. They are special people, they are leaders, they have a unique position to influence the lives of generations of young people. Thankfully we have many thousands of very good ones . . .

This local alliance between a school's parents, governors and headteacher does not have to be an 'unholy' one. An issue here, however, is the possibility of the headteacher-as-leader becoming detached from his/her staff and the consequent undermining of staff collegiality.

In the government's recent legislation (commonly referred to as the 'Baker Bill'), parent choice is one of the cornerstones. Schools are obliged to accept as many pupils as they have room for, giving parents a wider choice and a better — although not a guaranteed — chance of a place at the school they really want. Popular schools can expand; unpopular schools can contract and close. Given this drive towards parent power 'in theory' (in reality, they still have to *assume* power) there are two possible situations:

Situation 1: akin to Goodlad's change scenario (c), this situation holds the potential of a local partnership in which the teachers, parents and governors *collaborate* on behalf of *their* school. Parents and governors can then become involved in the shaping of the school's curriculum without the teachers having to relinquish curriculum control. As one headteacher was reported as saying (*Times Educational Supplement,* 28 November 1986):

> It's a renewal of credibility and trust. I feel that if we have the parents' consent they are more likely to back what we are doing.

The emphasis on parent power, which dates from the Taylor Report (1977) and which was given further backing in the 1980 Education Act, Circular 6/81, the 1986 Education Act and the so-called Great Reform Bill, need not be a recipe for partnership. The related emphasis on parents-as-consumers (as opposed to parents-as-partners) involves not only a shift of power in school government, but also the recommendation that parents are the best people to 'monitor the system'. Are parents, then, friends or foes?

- are they allies working with schools for internal development?
- are they 'agents' working to make schools accountable?
- are these roles compatible or incompatible?

Situation 2: similar to Goodlad's change scenario (b), this situation involves schools being opened up to the possibility of change through the mechanism of 'the market'. The operation of 'market forces' (hinging on parental expectations) involves *choice* and *competitition*. Peter Wilby (in *The Sunday Times,* 2 March 1986) surveyed the introduction of a market in schools and included in his discussion: talk of education vouchers; the expansion of direct grant (or grant maintained) schools; and the denationalization of education. According to what have been referred to as the 'business model' and 'free enterprise in education', successful schools are encouraged to flourish, while unsuccessful schools are allowed to go out of business. They can, of course, save themselves by their own efforts. In terms of this same mentality, 'neighbourhood schools' are potentially monopolistic; no schools should be allowed to rest on their laurels.

This model is currently receiving widespread attention in the United States. William Bennett, Education Secetary in President Reagan's administration, has tried to rekindle interest in voucher schemes. Furthermore, he has claimed that schools should be run like small businesses, with those unable to deliver what the public wants being shut down. In a speech (reported in the *Times Educational Supplement*), he said:

> We must have greater accountability in the schools. You know about accountability. You know that if your product isn't good, if your services aren't good, you're going to go out of business. We need something more like that in education . . . If a school works with students over a period of time and fails to educate them, those schools will be shut down. And if a school works effectively with students over a period of time, that school will be expanded and its teachers and its leadership will be rewarded for their efforts . . . If parents don't like the schools, if students are not learning in the schools, parents should be free to put their children in a school where they will learn.

In addition, Bennett restated the case for strong leadership in schools — if they are to be successful:

> Let's identify those people who can be great leaders in our schools and put them in there, whether they have had training and 14 or 15 courses in educational theory or not . . .
> Leadership is still a matter of grit and fibre and muscle and sinew and character. It is not something one picks up in graduate school.

Consequent to this speech, schools in New York City have been told to 'shape up or shut down' (*Times Educational Supplement,* 20 June 1986) and educationalists in the US have voiced 'private fears in the public sector' (*Times Educational Supplement,* 13 June 1986) in terms of their concern that market forces may be introduced in the classroom. They see the 'spectre of privatization looming' with the increased usage of private ancillary services and the suggestion (in the Carnegie Task Force Report, 1986) that certified teachers should go into business for themselves and contract with schools for their services. With 'market forces' providing 'incentives for improved performance and productivity', educational service companies, consultancy facilities and entrepreneurial developments generally could well receive much more attention.

In the experience of Garth Hill, these two *situations* are not necessarily incompatible. Given the reality of parent power, the onus is on the schools to promote a policy of inclusion which aims to combine accountability concerns with a partnership for development. According to the same headteacher quoted above (*Times Educational Supplement,* 28 November 1986):

> We decided that if we were really going to be accountable to parents and society at large we needed to take on board what they say about the curriculum.

Within such a vital dialogue, the character of a school can be forged, i.e. Deal's cohesive culture, our ethos or vision. Indeed, *schools of character* may well be the shape of the future. In a context of parent power and local choice and increased dialogue, *distinctive schools of some distinction* could well emerge.

It is interesting to note that in a recent article (in *The Sunday Times,* 14 February 1988), Caroline St. John-Brooks is able to describe not only the competition between schools ('uncomfortable demographic facts have already closed schools and left survivors competing for a limited pool of customers. Every school I visited was well aware of the need to attract parents'), but also, where there is direct competition, the emergence of very distinctive, alternative schools. In East Hertfordshire, for example, the reporter visited Broxbourne School ('traditional and formal') and Sheredes School ('one of the trail-blazing comprehensives with a "progressive ethos"'), both in receipt of strong parental support. Consequently, she says;

> Every school I visited seemed to be *good in its own way* (our emphasis), with a strong headteacher committed to giving pupils as good an education as possible.

Indeed, in terms very reminiscent of the Garth Hill story, St. John-Brooks describes another success story:

> One headteacher who has succeeded in turning round an unpopular school is Peter Evans, Head of St. Andrew's school in Leatherhead, Surrey. He took over nearly four years ago when the school could not fill all its places and was a candidate for possible closure. Now, parents are putting down their children's names two or three years in advance.
>
> 'I am very aware of market forces', he says, 'I had to raise the image of the school. The reputation of a school is made in the supermarket and on street corners. Communication is a vacuum. If I don't fill it someone else will, with rumour and innuendo'.
>
> Evans's conviction that parents matter affects how he runs the school. When he took it over he told the teachers: 'I want to run this school as if I were a parent. For the first month, I'm going to be walking this school as a parent'. At the end of the month, he called the staff together to plan improvements.

And for St. Andrew's read Garth Hill, for Peter Evans read Stanley Goodchild.

Yet St. John-Brooks concludes that all the effort being put into competititon, image-making and wooing parents is not necessarily improving the quality of education:

> But government policies to open education to market forces are not the answer. Headteachers will make ever more frantic efforts to sell their schools, but improved quality may not follow . . .
>
> Parents are easily taken in by symbols such as uniform which, while important, do not guarantee a good education. Government efforts to privatise education and treat it as a private investment, not a public good, will make things worse.
>
> When inspectors visited West Germany, they were struck by the fact that government, parents, teachers, employers and students all agreed on what the country was aiming for in education. Here, everyone pulls in different directions.

All current trends, however, are in the direction of the *independence* and *individualization* of schools. As in industry, schools are being urged to become champions and to be entrepreneurial. Central to this thinking is the promotion of Local Financial Management (LFM) — also referred to as Local Resource Management (LRM). What was originally an experiment in Cambridgeshire LEA is to be extended, we are told, to all schools. The experiment has received much attention in the press; *The Daily Telegraph* has included articles entitled:

'Schools given sweeping powers over spending'
'Baker to give schools control over spending'
'Cambridge diet of school home rule. Now the whisper about independent budgets has reached Baker'
'Tories to give schools choice over funding'
'What every head must learn about balancing the books'

Six aspects of LFM are worthy of mention:

- first, it provides for 'local' (i.e. school-site) budgetary control;
- second, it represents the devolution of power to individual schools and their governors by delegating decision-making covering resource-allocation;
- third, it can be construed as either 'free enterprise education' or 'worker participation in education' (according to the *Times Educational Supplement,* 14 November 1986) — our two situations described above;
- fourth, it has staffing implications and implications for role performance:

it (LFM) is making us into managing directors of units which have to produce education (quoted in the *Times Educational Supplement,* 14 November 1986).

> Some staff members have asked: 'Are we book-keepers, accountants or teachers, managers or educationalists?

- fifth, it can be used to serve educational purposes by operating alongside and supporting the staff's educational priority decisions.
- and, sixth, the administration of LFM produces its own costs. Such a scheme, therefore, would not necessarily lead to economies — the main finding of a recent report from management consultants Coopers and Lybrand (1988) and published by the DES. Though the estimated costs of 'local management in schools' (LMS) — the report's new name for local financial management — were outside Coopers and Lybrand's brief, the company does calculate where the main costs will fall: training, implementation, systems development, 'safety nets' for schools having to readjust to lower spending, management, and administration and support from the local education authority (as reported in the *Times Educational Supplement*, 22 January 1988).

The report says: 'It is difficult to say whether in the long run LMS by itself would lead to net savings or net costs; the position will vary considerably between LEAs. On balance, we would be surprised if there were net savings. However, we have stressed how important it is that LMS should not be seen as a means of cost reduction: its purpose is to produce a more effective and responsive school system, not necessarily a cheaper one'.

How LMS should work

The report's main recommendations:

'Local management of schools' is what is required as the changes are more than purely financial. A new culture and philosophy of educational organization at school level are needed.

Though the management of resources will be delegated to schools, the local education authority should still have responsibility for education as a whole in its area.

Most of a school's resources could and should be managed by governors and heads.

The l.e.a. role should be envisaged as that of a staffing agency, a contractor for goods and services and a landlord for school premises.

Complications could include the introduction of competitive tendering, changes in the role of advisers and inspectors and the community use of school premises. Restrictions on capital expenditure need to be relaxed to allow local management to operate with maximum effect.

Local education authorities will need to develop a formula with three components: pupil numbers, spending needs for premises and special activities. Schools should also be encouraged to bid for funds for particular projects.

The l.e.a. will need to monitor each school's performance and take action if required.

Management information is critical to the scheme's success.

Implementation will require staff time, cash and training. It cannot be rushed and a three to four-year timetable is reasonable. However, each l.e.a. should develop and define its scheme within 12 to 18 months.

Times Educational Supplement 22 January 1988

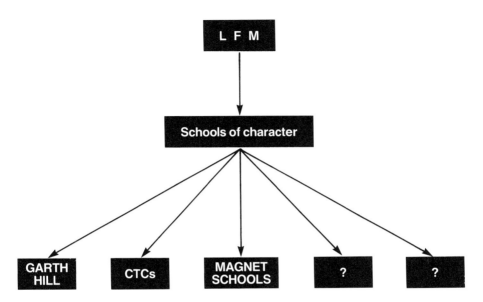

What is significant about the debates concerning LFM or LMS is its promotion of self-management in schools. This is, of course, very much Kenneth Baker's agenda:

> If we can build the authority of our schools as self-managing, self-governing bodies, we can do an enormous amount to enhance their status. The thrust of our policy is to put responsibility on to the schools, their heads and their governing bodies.
>
> (quoted in *The Sunday Times*)

And in a recent publication entitled *The Self-managing School* by Brian Caldwell and Jim Spinks (1988), an Australian LFM scheme is described that allows heads to put education before accountancy. The scheme is very much like some of the school self-evaluation exercises launched in the U.K. (for example, the GRIDS scheme) and, according to Virginia Makins, it is

> A tested system for local financial management for schools that focuses on teaching and learning, rather than on administrative and financial arrangements . . .
>
> The authors, Brian Caldwell and Jim Spinks, argue that their procedures allow heads to act as educational leaders, unlike more

227

narrowly administrative arrangements which turn them into accountants and purchasing agents.

The plan comes as a welcome breath of educational air in the welter of bureaucratic difficulties and intricacies outlined in the recent Coopers and Lybrand report on the local manangement of schools. (*Times Educational Supplement,* 22 January)

The Australian scheme was based on existing research into effective schools in several countries, which revealed that their success was based on positive educational leadership and a sense of ownership by teachers.

It claims to allow for the involvement of the whole school community — governors, teachers, students, parents and employers — in policy-making in a manageable way that does not end with wodges of paper policies and little action.

The book outlines detailed procedures for the development of policies and programmes for the different subject areas and for whole school matters like special needs, homework, reporting to parents and discipline.

The system has now been introduced in Tasmania, and more recently in Victoria, where schools have been given considerable responsibilities for self-management.

Themes that are familiar in this present volume emerge in this report:

- the central importance of the improvement of teaching and learning processes;
- positive educational leadership *and* teacher ownership;
- the involvement of the whole school community in deciding *their* future;
- the potential of self-management.

It could be argued, of course, that Garth Hill — given the massive influx of funds over the months — has much experience of LFM-type arrangements. A reflection of this is the appointment of not only the business manager but also a 'school bursar and office manager'. The advertisement for this post read as follows:

This is a new and exciting post for a person with vision and initiative. The successful candidate will be responsible for managing the finances of the school under the direction of the Principal, and for leading the team of office staff. Ideally, applicants should have a qualification in accountancy and be able to demonstrate leadership qualities in managing a busy office.

It could also be argued that Garth Hill not only has experience of LFM but has proved something of a 'magnet school' and a fore-runner, in style and curriculum anyway, of the City Technology Colleges (CTCs).

According to Bruce Cooper (1987), magnet schools — as experienced in the USA — are typified by *specialization* (a *distinct curriculum orientation,* for example, technology, around a common core curriculum) and *devolved management* (i.e. decentralized budgetary control as with LFM). Cooper maintains that they can be instituted within 'privatization' (i.e. the 'total denationalization' and decentralization of the educational system with each individual enterprise being independent) or 'partial decentralization' within State education (i.e. nationally funded) but 'privately run'. Magnet schools, says Cooper, share most (or all) of the following considerations:

  (i)   theme-based programmes; specializing in science, mathematics, technology, computers, the arts (music, dance, drama, fine arts, design, etc.), vocational/technical education etc;
 (ii)   the opportunity for parents to select them voluntarily, i.e. no 'zoning' stipulations;
(iii)   the chance for schools to set many of their own policies;
 (iv)   the goal of desegregating the school district.

Above all, says Cooper, 'magnetization' has the power to change the entire local system — leading Anne Sofer (*Times Educational Supplement,* 17 October 1986) to remark that the problems magnet schools are intended to solve seem to be more social and political than purely educational.

As a consequence, Bruce Cooper highlights the 'common ideology' of 'going magnetic'; the schools aim to combine the following:

- choice, competition and excellence;
- private, entrepreneurial, and competitive approaches to change;
- enterprise as opposed to welfare;
- the avoidance of 'risk-averse bureaucracies (which) are unsatisfactory sources of economic dynamism';
- the instigation of market-driven, anti-monopolistic approaches;
- the pursuit of productivity;
- the introduction of alternative schools which do not have a 'captive, client group' and which have to work actively on recruitment, publicity and the distribution of information;

Such schools embody one interpretation of the 'enterprise culture'.

When asked about CTCs, Stanley Goodchild, knowing that his school has been considered a forerunner in this area, says that many people, both in the private and State sectors, believe in the CTC philosophy and, if the pilot scheme is successful, he believes that they will become an integral part of the State system, thus (as with TVEI before them) potentially benefiting all students in the U.K.

By and large CTCs are to be technologically-oriented magnet schools. They are intended, according to Cyril Taylor (*Times Educational Supplement,* 22 January 1988), to be 'exemplar schools whose lead will be followed at a later stage by local education authorities. Other projected characteristics include the following:

- a close relationship with local employers;
- regular and continuous work experience so that CTC pupils will develop an understanding of, and be prepared to enter, the world of work;
- job exchanges involving CTC teachers and their industrial counterparts;
- core and foundation subjects, plus *technology* in all its forms.

Computer literacy and the use of word processors across the curriculum will be considered basic, while there will also be, says Cyril Taylor

> technology courses in such subjects as robotics, automation, control of manufacturing, programming machine tools and robots, data processing and computing, biochemistry, microbiology and enzymeology, and even hotel management, marketing, fashion and retailing. These subjects will not only help pupils to learn marketable skills, but encourage them to think clearly and to solve problems.
>
> Through the support of sponsors, a well as a more efficient use of state funding, CTCs will enjoy use of the latest hi-tech equipment, including computers, word processors, electronic mail, robots and computer-assisted design equipment. All staff will be expected to become familiar with the use of this equipment.

This is basically the curriculum that has been tried and tested at Garth Hill. No wonder, then, that the advocates of CTCs have been queuing up to have a look at a CTC type curriculum in action. If the aim of magnet schools and CTCs is to implement the enterprise culture in education, one school has been there already and thrived on the experience.

The Enterprise Culture in Education

This concluding section will focus on the **enterprise culture.** The first point to make is that the enterprise culture is pervasive and is operative in various overlapping spheres of activity; it is the enactments:

an economic philosophy
a social philosophy
a political philosophy
a management philosophy
an educational philosophy

In 1968 the Institute of Economic Affairs (which itself has done much to disseminate the theories embodied in the enterprise culture) published — in translation from the French — *The Enterprise Ethic* by Octave Gelinier. In this book Gelinier advocates the *discipline* of competition, competitive markets and choice. He argues that competition:

- effectively eliminates inefficiency, complacency and routinism;

- is neither about laissez-faire nor authoritarianism;
- is about innovation, freedom of action, and the *creation of enterprise;*
- rests on four freedoms: freedom of consumption; freedom of investment; freedom of contract; and freedom of mobility.

There are also eight rules for competition:

- the elimination of violence;
- the elimination of fraud;
- the elimination of monopolies;
- stimulation of competitive initiatives (sometimes by the State, albeit temporarily);
- aid to resolve difficulties of transition (again, the State can have a role to play here);
- resistance to pressure groups and vested interests;
- action through the 'rule of law' (general laws of democratic societies) as opposed to the administrative fiat of authoritarian bureaucracy;
- the application of the principle of generalized competition, for example, the operation of the 'price' mechanism and the emphasis on quality of production;

'To sum up', he wrote, 'the law must encourage competition in every form. Under such a system of generalized competition, it is impossible for a country's economy to slumber for long under bad management.'

Traditionally, he wrote, when an industry ought to be reorganized, too often it has been subsidized, thus encouraging dependency, ossification and stagnation rather than adaptability and enterprise. The government's responsibility is to extend the limits of competition (and institute what could be called *democratic enterprise*) by being non-authoritarian:

> Competition is not a dogma, but an efficient tool . . . competition compels the enterprise to progress.

But competition cannot prosper without a sympathetic culture within which to work. Gelliner concludes:

> There can be no moral and cultural progress without an economic foundation, no economic progress without some moral and cultural foundation . . .
> The most significant and stable factor in a nation's economic development must be found . . . in the framework of rules which order its population and government.

Thus the importance of galvanizing *an enterprise culture* within which *an enterprise economy* can flourish. Again, the State has a triggering role:

> In some sectors of the economy, legally subject to competition, competitive initiatives are rare and weak, which relaxes the discipline on management and incentives to growth and efficiency. In such cases,

the State must stimulate competition by spreading information, developing technical education, introducing foreign competition, lowering tariff barriers or attracting foreign firms.

And in this passage Gellinier merges the economic, the social, the political and the educational. What is significant about his writing is his interpretation of 'democratic' which revolves around the freedom and enterprise of open competition; it is the economics and politics of self-help and self-responsibility as opposed to self-interest.

The so-called New Enlightenment (see Graham and Clarke, 1986) has built not only on Gelinier but also on the classical liberalism of David Hume and Adam Smith and F. A. Hayek and the Mont Pelerin Society. Such ideas are popular amongst the so-called Neo-Conservatives in the USA and have gained many British converts. One such is Keith (now Lord) Joseph.

Recently, in what has been referred to as an 'acclaimed maiden speech' in the House of Lords (reported in *The Independent,* 20 Feburary 1988):

the former Sir Keith Joseph looked forward to a greater 'embourgoise-ment' of British society with choice expanded through higher earnings.

During a debate on the Government's 'Enterprise Initiative', he said:

Free enterprise, if it is given the chance, is the least bad method yet invented to create for virtually all, jobs, prosperity, social and public service and freedom.

Lord Joseph maintained that he had entered politics 'to try, however modestly, to reduce the widespread poverty of many British people', but that he soon realized that 'statism' is not the answer:

I have come to realize over time that the state can perhaps do better by setting the right framework and by intervening little . . . It is free enterprise with the decentralization of ownership and decision-making and, subject to the law, business competition which makes 'embourgeoisement' possible. We need to go farther yet into the hitherto no-go areas . . . For me the magic ingredient is freedom of choice.

This debate in the House of Lords was concerned with Lord Young's Enterprise Initiative and the remodelling of the DTI as the 'Ministry for Enterprise'.

The language is clearly important. The term 'enterprise' is crucial, as are the terms 'freedom', 'choice', 'competition', 'initiative', 'opportunity', 'entre-preneurialism' and 'innovation'.

This new philosophy explores the potential power of spontaneous, uncoordinated action by individuals, who, through their independent actions, are seen as a greater force for good than most blueprints for social organization. According to Gilder (1986), an advocate of this philosophy,

Enterprise is unstoppable. The entrepreneur is on the leading edge of an instinct we all have. It emerges wherever it can and goes off on its poverty-slaying mission.

Peter Drucker (1985) has taken a rather different line. Whereas Gilder sees entrepreneurship as a natural 'spirit' which is both creative and spontaneous — almost effortless (if it does not well up in an organization, then it's being stifled) — Drucker argues that 'entrepreneurship is not "natural"; it is not "creative". It is work'. It has to be done by capable people; it has to be consciously striven for; and it requires effort:

> Entrepreneurial businesses . . . are disciplined about it . . . they work at it . . . practise it.

And the task of management, according to Drucker, is to build an *entrepreneurial climate,* a receptiveness to innovation — with change perceived as an opportunity not a threat. Management, therefore, can promote enterprise:

> The manager is the dynamic, life-giving element in every business. Without his leadership 'the resources of production' remain resources and never become production. In a competitive economy, above all, the quality and performance of the managers determine the success of a business, indeed they determine its survival. *For the quality and performance of its managers is the only effective advantage an enterprise in a competitive economy can have.*
>
> According to Harvey-Jones (1988):

> In this world the firm begins to seem to have a different function from firms of old. The old firm was a hierarchy run by a boss. A new firm is a machine for increasing the exchange value of individuals' skills and abilities, providing a framework, within which employees can realize their best creative potential. The firms are people-oriented . . .

In addition, Harvey-Jones raises the same point as Gilder (1986) and Wiener (1985). Culturally-speaking, he says,

> Industry is widely misunderstood in the world today . . . the purpose of industry is to create wealth . . . Without wealth, they (social problems) cannot be tackled at all.

But, as Gilder (1986) maintains, traditionally, there is an intellectual disdain for all things industrial. This leads, he says, to the depletion and demoralization of the 'culture of capitalism':

> It leads to a failure to pass on to many youths a notion of the sources of their affluence and the possibilities of their lives. It leads to a persistent illusion on the part of intellectuals that we live in an age without heroes. It leads to a widespread sense of entitlement to the bounties of 'society', to a 'social surplus', which in fact is the product of the labour and ingenuity of particular men and women. Society is always in deep debt to the entrepreneurs who sustain it and rarely consume by

themselves more than the smallest share of what they give society.

In fact, says Gilder, the comforts of life are *made* by the 'specific exertions and sacrifices of men and women on the frontiers of enterprise'. Such 'hero innovators' make it happen:

> From their knowledge of failure, they forge success. In accepting risk, they achieve security for all. In embracing change, they ensure social and economic stability . . . They overthrow establishments rather than establish equilibria. They are the heroes of economic life.

Yet, says Gilder, a hostile, resistant culture wants 'capitalism without capitalists' and 'enterprise without the coarse bustle of business and trade'. Wiener (1985) describes this resistant culture as a distinctive complex of social ideas, sentiments, and values, which embodies an ambiguous attitude towards industrial life and which arose in the nineteenth century:

> In the world's first industrial nation, industrialism did not seem quite at home. In the country that had started mankind in the 'great ascent', economic growth was frequently viewed with suspicion and disdain. Having pioneered urbanisation, the English ignored or disparaged cities.

There is, Wiener says, a cultural 'cordon sanitaire' encircling the forces of economic development. Recent surveys (the findings of which were published in the *Times Educational Supplement*) confirmed that many pupils still have a depressing image of industry. One of the biggest deterrents to working in industry was that they thought it would be 'too routine and boring'. Furthermore, according to a speaker at a CBI conference in Glasgow (reported in the *Times Educational Supplement,* 6 November 1987), the 'school ethos' is 'anti-business' and most teachers 'have actively decided against industry and commerce; they are a much greater barrier than their students in building up a strong spirit of enterprise'.

An editorial in the *Times Educational Supplement* (11 September 1981) proclaimed that education is 'anti-entrepreneurial, anti-industrial, anti-productive'. The editor referred to Corelli Barnett's RSA paper (delivered in 1979) and Wiener's work and quoted from Professor David Marquand's article which had appeared in *The Times* the previous week:

> One of the main reasons for Britian's failure to keep pace with competing economies is that, for more than a century, our elite culture has been anti-entrepreneurial, anti-industrial and, in a profound sense, anti-productive, esteeming the possession and tasteful consumption of wealth but disparaging its creation and creators.

The editorial continued by describing the 'modest' educational programme of the DTI and the Education for Capability movement launched in the summer of 1981, at which point 'most politicians, civil servants, local authority administrators, heads and primary and secondary school teachers look, ostentatiously, in the opposite direction'.

Consequently, this editorial concludes that;

> This is because the argument goes far beyond and behind the schools. If the ambience of the English elite culture is what the critics say it is — and most fair-minded people would probably agree that it is — *then the schools are the prisoners of this culture as well as its celebrants* . . . schools cannot by themselves change the reward systems by which society underwrites present values.

This anti-entrepreneurial high culture, according to Sir Geoffrey Chandler (*Times Educational Supplement,* 3 January 1986) determines that:

> nothing fundamentally changes. The reason is that the supposed causes of our poor performance are in fact symptoms of a set of attitudes and an inherited culture which put industrial activity at the bottom of the social pecking order. Our industrial performance reflects the low esteem in which society holds it.
>
> Our education has reflected this anti-industrial culture: it has been predominantly academic, leaving children in ignorance of how the country earns its living and failing to develop the talents of making and designing. The fundamental connection between standard of living/quality of life and industrial success is therefore not understood. On emerging from full-time education too many young people are doubtful about the value of pursuing a career in industry.

Chandler wrote these comments at the beginning of Industry Year (1986) which he called a 'lever for change, not an end in itself'. He continued:

> Industry Year cannot reverse the attitudes of a century and more in 365 days, but it can do three things:
>
> - improve awareness of industry's essential contribution to the community and of the fact that it provides a service in which the participants should be able to take pride;
> - strengthen, add to, and multiply the growing number of initiatives designed to bridge the divide between education and industry. Links between schools and companies, the broadening of teacher training, and modification of the curriculum are central to this; and
> - encourage industry itself to articulate its role more clearly; to recognize that the simplistic response 'we are in business to make money' fails to reflect the very real set of obligations to which any successful company and manager must respond; and to understand that the lack of a corporate industrial ethic is a positive deterrent to a critical and idealistic student population.

In a vituperative article by Paul Johnson in *The Daily Telegraph,* he voices similar sentiments and, influenced by the writing of Gilder and the

Neo-Conservatives, announces that all aspects of British culture should be exposed to the discipline of the market. Declaring that the cultural flavour of British life has never been more hostile to success in wealth-creation, he maintains that,

> A reformed schools system, geared to producing skills, elites and high flyers, will not in itself make Britain a competitive nation. We need also to create an enterprise culture.

He singles out the British universities for particular criticism (they are 'isolated in virginal purity from the real world of the market place' and are the 'primary source of our anti-enterprise culture') and demands that the Government expose these 'cultural citadels to the educative discipline of the market' and make them 'work for their survival'. He concludes that

> What is essential is the principle: that no element in our culture has an automatic entitlement to a living from the state . . . and to flourish they must develop the same responsible appeal and functional efficiency as any other enterprise.

And then along came the announcement (*Times Educational Supplement*, 23 October 1987) that there is an '"Enterprise" future in store for students'. This article described the 'long-awaited plan' for the MSC to 'vocationalize' higher education. This scheme, which offers universities, polytechnics and colleges the necessary finance to provide training in management and business skills, and work experience for all their students, aims to ensure that the participants will 'acquire competence and skills and develop attitudes and qualities appropriate for an enterprise economy'.

During 1988 the pressure has continued to mount. 'Baker lists ways for business to put goals across' (reported in the *Times Educational Supplement*, 5 February 1988). The list included:

- visiting schools and talking about the curriculum;
- volunteering to become governors;
- helping with LFM arrangements;
- getting into schools and explaining to the pupils about industry and wealth creation.

The DTI's White Paper has been thoroughly discussed, especially its educational implications (*Times Educational Supplement*, 22 January 1988). With its aim of 'encouraging enterprise', the DTI was described as the new bridge-builder between industry and education. Its intentions were seen as the fostering of new links between employers and the schools, the promotion of work experience and the use of new technology. The White Paper received this coverage in the 'Comment' section of the TES:

ENTERPRISE
Lord Young's new-look Department of Trade and Industry has 'encouraging the growth of links between schools and the world of

work' among its objectives. The educational programmes figured prominently in last week's DTI White Paper.

Three specific commitments are set down. The DTI will work towards getting each year 10 per cent of the teaching force to spend some time in gaining personal experience of the world of business. It will aim to get to a stage when all pupils will have had two or more weeks of work experience by the time they leave school. And it will ensure that everyone training to be a teacher gains an appreciation of the needs of employers and of the importance of links between schools and employers.

These aims are set out in typically general terms which bear the authentic David Young hallmark. Not that this is a substitute for action.

What he has done is to serve notice on his own department and on the Department of Education that he wants things to happen. He has deliberately refused to get bogged down in the mechanics of how to do it, because he knows that the normal inertia of the 'system' can always defeat him.

The unanswered questions, however, abound. Some reports have suggested that the teachers are to get their work experience in the school holidays. This suggests certain elementary difficulties. Is the DTI scheme to be written into the Baker contract? Who is going to pay for supply teachers if 10 per cent of regular teachers are going to be away for some weeks each year at Lord Young's behest in term-time? And as for more work experience for secondary pupils, how is this going to make headway against the pressures of the national curriculum?

What is quite clear is that Lord Young still nourishes ambitions. His translation to the DTI has not muted the interest which he showed at the Manpower Services Commission and the Department of Employment. He believes the seeds of an enterprise culture have to be sown in the schools But the DES may well be unenthusiastic at the very time it is staging its grand Whitehall comeback.

Lord Young then has become the 'champion of enterprise'. It has to be remembered, of course, that his enterprise crusade is based on an economic and political philosophy. Liberal democracy, as we have referred to it, aims to reduce the role of the state, with the task of government being limited to do what 'the market' cannot do. Liberty is all important as is the faith in the market system. Economists who argue for this position take the line that the more markets are allowed to do, the less government has to do. It is an individualist philosophy. And the extension of this philosophy to education reads like this:

> Given the maximum of parental free choice, pressure will be brought to bear on the least satisfactory schools so that they are constantly prodded

into matching the services of competitors threatening to attract or already attracting clientele. In these conditions, there would be every reason to expect efficiency in schools to continue rising until they all exceed standards originally specified by the state. (West *Education and the State*)

Lightfoot (1983) seems to agree when she argues that:

> . . . in trying to protect against inferior schooling, these 'central authorities' have limited the freedom of the better schools and distorted the essential human encounters that shape education.

Drucker (1985) has also criticized the lack of initiative in public (i.e. state) schools and their 'dependency' mentality. Yet, he argues, if they do not adapt, they will not survive:

> The public school in the United States exemplifies both the opportunity and the dangers. Unless it takes the lead in innovation it is unlikely to survive this century, except as a school for the minorities in the slums. For the first time in its history, the United States faces the threat of a class structure in education in which all but the very poor remain outside of the public school system — at least in the cities and suburbs where most of the population lives. And this will squarely be the fault of the public school itself because what is needed to reform the public school is already known.

His recipe for success is a straighforward one. Schools have to learn how to build entrepreneurship and innovation into their internal processes and to remember what schooling is for:

> Perhaps the time has come for an entrepreneur to start schools based on what we know about learning . . .

According to George Walden (in an article in *The Daily Telegraph,* 18 January 1988), in the USA 'enterprise does not have to be preached — it is in the air'. So much so, in fact, that public figures like William Bennett and Allan Bloom, author of the best-seller, *The Closing of the American Mind,* are more concerned about the need for 'moral literacy' and 'cultural decomposition'. They are worried about the effects of 'bureaucraticized liberalism' and want to return to an education which considers 'cultural canons' and appeals for 'greater individual moral and cerebral effort'. 'What seems to matter most to Bennett', says Walden, 'are the ethical and cultural values of education and plain old-fashioned character-building'. This emphasis on personal morality is an interesting one. Presumably, the more that emphasis is placed on energetic, thrusting and powerful individuals, the more that these individuals need to have a moral grounding to govern their forceful actions. As Walden concludes, this crusade

> could all come to nothing . . . Yet is is also just possible that this may be the beginning of the cultural re-emergence of America — an event not without significance for ourselves.

It is this same area, however, which gives doubts to 'social democrats' in and out of education. In a recent volume significantly entitled *The Unprincipled Society*, Professor David Marquand has warned that it is not a case of the State doing less; what is required is for the state to do more — thus becoming a 'developmental State', the energies of which have to be channelled to economic success. He talks about the 'philosophy of public purpose' based on negotiation, consent, a sense of community, mutual obligation and partnership. The aim, he says, is to avoid the unrestrained pursuit of sectional greed and adversarial politics; the answer is to turn Britain into 'a classroom, a debating chamber, a Quaker meeting or a Jewish Yeshiva'. Like Marquand, some comprehensive school headteachers are alarmed at the spread of the entrepreneurial version of the enterprise philosophy. Bernard Barker has argued 'for an open dialogue between teachers, pupils and parents as the mainspring of a *democratic, co-operative enterprise*. He warns against the dangers of the 'new managerialism', which constitutes a political and ideological movement masquerading as industrial psychology which demands 'competitive, tough, innovative but undemanding citizens'. What are required by this ideology are 'changed attitudes, not critical ideas'. His fellow head, George Walker, has also warned against the (over)-instrumentalization of education — the view that education can become the programme for economic survival — and the individualization of enterprise initiatives. Moreover, Walker voiced his anxieties concerning the 'increasingly entrepreneurial aspect of education funding'. He commented:

> I'm beginning to feel I've missed out, somehow. I feel I don't know the new rules. I'm not smart enough.

It seems, then, that there are two philosophies at work here — for want of better descriptions, the 'liberal democratic' and the 'social democratic', with each one aiming to compensate for the shortcomings of the other. A recurring theme in this book, however, is that 'Enterprise' (usually interpreted as individualistic and entrepreneurial) needs to permeate — and be supported by — the organizational 'Culture'. This is vital to prevent the organization being stultified by its dependency on an un-enterprising culture.

Fullan (1988) has recently produced a stimulating 'thought-piece' in which he claims that the 'system' fosters dependency on the part of heads/principals. Heads, he argues, are pressurised from below (by the 'pull' of teacher expectations and the informal culture of the school) and from above (by the welter of externally imposed directives). In a powerful passage Fullan elaborates on those points:

> Paradoxically, dependency is fostered both by emphasis on tradition and by demands for innovation. The role of principals in implementing innovations is more often than not a case of being on the receiving end of externally initiated changes. Dependency is created through the constant bombardment of new tasks and continual interruptions on the job which keep principals occupied or at least off balance. Overload fosters dependency. Principals are either overloaded with what they are

doing or overloaded with all the things they think they should be doing. Dependency, I will argue, may also be internalized or too easily tolerated by principals themselves.

By dependency I mean that one's actions are predominantly shaped, however unintentionally, by events and/or by actions or directions of others. Empowerment, taking charge, and otherwise playing a central role in determining what is done is the opposite of dependency. Taking charge does not mean that one eschews inter-dependencies. As will become clear, effective empowerment and interdependency go hand in hand.

To ward off dependency, says Fullan, heads and their schools must reject the notion of isolated autonomy. In going it alone, heads need all the help they can get; they need to be autonomous but supported, pioneering but interdependent. It is very much a case of 'Enterprise for the Enterprise'.

Chapter Six

Enterprise for the Enterprise

We must fix our horizons not on the mandates of atrophying institutions but on the successes of burgeoning new enterprises.

(Bennis and Nanus, 1985)

In this concluding chapter we would like to return to four themes which have recurred throughout this book. In so doing, we will highlight some of the major issues as we see them.

Theme 1:   Garth Hill: The School For Enterprise
Theme 2:   The Management Culture in Education
Theme 3:   The Incorporation of Schooling
Theme 4:   The Developing School

Theme 1:   Garth Hill: The School For Enterprise or 'The World According to Garth'

'I am no longer a teacher, I am a company manager'

'We run the school very much like a business.'

'If you know where you're going, be prepared to waver, but no U-turns.'

'I told them what we were going to do five years ago — they thought I had my head firmly stuck in the clouds.'

'Lead from the front — demonstrate you mean business.'

'Have a clear vision, be prepared to use pressure from the outside . . . know your staff and don't make promises you can't keep; don't be two-faced but be direct. Be compassionate but show you won't be taken for a ride.'

'I wouldn't avoid confrontation if it was for the school.'

'I try to make people feel important.'

'I teach six periods per week; as the managing director of the school, it is difficult to find the time for this but, for multiple reasons, it is very important.'

'One of my routine priorities is to attend my assemblies.'

'An idea is a gimmick if it's in isolation. There's been a common theme to everything we've done here — when ideas are up and running they need to be dovetailed . . .'

'I'm prepared to accept I'm wrong.'

These quotes from interviews with Stanley Goodchild relate to some of the dimensions of his leadeship style and the style of Garth Hill's rise to success. It's very much a case of

- 'doing the business' — and the business is education;
- providing the vision — and weaving towards it;
- attending to the continuum of pressure . . . direction . . . honesty . . . integrity . . . caring . . . consideration;
- ensuring that the school culture is ethos-led (i.e. formally-based) rather than culture-led (i.e. informally-based) and that there is congruence between the rhetoric and the reality;
- providing fusion for the various initiatives by ensuring that there is thematic consistency;
- combining self-confidence and humility.

Garth Hill is *the* school for enterprise; entrepreneurship is its hallmark. It has proved to be enterprising in so many different ways:

- possible closure has been turned into outright success.

It is interesting to note that when, at a recent conference, the participants were warned of the 'trauma faced by teaching staff who may suffer loss of status and significantly damaged career prospects' caused by school closures, the list of moves deemed necessary to ameliorate the situation did not include fighting to keep the school open and winning. And it is not necessarily a case of the 'survival of the fittest'; once 'saved' and with an intake that has doubled, Garth Hill has resolutely clung to a 'ceiling' of seven forms of entry — despite pressure to take more pupils at the expense of other schools.

> Just five years ago, the school's reputation and morale was so bad that parents did not want to send their children there and Berkshire education authority was considering closure.
>
> Now, under a dynamic headmaster — but with many of the same staff and no extra local authority resources — parents are queueing up to send their children there.
>
> And there are three other schools within two miles of Garth Hill.
>
> (*Nottingham Evening Post,* 9 October 1987)

And, in the same newspaper article, comes the central question — what has caused such a transformation?

> Pupils at Garth Hill Comprehensive School in Bracknell are used to being filmed and photographed.
>
> In recent years, no fewer than fifty-five television crews from all over the world — including Japan — have visited the school.
>
> What they are all clamouring to know is how it has been transformed from a school no one wanted — into one of the most high powered and technologically advanced in Europe.

One factor has been the intuitive understanding of the importance of 'ecological niche' — the attainment and maintenance of a sufficient share of 'the market'. Stanley Goodchild, once weekly, institutes his informal policy of 'testing the water' by talking to teachers, pupils and parents about their opinions of the school's current situation. Most times the news is good. Once recently, however, the alarm bells were set ringing when one pupil said that the GCSE examinations are going to be chaotic ('even the teachers say they don't know what's happening') and another said that 'my father thinks that the school spends too much time raising money' Both these comments sent shock waves down the system at Garth Hill — mainly because both comments went to the heart of its enterprise spirit.

- the belief at Garth Hill is that if something is worth doing, it is worth doing it well. GCSE is a case in point. Garth Hill has championed the cause of GCSE; so much so, in fact, that some of its pupils were interviewed on television and extolled its virtues. During this broadcast the pupils argued that:
- having an element of continuous assessment, is 'fairer'; it gives each candidate more of a chance and discounts the influence of 'exam nerves';
- examiners will be lenient the first time through!
- CSE has always been underrated; GCSE brings the CSE and 'O' level together;
- GCSE is more practical, more relevant and, therefore, more enjoyable. The marketability of GCSE was also emphasized in an interview with 3M's personnel manager. The psychology of the situation is important as the message from the school; for GCSE to be a success everyone — teachers, pupils, parents and employers — has to believe in it. Doubts and confusion will only serve to undermine confidence and credibility. 'Think positively' is the message. What is required is *reassurance:* GCSE is in place and will be a success.
- the comment about fund-raising touched a raw nerve. Garth Hill has achieved success through sheer hard work and the resources this hard work has brought to the school. Writing in the *Times Educational Supplement* at the beginning of 'Industry Year' (17 January 1986), Stanley Goodchild had this to say:

The achievements of the last three years have been made possible by the sheer hard work and dedication of the Staff and pupils. Garth Hill school has always provided a good, sound education for its pupils but it was not until 1982 that it focused on its image as seen by the community, industry and commerce at large. Our experience shows that a school ignores at its peril the views of the community and industry it serves. Bracknell is a 'high tech' area and yet our curriculum did not reflect this. Three and a half years ago the school had a 380z computer and a great deal of wire; it now has equipment worth over £200,000 supplied not only by local but national organizations . . .

Before the school could hope to attract the help of industry and the community, it needed to gain their confidence and demonstrate that it was not only prepared to help itself but also to listen and act upon suggestions made, have an action plan and be prepared to give as well as to take.

As part of the school's strategy more than sixty evening meetings were held over a period of six weeks comprising small groups of parents and representatives from the community and industry, asking them how they felt about education and the development of Garth Hill . . .

Although teaching staff are the most important resource, the school also needed finance if the education provided was to reflect the technological world in which the school leaver finds himself. Staff, parents and pupils all devised projects to raise money for a computer centre costing £24,000. It seemed an impossible task but to everybody's amazement, £12,000 was raised within 10 months and it was decided to go ahead with the project, completing it as and when the remainder of the money became available. The centre's furnishings were built under the direction of a senior member of the CDT department.

The resources, galvanized by the efforts of the Garth Hill 'community' of teachers, parents and pupils, are the basis of its success. They are also a reflection of the esteem in which the school is held by employers and industrialists alike. Firms invest in Garth Hill because it is a 'going concern'. Everyone now agrees that Garth Hill is

Europe's leading exponent of information technology in the school environment.

Information technology lies at the heart of Garth Hill's success; it is the *content* of its rise to fame; it is the basis of its new curriculum. This description of Garth Hill's IT curriculum appeared in the 'Education' section of *Your Computer* in September 1986:

Educational software for most subjects is available via the terminals in the centre and all the students can work there and learn more about computing from an early age.

In their first two years, all pupils attend computer awareness courses, designed to give a gentle introduction to information technology. In the third year they study an IT business course before choosing their final options for the fourth year . . .

Garth Hill has converted one of its classrooms into a high-tech office so that pupils may become familiar with the type of equipment used in the fast-changing office environment. Pupils from the third year onwards, studying any of the school's business and information technology courses, gain experience of word processing, data processing, business computing and electronic mail, in addition to the more traditional subjects such as typing, audio-typing and general office management. Goodchild explains:

'We believe all our pupils, on leaving school, will require keyboard skills in their work. The traditional idea of the business studies room is one where there are rows upon rows of typewriters and that is often divorced from the real world. Our high-tech office is based on a completely different concept. It has been developed after close consultation with the world of industry and commerce. We believe it is a more realistic way of preparing young people for the modern world' . . .

The Headmaster is adamant that other subjects in the curriculum do not suffer as a result of the commitment to computers in education.

'It is not our aim to produce programmers. Our objective is to make full use of information technology as part of the teaching and learning process. That will ensure that our pupils are better-equipped to find jobs,' he says.

There can be little doubt that the system works. Three years ago more than thirty pupils failed to find jobs before September. Last year the figure fell to two.

The string of Garth's 'firsts' has arisen from this same strength — information technology. The Computer Centre (1983), the Hi-tech Office (1984), the launch of The Times Network System (TTNS) in 1984, the direct computer link for parents (1985), the Business Centre (1986) and the Hi-tech Library (1987) are all variations on the same theme. No wonder, then, that Garth Hill has been the site of the only 'outside' broadcast of Micro-live (BBC Television). It is this intensity of impact which has led to the international acclaim. The emphasis on information technology is tantamount to it becoming a 'natural part of everyday lives'. Consequently, says Stanley Goodchild, 'it is vital for schools to be equipped in this way'. This central part of Garth Hill's enterprise culture has very much its own language: networks, peripherals, disc-drives, printers, spreadsheets, word-processors, keyboards, electronic mail, floppy discs, etc. It's not all electronic wizardry, however; prior to GCSE, success in the business and information studies course was recognized in terms of 2 'O' level passes and a 'hard day at the computer office' is seen as genuine work experience. Indeed, Garth Hill has pioneered the concept of *school-based work experience:* the world of work being experienced inside the school. The 'Young Enterprise Scheme' has a similar intent. The pupils who work for Extra Special Products (ESP) Ltd. have direct experience of share-holding, board meetings, local sales drives, etc. This 'practical experience' gained at Garth Hill, according to a Thames TV special, is 'far from a game'. It provides a winning combination of practical, experiential learning plus examination credentials; moreover, 'employers recògnize it'. Given the context of shrinking youth employment prospects, Garth Hill pupils must feel privileged that *their* curriculum offers them wide educational opportunities plus marketable skills. Stanley Goodchild delights in the story of a local bank which reduced its entry qualifications in order to obtain the services of a Garth Hill pupil. And now the information revolution at Garth Hill has encompassed the Hi-tech Library with its computer terminals, its facilities for tracing articles worldwide, its 18,000 books and opportunities for resource-based learning (so vital in GCSE coursework). These resources have implications right across the curriculum and are 'pioneering (school) libraries of the future'.

Another cornerstone of Garth Hill's enterprise culture is provided by the school's links with industry. And these relationships are by no means one way — as reflected in the newly-appointed Business Manager (another Garth 'first'). This appointment symbolizes Garth Hill's emphasis on:

- marketing the school;
- 'going commercial' — and ploughing the profits back into education;
- maximizing the school's resources;
- linking with small businesses and offering training facilities for computer education and hi-tech office procedures;
- providing the teaching staff to consultants to industry; taking business to the business world.

The reactions of the press to this appointment are of some relevance here. Under the headline 'Business of state education' (*The Times,* 8 September 1987), the report described the intention of

> selling the school's high-tech facilities to industry and commerce.

Mentioned in the report were the 'three computer centres', the new hi-tech library, the restaurant, and conference facilities — the 'untapped potential of schools' which can be utilized if schools are 'run like a business'. In the *Today* newspaper (15 September 1987), the reporter announced that

> A top businessman went back to school yesterday to unleash his boardroom skills in Britain's most enterprising comprehensive . . .
> The appointment will impress Education Secretary, Kenneth Baker, who sees Garth Hill as a blue-print for the future.

Stanley Goodchild was quoted as saying that 'we see the school very much as a business — where the business is educating young people'. Alternatively, he said in the press release (sent out prior to the press conference at which Alan Watts was introduced to reporters):

We are sitting on a valuable resource which is not being used to full effect. If we are able to provide a service for local industry and commerce and at the same time increase the resource available for our students then I would be a very foolish Head not to take advantage.

Press releases; press conferences — this is a new deal for state education

Press Release
Royal County of Berkshire   Date 4 September 1987   No.919
BUSINESS MANAGER APPOINTED AT BERKSHIRE SCHOOL
Alan Watts who has spent his lifetime in senior management private industry, is next Monday (September 14) becoming what is believed to be the first-ever Business Manager at a local authority school in the UK.

Mr Watts previously Senior Manager of Hewlett Packard (UK), will be responsible for seeing that the resources of Garth Hill Comprehensive School in Bracknell are used to maximum effect when not required by staff and pupils.

In addition some staff will have the opportunity to be involved in providing industrial consultancies for those companies using its facilities.

This innovation is yet another chapter in the history of Garth Hill School which is renowned worldwide for its approach to management and teaching of information technology.

Above all, of course, Garth Hill's enterprising spirit owes a great deal to its 'dynamic' headteacher. According to the *Nottingham Evening Post,*

What soon becomes apparent is that Garth Hill's success is due entirely to one man's vision, determination — and acceptance of the changing role that all headteachers may have to come to terms with in the years ahead.

Stan Goodchild has a simple but determined philosophy. He runs the school as a business, with himself as managing director rather than headteacher.

He's also a salesman, persuading local and multi-national companies, including IBM, Prestel and Acorn, to invest in his school to the tune of nearly £½m a year. He gained his know-how with a business management degree from the Open University . . .

Mr. Goodchild's unique career path has helped him break the psychological mould of seeing himself first and foremost as a teacher. Now 44, he was a deputy head at 27, then an adviser, chief inspector and chief education officer for the London Borough of Bexley.

'In those years I got fed up with heads telling me what they could not do. I set out to do it.' He makes no effort to conceal his satisfaction when he adds: 'I delight in telling those heads now . . .'

He added: 'Heads are riddled by guilt. They have to decide what their job is. My job is to facilitate good teaching by others. A head with a heavy teaching schedule is an overpaid Scale One teacher'.

Neither is Mr Goodchild a remote figure communicating only by hi-tech. He believes in morning assemblies and walks around the whole school every day — often with visitors.

What emerges from this article is the combination of dynamism, opportunism, 'managerialism' (thus breaking the 'teacher mould') and MBWA that characterizes his leadership style. And judging from the success of Garth Hill this is a winning combination.

Stanley Goodchild has been the 'change leader' at Garth Hill. He has led the changes. What strategies have been used to promote change in the school? Stanley Goodchild talks in terms of using 'high risk' (as opposed to 'low risk') strategies, but he seems to mean several things by this. For instance

- he went 'beyond the staff' and invoked 'parent power' and the interest of the local community in support of change initiatives;
- he put his 'neck on the block' and, on his first day in the school, directed that much of the graffiti-covered classroom furniture be destroyed. This symbolic gesture heralded his arrival at the school, but it 'could have back-fired on him from the beginning';
- he was prepared to use the media in the interests of the school, knowing that 'they'll pull you up — or down';
- given the immediate situation (falling rolls, imminent closure, etc) he was quite prepared to exploit the need for urgent action — for the sake of the school. He demanded rapid, drastic changes to pull the school around in as short a time as possible. His view, apparently, is that high risk strategies are synonymous with rapid change, while low risk strategies are equated with slow, gradualist approaches to change.

These points require some elaboration. Given that he found the inertia of the staff rather 'depressing' ('they seemed oblivious to the situation' and were 'firmly stuck in the same mould'), following an initial staff meeting in which he 'enthused' and 'they found every reason under the sun why these ideas wouldn't work', Stanley Goodchild decided to create external pressure for change by meeting with parents and representatives from the local community and instigating 'client-led' changes, for example, the reintroduction of the school uniform.

Buchanan and Huczynski (1985) have drawn attention to Harold Leavitt's scheme for organizational change:

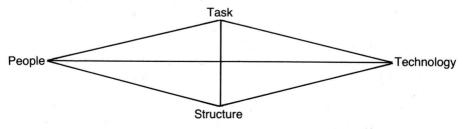

Leavitt's four 'entry points' (technology, task, structure and people) can be, individually or collectively, *levers for change*. At Garth Hill, while 'technology' (i.e. resource-led change) has often been the entry point, 'people' have been seen, quite rightly, as the 'makers and breakers' of change initiatives. As Buchanan and Huczynski explain, however, 'people' can be used as levers for change in two basic ways. First, key individuals can be seen as 'champions', 'promoters' of change and entrepreneurs. They make change happen.

The American economist Joseph Schumpeter has referred to the drive of such innovators as the 'entrepreneurial spirit'. To thrive, however, such change leaders need an organization that is sympathetic to their preferred style of action, i.e. entrepreneurialism.

The entrepreneur, in the classic definition of the term offered by Joseph Schumpeter, is an innovator; someone who introduces new ways of doing things:

> For actions which consist of carrying out innovations we reserve the term Enterprise; the individuals who carry them out we call Entrepreneurs.

In his description of the Entrepreneur as Innovator, Schumpeter is careful to separate this role from that of the risk-taker and/or founder. These roles may or may not overlap, he says.

Second the 'whole staff' can be seen as the agency for change; but, for this to happen, participative decision-making, consultation and negotiation have to be built into the internal processes of the organization. When Stanley Goodchild says that 'I was a despot; I'm now a democrat', he is referring to the phases of development through which the school has travelled since his arrival. Given the urgency of the situation in 1982, his main stance was a directive, authoritarian one — there was not time for such consultation. Moreover, at that point the school was in no state of readiness to become 'democratic'. During his 'succession', Stanley Goodchild 'took up the reins' and, during this period of directive leadership, he acted as the 'founder' and innovator; key people in the institution were also identified to help lead the changes. This group of 'innovators' was strengthened by the influx of seven new appoinments in key positions. This phase of dynamic, entrepreneurial, *person*-dependent approaches to change is now in the process of overhaul. The school is ready for the next stage in its development — involving more organic, *staff*-dependent, participative and democratic change strategies. As Stanley Goodchild stresses, staff involvement will be the key to Garth's future successes.

But the organic nature of this involvement, according to Bennis (1969), could well be interestingly different:

> The social structure of organizations of the future will have some unique characteristics. The byword will be 'temporary'. There will be adaptive, rapidly changing, temporary systems. These will be task forces organized around problems to be solved by groups of relative strangers with diverse professional skills. The group will be arranged

on an organic rather than mechanical model; it will evolve in response to a probelm rather than to programmed role expectations. The executive thus becomes coordinator or 'linking pin' between various task forces . . . People will be evaluated not according to rank but according to skill and professional training . . .

Adaptive, problem-solving, temporary systems of diverse specialists, linked together by coordinating and task-evaluating executive specialists in an organic flux — this is the organizational form that will gradually replace bureaucracy as we know it. As no catchy phrase comes to mind, I call these new style organizations adaptive structures.

I think that the future I describe is not necessarily a 'happy' one. Coping with rapid change, living in temporary work systems, developing meaningful relations and then breaking them, all augur social strains and psychological tensions. Teaching how to live with ambiguity, to identify with the adaptive process, to make a virtue out of contingency, and to be self directing — these will be the tasks of education, the goals of maturity, and the achievement of the successful individual.

Building on the work of Leavitt (1986) and Patterson *et al* (1986), Fullan (1988) has suggested that heads/principals need to sort out 'What's Worth Fighting For In the Principalship' and, in doing so, adopt three integrated strategies:

- Managing the Organizational Culture
- Strategic Planning
- Empowerment

We would suggest that these three strategies are much the same as Leavitt's tripartite arrangement for corporate pathfinding:

- Pathfinding   Key-word: Mission
- Problem-solving   Key-word: Analysis
- Implementation   Key-word: Action

The linkage between these three interrelated spheres of activity has been explored in the previous chapters.

The following points need restating in summary form:

- Strong, assertive leadership (to the fore in pathfinding) can be used to invoke participation (in planning/probelm-solving and implementation). Leadership and participation are not incompatible.
- One of the central tasks of management is to encourage individuals and groups to march to their own drummers while still working as collaborative members of the organizational team. What is required is the generation of a school's capacity to accommodate, support, blend together and capitalize upon various kinds of endeavour and creative innovation.

- One route forward is the use of 'chunking': teams of people (small interest groups) exploring various key focus areas on behalf of their colleagues. Such an approach rests on the flexibility of temporary groupings and the constant reinvigoration of the organization through 'championing behaviour' (Leavitt, 1986)
- Transformative leadership mobilizes the activity necessary to translate ideas (pathfinding) into plans (problem-solving) into action (implementation). Equally, it is the pivotal force which activates culture-building, strategic planning and the empowerment of others in the organization. According to Bennis and Nanus (1985), 'the new leader . . . is one who commits people to action, who converts followers into leaders, and who may convert leaders into agents of change'.

Such leaders encompass both the initiator style (discovered by Hall *et al* 1984), which involves decisiveness, the setting of high expectations and frequent contact with colleagues, and the stance of *systematic problem-solver* identified by Leithwood and Montgomery (1985), but which Fullan says is rarely found in practice. Above all, however, Bennis and Nanus (1985) argue that transformative leadership sustains a vision that encompasses the whole organization and which is translated into a living reality. This is achieved, the authors maintain, through four leadership strategies:

- attention through vision (providing a focus);
- meaning through communication;
- trust through positioning (having decided on a course of action, sticking with it);
- deployment of self (MBWA).

Leavitt (1986) and Bennis and Nanus (1985) make much the same point: that developing organizations need to mix three orientations or styles: the personalistic (to the fore in pathfinding), the formalistic (the orientation of problem-solving) and the collegial (participative and supportive implementation). These three emphases form the three 'faces' of organizations. We would argue that Garth Hill has experienced the personalistic 'stage' and is now heading towards a more collegial style via more formalized arrangements (for example, the emphasis on management 'structures', management-by-objectives and role descriptions), i.e. a management culture.

Theme 2: The Management Culture in Education

With the publication of the Coopers and Lybrand report on 'Local Management of Schools', the editorial in the *Times Educational Supplement* was given the title 'Towards a management culture'. The message, according to the editor's reading of the management consultants' report, is clear; the changes implicit in LFM entail a massive upheaval which redistributes a range of managerial and administrative tasks.

Self-management and budgetary control are certainly no novel experiences for schools like Garth Hill. They know that the *right* of self-development is matched by the *responsibility* of self-management. And to maintain this balance, schools like Garth Hill have had to develop a 'business mentality' and a management culture. Stanley Goodchild's instinctive realization of the importance of securing an 'ecological niche' and his informal policy of 'testing the water' are good examples of his business acumen. His championing of entrepreneurial, innovative small team enterprise (skunkworks) is another example. Tom Peters and Karl Weick would be proud of Garth Hill's unconventional, enterprising spirit. Indeed, the ideas that have made Garth Hill so innovative and 'ahead of the pack', haven't just appeared as if from nowhere. As Tom Peters argues in his latest book, *Thriving on Chaos* (1987),

> In today's ever-accelerating business environment, you must become a determined copycat, adapter and enhancer.

Successful enterprises, he argues, keep asking: who is the competition? what is the character of the competition? how can we learn more about the strengths of this competition? In his usual swash-buckling style, Peters says that innovators/entrepreneurs need 'to be swipers, askers, note-takers, learners'; in fact, he contends, they must be 'shameless thieves' indulging in 'creative swiping'. In rather less evocative language, Peters hits the mark by saying that entrepreneurs find ideas and *take, adapt,* and *enhance* them to fit their particular circumstances. This has been Stanley Goodchild's greatest gift to Garth Hill: his ability to seize on ideas, put them together and come up with a 'cocktail' that is truly Garth's. It is the quality of the synthesis, the concoction, that is all-important. And, as Peters argues, a major breakthrough (for example, the IT revolution at Garth Hill) arises from an accumulation of scores of small changes - another case of discontinuous (yet effectively cumulative) in-crementalism. Peters quotes the case of Sony's entrepreneurial exploitation of the idea of the video cassette recorder. Seven points — six are his, the seventh ours — arise from this example:

- first, as Peters points out, Sony's employees had 'new thoughts' and 'moved fast';
- second, they put the 'consumer first';
- third, they thought 'small', with lots of early experimentation;
- fourth, they heeded the advice not to stand still and were determined to supercede their own best ideas before someone else did;
- fifth, the innovative, experimental work was entrusted to 'skunk-works' — semi-independent, informal and small teams of six-eight people;
- sixth, they broke with the 'mindset of mass production'. This 'disastrous' mentality, says Peters, encourages the specialization of

labour to the point where 'people' are eliminated. It was, of course, the same in education in the early 1970s with the formulation of 'teacher-proof materials'. Cuban (1984) has written persuasively about the temptation to short-circuit the 'human' dimension. Peters agrees with Harvey-Jones; there is no alternative — people must be involved and given room to grow.

- and seventh, schools have long realized this fact and, as Handy (1984) and Torrington *et al* (1987) have pointed out, they have much experience of the management of *professional organizations.*

Everard (*Times Educational Supplement,* 12 September 1986), in arguing the case for the relevance of industrial experience for educationalists charged with the responsibility of 'Managing change', contended that schools have:

- no skills of implementation;
- no understanding of human and organizational behaviour;
- no systematic or structural approaches;
- no diffusion of management style throughout the system;
- no appreciation of the importance of common vision;
- no understanding that educational problems are deeper than resource provision;
- no ability to 'stick to the knitting';
- no resolve to allow leadership skills to emerge throughout the system.

While not wanting to endorse this list of indictments — indeed, our point is that schools have much to offer other kinds of organizations in terms of their experience of orchestrating and managing professionals and their endeavours — the point remains that there has been no systematic attempt (beyond the valiant efforts of the National Development Centre based at the University of Bristol) to train teachers for the rigours of headship. Trethowan (*Times Educational Supplement,* 21 March 1986) has claimed that there is a 'Hole at the top' in terms of both management training and the appraisal of headteachers and Rowe (*Times Educational Supplement,* 18 July 1986) has resuscitated the demand for a staff college.

> Running a school is a very different activity from being even a very senior member of staff . . . If, as we all know, headteachers shape our schools, why do we not take a great deal more trouble to shape them?

And given the increased power and financial obligations now being devolved to heads and the fact that they are key people in Kenneth Baker's educational reforms, no wonder that Rowe's suggestion is currently receiving wider recognition. Any moves in the direction of a staff college, however, must bear in mind Handy's recent advice (contained in his MSC/NEDC report entitled *The Making of Managers*):

- any staff college should be a 'real life school' for managers;
- the courses should be more flexible and more closely related to actual

work problems and career needs; in other words, they should be relevant and practical;

- they should be 'centred on the work-place' and involve negotiation of course content. Targetting (i.e. tailoring to individual needs) is clearly important.

And, judging by Stanley·Goodchild's experience, courses should enable participants:

 (i)   psychologically, to break with the teacher role;
 (ii) to merge the theory and practice of management;
 (iii) to investigate the value of experience, intuition and instinct in managerial decision-making;
 (iv) to understand that it is more important to be a practitioner of the 'art' (rather than the science) of management;
 (v)   to appreciate that management development is a major form of in-service training and that it should take the form of 'Applied INSET' (see Holly, James and Young, 1987).

This move towards management courses which have as their content 'company-based projects' and other 'real-life', experiential learning opportunities is similar, then, to the growth of 'Applied INSET' and school-focused INSET in the educational sphere. Indeed, one of us is currently involved in running a part-time advanced diploma course entitled 'The Developing Secondary School' in which the content of the course is negotiated, and therefore tailored to the developmental needs of the schools concerned. The aim, as with the new management courses, is to knit the training far more closely to the organization — the company or the school — which remains the focal point of all the activity.

Such changes reflect two major issues already touched upon in this volume.

- First, in the new change scenarios (characterized by the rapidity, quantity, and ambiguity of the changes), 'managers' are having to approach their work with different attitudes, using different skills and with new perceptions of their management roles. When Peters (1987) titles his new book *Thriving on Chaos* he is describing not only that nature of the management task but also the qualities demanded of the 'role incumbent'. Management will not be the same again. When the emphasis was placed on the *management of change,* it was expected that managers would be responsible for *planning, coordinating, controlling, supervising, evaluating, predicting* and *holding together.* In loosely-coupled, professional organizations in which *management for change* is the emphasis, managers have to cope with risk and uncertainty and are responsible for *initiating* changes at the core of the enterprise and then *supporting,* equipping, facilitating, emboldening and healing the wounds of their innovative colleagues. They are responsible for inspiring and motivating their colleagues 'to boldly go where no man has gone before'. They have to create the climate for 'space treking' — in terms of Handy's 'doughnut thinking'.

- Second, a recurring theme in this book has been the importance of recognizing the value of 'intuition', 'instinct' and 'feel' on the part of school managers. Stanley Godochild always emphasizes the importance of experienced, intuitive management, which is vastly preferable, he says, to 'managing by the rule book'. Schon (1983) echoes this stance when he argues that practical competence (and 'professional artistry') constitutes a vital way of 'knowing'.

Notions of 'professional mystique' need to be jettisoned, Schon argues, in favour of attempts to unpack intuition and to investigate the kinds of 'knowing' in which competent practitioners engage. Basing his approach on the writings of Polanyi, Schon charts the territory of 'tacit knowledge' ('we know more than we can say') and the capacity to reflect on this 'knowing-in-practice' in order to cope with unique, uncertain and conflict-laden practical situations.

> When we go about the spontaneous, intuitive performance of the actions of everyday life we show ourselves to be knowledgeable in a special way. Often we cannot say what it is that we know. When we try to describe it we find ourselves at a loss . . . Our knowing is ordinarily tacit, implicit in our patterns of action and *in our feel for the stuff with which we are dealing* (our underlining). It seems right to say that our knowing is in our action . . . the workaday life of the professional depends on tacit knowing-in-action. It is this entire process of reflection-in-action which is central to the 'art' by which practitioners sometimes deal well with stituations of uncertainty, instability, uniqueness, and value conflict.

'Training', says Schon, is often designed according to ideas of 'technical rationality' as opposed to his mode of 'reflection-in-action'; 'students' are taught how to manage rather than how to unpack and build on their experience and 'grasp' of 'doing management'. Extending William Bennett's assertion that managers like Hogans and Goodchild are not course-produced (that they are 'graduates of the school of life'), it becomes clear why those responsible for course-provision are beginning to promote the efficacy of experience-based activities which recognize that the expertise has to be discovered (from the inside) rather than imposed (from the outside). Management courses which explore the tacit knowledge of the participants are very different in shape, style and scope from their more traditional counterparts. The role of experience (of management) in *educating* intuition also explains the importance of Stanley Goodchild's 'unique' (i.e. management-based as opposed to teaching-based) career pattern. Managers learn how to manage through the experience of managing.

Moreover, by recruiting heads from the ranks of teachers, it could be argued that it is that much harder to 'break the mould'. Indeed, some commentators would argue that being a teacher is not a very good preparation for being an effective principal/head. Lortie (1987), for instance, has claimed that there are four powerful built-in tendencies toward stabilizing the principal's role:

- recruitment and induction which encourages narrowness of experience and limited exposure to new ideas;
- role constraints (the need for school maintenance and stability) and the lack of rewards for trying to make improvements;
- system standardization which forces schools into line, creates uniformity across schools and inhibits the impulse for school individuality and enterprise;
- anxiety concerning career aspirations and the awareness of the opinions of others (for example, the parents)

Ultimately, says Fullan (1988), heads can end up tolerating rather than shifting the *status quo*.

Theme 3: The Incorporation of Schooling

One of the lessons that schools can teach business organizations is the power of a 'corporate culture'. The 'incorporation of schooling', within an ethos-led culture, is the greatest asset of schools as synergistic enterprises. As Torrington *et al* (1987) have discovered in their UMIST-based research, schools recognize that success comes from the successful incorporation of ethos, spirit and individual commitment:

> Many industrial companies devote considerable energy and funds in the development of organizational culture to overcome deep-rooted problems such as the them-and-us alienation and a lack of commitment to organizational goals. Most schools accomplish with ease what these companies seek, because schoolteachers know that their efforts can only succeed within an organization that is a community with ethos, spirit and individual commitment.
>
> Much of the emotional and intellectual development of their pupils can only come from the wholeness of the school. Any managing director could learn more about effective organizational culture from an hour's chat with members of a school staff than through spending a small fortune with a firm of consultants. (*Times Educational Supplement,* 30 October 1987)

Effective schools, as Deal (1985) has argued, have strong, cohesive organizational (or corporate) cultures, which create a sense of community and the social organization within which the curriculum can prosper (see below).

Attributes of Effective Schools	
Social Organization	*Instruction and Curriculum*
Clear academic and social behavior goals	High academic learning time (ALT)
	Frequent and monitored homework
Order and discipline	Frequent monitoring of student progress
High expectations	
Teacher efficacy	Coherently organized curriculum
Pervasive caring	Variety of teaching strategies
Public rewards and incentives	Opportunities for student responsibility
Administrative leadership	
Community support	

Deal and Kennedy (1983) have argued that many school principals/heads spend considerable time building cohesive school cultures and the 'wisdom of their efforts is supported by educational researchers who have documented the power of culture'. They mention Rutter *et al's* work (1979) linking 'ethos' to student achievement and they conclude:

> Ethos, another term for culture, can produce dramatic results when it channels energy in positive directions. The problem is to make something powerful and ill-defined work for us and to show that building strong school cultures is intimately tied to improving educational performance.

There is another problem. Building on the work of Sarason (1982), Deal and Kennedy point out that

> school culture can undermine innovation when culture works against you, it's near impossible to get anything done.

Golzen in *The Sunday Times* (15 November 1988) has shown 'How "corporate culture" can be carried too far'. Basing his comments on David Mercer's insider study of 'IBM: How the World's Most Successful Company is Managed', Golzen charts the comparative decline of IBM (in 1982 singled out for excellence by Peters and Waterman) and argues that IBM's problem lies in the strength of its corporate culture — the very thing on which the company most prides itself.

> IBM is controlled by its culture, rather than by management.

And at the heart of its corporate culture lies the company's appraisal and counselling system. Every employee is appraised annually by his/her superior and has to agree in writing with the appraisal — or launch an appeal to corporate headquarters. Alongside this formal system, however, is an informal arrangement by which subordinates report on managers. Taken together, these arrangements have led to stultification. No one dares shake the tree; the company has become 'rooted' in its own internal culture.

Extending our discussion in chapter 2, it is possible to sketch three hypothetical change scenarios:

Scenarios	Culture	Filtering	Degree of innovativeness	Likelihood of successful implementation
A	STRONG (CLOSED)	STRONG/ NEGATIVE	WEAK	LOW
B	STRONG (OPEN)	MODERATE/ POSITIVE	HIGH	HIGH
C	WEAK	WEAK	PARTIAL	PARTIAL

Scenario A involves a strong, resident culture which 'encultures' change initiatives through a negatively-disposed process of filtration, thus leading to weak levels of both innovativeness and implementation

Scenario B involves a strong, but open culture which has a moderate (but positively oriented) filtering influence, thus leading to potentially high degrees of innovativeness and implementation

Scenario C involves a weak, atomized, informal array of sub-cultural affiliations which produces random filtering (according to the values of the sub-groups) and partial, haphazard amounts of innovativeness and implementation.

It could be argued that Garth Hill, over the last five years, has travelled from Scenario C to Scenario B but, like all successful organizations, needs to beware of stagnation and a retreat into Scenarios A or C.

Heckman (in Goodlad 1987) has explored the 'cultural regularities' which induce resistance towards alternative practices. Consequently, he argues,

> . . . those interested in improving schools confront the culture of the school and the problems involved in changing the culture.

Heckman makes several points in relation to the cultural perspective on school improvement which are similar to our own in this present volume:

- within school improvement efforts, teachers should examine the 'total setting' in which they work as they embark on the process of renewal;
- there is an urgent need to agree on a 'hard-rock agenda for change';
- change and improvement initiatives need to focus on both the substance and on the process of improvement, not one or the other;
- part of the 'hard rock agenda' will be school-specific, but some of the elements will be common to all schools; like, for instance, the current and wide-spread interest in new approaches to teaching and learning. According to Heckman,

> During the hey-day of organizational development, needs assessment took place in many schools. Teachers, students,

parents stated preferences for the kinds of programs on which schools should focus. Each school assessed these stated preferences and selected the few preferred by most people. Frequently, one area of focus was viewed to be as good as any other so long as the process was one that involved the whole staff . . .

I propose a paradigm that joins process with substance, eschewing a choice of one over the other. Furthermore, each school engaged with this paradigm will confront some long-standing, persistent issues that are common to most schools.

- building on Sarason and Goodlad, Heckman argues that the very cultural apparatus that helps to explain resistance and the lack of change can be employed by school-based groups to produce change;
- what are required are changing teacher perspectives, which enlarge their perceptions, terminate their isolation and encourage *dialogue, collaboration,* a concern for *sharing* and *openness.*

According to Heckman, their perspectives will *evolve* during the *process of talking* and *group decision-making initiated by the head/principal;* a 'healthy' school (development) culture, says Heckman, promotes 'the *incorporation* of new concepts into teachers' current perceptions.' This development culture rests on three principles:

(i) when teachers work together they *create new cultural norms* of collaboration and *collaborative inquiry* (see also Lieberman, 1986);

(ii) the teachers must be open to new ideas from outside the school and ways have to be developed deliberately to bring these ideas to the school;

(iii) ways have to be found to examine the value differences (which arise when the new and old concepts struggle with each other) without the school or the individuals in it being torn apart. Heckman says that the head's/principal's leadership role is crucial here.

These three features require cultivation for the development culture to be activated.

Several years ago, during a speaking engagement in Britain, Kurt Vonnegut, the novelist, was asked about his opinions of today's society. He replied that, while he is optimistic about people, he is pessimistic about their culture. In this book we have charted the importance of cultural factors in schooling. We have come to a rather more positive conclusion — that a *development culture,* which accommodates the pursuit of continuous improvement, rests on the articulation of a school's *vision.* According to Peters (1987):

The vision is thus paradoxical. It is relatively stable . . . but it is dynamic in that it under-scores the constant improvement . . .

Indeed, Peters argues that it all begins with a vision; a vision that inspires, empowers, challenges, and provokes confidence enough to encourage risk-taking entrepreneurs/innovators within the organization. For the vision to have this kind of impact, however, it has to be 'lived' by the senior management team. Leading by example, says Peters, is more important than ever before. For organizational members to be empowered to take action to the 'front-line', they need to receive two kinds of crystal clear signals; they need to know that

(a)   their leaders are four-square behind them;
(b)   the agreed priorities — arising from the vision — are to be pushed hard — over time.

Leaders, says Peters, must not only 'ensure that the frontline people — the implementers, the executors — know that they are the organization's heroes', but also 'learn the subtle art of delegtion anew . . . True delegation means Really Letting Go'. Delegation, argues Peters, needs to be accompanied by MBWA, which involves:

getting out of the office;
listening to and 'honouring those who matter';
engaging with those on the 'front-line';
being facilitative rather than giving commands and 'doing' inspections.

Indeed, stresses Peters, MBWA is all about supporting, 'not close, over the shoulder, supervision'. It is about encouraging implementation, not stifling it. Peters concludes that 'success will come to those who love . . . constant change — not those who attempt to eliminate it'. Success, he says, is ensured by being 'fleet-of-foot', thriving on uncertainty, by not being continuously 'in control' and by the urge to 'create new worlds'.

The acclaimed management consultant, Rosabeth Moss Kanter, has argued — in very similar terms to Tom Peters — an enterprising organization needs a 'culture of play, irreverence and challenge', which is activated by an inspiring (yet realizable) *vision,* capable of sustaining people over time. She argues that we can become the masters (not victims) of change by anticipating and leading changes and by securing the active cooperation and enlisting the *power* (i.e. empowerment) of those responsible for the implementation of new ideas. This *coalition,* she says, sustains people during implementation, when 'everything looks like a failure in the middle'.

Kanter (1983) concludes by emphasizing the importance of a culture which sustains enterprise and innovation:

It is thus the whole context, the whole system at the more innovating companies . . . that generates the enabling conditions for managerial enterprise . . . Such expectations or cultural norms guide behaviour in a holistic sense.

The highest proportion of entrepreneurial accomplishments is found in the companies that are least segmented or segmentalist, companies that instead have integrative structures and cultures emphasizing pride, commitment, collaboration, and teamwork . . . They (the members) are encouraged to take initiative and to behave cooperatively.

The greatest task facing a pathfinding leader is the transforming and rebuilding of the old (and probably tired) organizational culture — upon which many people have become dependent. According to Leavitt, three supportive pressures act to ease this (for many) painful process:

- crises: these are effective 'looseners of old cultures';
- the sheer force of personal style: the use of transformative leadership to turn around the organization;
- personnel changes.

Indeed, the old, informal (and, probably, deeply entrenched) culture may well prove so resistant to change that a combination of these pressures is required. No-one should underestimate the enormity of the task. Bennis and Nanus (1985) point out that what was once a strength can become a major obstacle to future success:

> In our experience, the reasons so many experiments in organizational change fail is that the leaders have failed to take into account the strong undertow of cultural forces . . . In short, when management attempts to shift the goals of the organization, to adopt new work methods, or to create any fundamental change, the culture may not only fail to support these changes but may actually defeat them.

Bennis and Nanus go on to differentiate between four dimensions: the 'manifest' (the formal rhetoric — what we refer to as the ethos); the 'assumed' (as perceived as existing — the climate); the extant (as revealed through systematic investigation — the informal culture); and the 'requisite' (the reality of the ecological situation in which the organization exists). Consequently, they argue,

> The ideal but never realized situation is that in which the manifest, the assumed, the extant, and the requisite are aligned as closely as possible with each other. Wherever these four organizational concepts are in contradiction, the organizational culture is such that its identity is confused and integrity difficult to achieve.
>
> Indeed, taking our break-down of ethos/climate/culture described in chapter 2, Leavitt's pathfinding/problem-solving/implementation and our comments on manangement for change in chapter 3 (that the baton needs to be passed across the staff through mechanisms such as team-based collaborative inquiry or, as some schools are beginning to use, 'contact groups' linked to a staff development committee), we would suggest the following composite diagram has some relevance to the themes of this book in general and this chapter in particular.

Theme 4: The Developing School

In Heckman's own research on the development culture, (in Goodlad, 1987), he discovered five school-focused characteristics which distinguished more or less (self-) renewing schools:

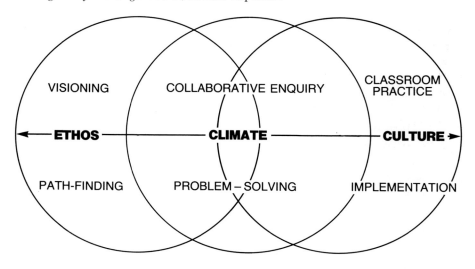

- principal leadership;
- staff cohesiveness;
- a 'take-care-of-business' attitude;
- staff problem-solving processes;
- adequate assistance.

Yet, in schools where all five factors were present and actively being pursued, an interesting conundrum came to light (as evidenced by Holly, 1984, in similar research on the GRIDS Project):

> An interesting dilemma emerges. On the one hand, it appears that relationships existed between renewal and certain school-focused variables. Schools that had principals who promoted openness and problem-solving, and staffs that took care of their business, solved their problems, and had adequate support (assistance and resources) appeared more renewing at the schoolwide level than did schools not possessing these characteristics to the same degree. Yet, on the other hand, the critically important place where teachers and students spend most of their time showed few signs of renewal. Classroom practices, on the average, remain very stable over time. *School renewal appeared to have little impact on classroom renewal,* even though one would expect that school-wide renewal would carry through into the classrooms. If certain elements of school culture are amenable to a good deal of change but classroom elements are not, then the challenge before us becomes clear. How do we bring the problem of improving classroom practices into the larger context of school culture and open up these problems to close staff scrutiny?

This, of course, is the dilemma posed in chapter 3. How to achieve fusion between the classroom and the organization, the individual and the whole staff; how to create a balance of interests and impact? Heckman, like Lieberman (1986) and Holly (in Southworth, 1987), claims that what are required are strategies that focus on ways of renewing both the school *and* classroom, for example, collaborative enquiry. He argues that this process has four characteristic features or 'stages':

(i) teachers meet to describe *what* they do in classrooms;
(ii) teachers explain *why* they do these things;
(iii) teachers seek new knowledge concerning how to facilitate the learning process;
(iv) teachers *match* these new ideas with their existing practices.

Having successfully instigated this kind of staff collaborative enquiry, Heckman concludes that there are six conditions for school renewal:

- first, schools need help from the outside within a *partnership* of collaborating schools;
- second, the effort must be *school-focused;*
- third, while there has to be an internal change agenda, there has to be a mechanism by means of which new ideas can be fed into the process;
- fourth, it has to be recognized that every solution to a significant pattern will have repercussions throughout the school as a social system;
- fifth, there is a requirement for the tools of collaboration — the skills/resources for renewal; i.e. what teachers use to be able to collaborate;
- and, sixth, once the teachers have decided that their present practice needs to be improved, they will need external advice on what to do next.

What emerges from these six points is that the developing school is aiming for self-renewal within an internal process which is greatly enhanced by several different kinds of external support.

Two 'structures' have been offered for the process of collaborative inquiry in schools: one is the 'classic' action-research cycle offered by Kurt Lewin and the other is the GRIDS cycle (see McMahon *et al*, 1984):

Whatever 'cycle', scheme or set of procedures is adopted, the central tasks are to energize the enquiry and to empower the participating teachers. Goodlad (1987) makes the point that:

Empowering principals and teachers — those closest to the processes of students' learning — to create the best possible school settings is not likely to result from mandating the rules and procedures to be followed.

It would appear, rather, that this empowerment and everything one might expect to follow from it are more likely to occur when those

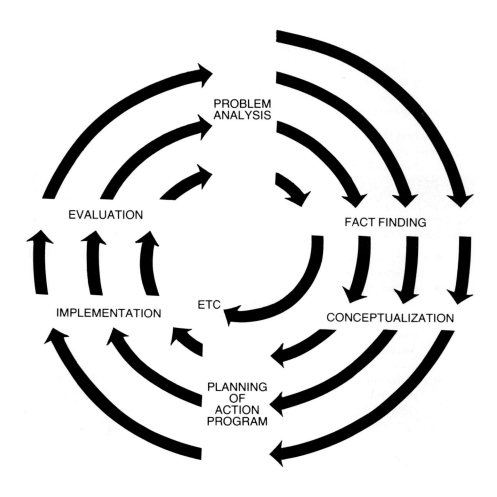

PROBLEM ANALYSIS

EVALUATION

FACT FINDING

IMPLEMENTATION

ETC

CONCEPTUALIZATION

PLANNING OF ACTION PROGRAM

in authority create policies designed to provide the time and resources deemed necessary for on-site professional and institutional renewal.

Those who argue that teachers are too 'immature' to accept the responsibility of developing *their* school need to reflect that, without their commitment, development will be a non-starter. Goodlad says it is easy to alienate and reduce the potency (and maintain the 'immaturity') of those best suited to make a difference. It is Cuban's point revisited. He says that teachers are too often seen as 'the problem' or 'the scapegoats' (for lack of success). 'Few scapegoats', says Cuban (1984), 'have been noted for volunteering'. Holly (1986) has differentiated between three kinds of collaboration in schools:

> *instrumental collaboration,* which is mandated according to someone else's agenda;

THE FIVE MAIN STAGES OF THE GRIDS CYCLE

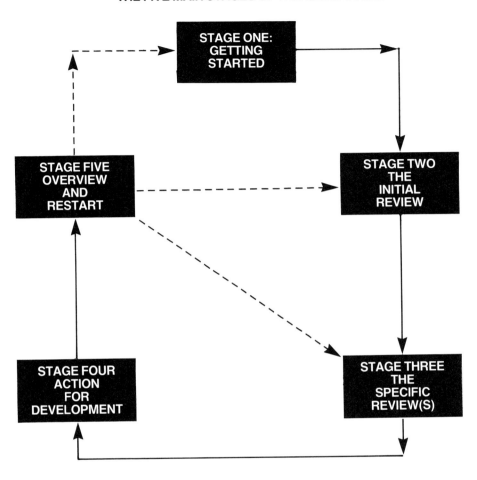

factional collaboration, which involves the competitive rivalry of small groups;
and *collegial collaboration,* which is based within and across the staff.

And it is not a case of saying that one of these forms of collaboration is superior to the others. Instrumental collaboration is activated by *leadership pressure;* factional collaboration is energized by the *loyalty and commitment* of individuals and small teams; and collegial collaboration involves more whole staff *involvement and support.* At various times the developing school needs all these features — pressure, loyalty, commitment, involvement and support — in order to succeed. And, echoing Bernard Barker's point, the conception of a developing school is not a political ideology masquerading as an improvement process; it is neither exclusively individualistic nor collectivist; it is both.

Similarly, it is not the exclusive preserve of either 'hero innovators' or staff collegiality; both have a vital role to play. The 'enterprisers' are as important as 'the enterprise' and vice versa. Up till now Stanley Goodchild has been Garth Hill's enterpriser-in-chief. But Garth Hill is a developing school and, during the next phase of its development, the staff members — whether acting as individuals, small teams or in concert — will surely provide the spirit of enterprise. In doing so, they will need to emphasize:

- the 'collaborative' rather than the 'individualism' (in collaborative individualism);
- doing collaborative enquiry in the form of self-evaluation of the learning process in the classroom; thus investigating the effectiveness of the internal curriculum.
- looking at the effective curriculum in Information Technology, for example, and asking themselves, 'has the revolution actually occurred?'

Garth Hill School, however, must never be allowed to lose its sense of adventure. It has 'boldly gone where no school . . .' and must keep 'boldly going'; but with one vital exception. Stanley Goodchild has been the manager of change; the staff now have to join him in providing management for change.

Bibliography

Articles from The Times Educational Supplement

Editorial 'Anti-entrepreneurial, anti-industrial, anti-productive . . .', 11 September 1981.

TRETHOWAN, D. (1983) 'Managing to learn', 6 May.

'Staff say they hope new heads will be like Moses', 6 September 1985.

REYNOLDS, D. (1985) 'The effective school', 20 September.

CHANDLER, SIR GEOFFREY (1986) 'Industry year. The lever for change', 3 January.

'Fewer want to become heads', 17 January 1986

'Push to offer vocational courses at 'O' and 'A' levels', 21 February 1986.

TRETHOWAN, D. (1986) 'Hole at the top', 21 March.

Editorial 'Department of bright ideas . . .', 4 April 1986.

'Heads can be "magic wands": Sir Keith', 11 April 1986.

'Study spotlights way some primaries reach pupils that others cannot', 18 April 1986.

'Where learning is a cardinal virtue', 23 May 1986.

SAYER, J. (1986) 'Listen to the auditors', 23 May.

'Ten year programme to extend TVEI', 4 July 1986.

EVERARD, B. (1986) 'Managing change', 12 September.

'New heads on unready shoulders', 3 October 1986.

'Beleaguered London heads start helpline', 17 October 1986.

LEACH, M. (1986) 'TVEI will fail', 31 October.

TAGG, H. (1986) 'Control of the purse-strings', 14 November.

'Enterprise pilot will urge young to boldly go', 19 December 1986.

'Complex views from the top', 9 January 1987.

'ILEA chief sees onward march of the modules', 9 January 1987.

'Enterprise future in store for students', 23 October 1987.

GREENALL, J. (1988) 'How to improve your image', 15 January.

'Baker lists ways for business to put goals across', 5 February 1988.

References

AUSTIN, G.R. and GARBER, H. (Eds) (1985) *Research on Exemplary Schools,* Orlando, FL. Academic Press.

BENNIS, W.G. (1969) *Organisation Development: Its Nature, Origins and Prospects,* Reading, MA, Addison-Wesley.

BENNIS, W.G. and NANUS, B. (1985) *Leaders,* New York, Harper and Row.

BERGER, P. and KELLNER, H. (1965) 'Arnold Gehlen and the theory of institutions', *Social Research,* 32,1.

BLAKE, R.R., AVIS, R. and MOUTON, J.S. (1966) *Corporate Darwinism,* Houston, TX. Gulf Publishing.

BLOCK, P. (1987) *The Empowered Manager,* San Francisco, C.A. Jossey-Basse.

BUCHANAN, D.A. and HUCZYNSKI, A.A. (1985) *Organizational Behaviour,* Englewood Cliffs, NJ, Prentice Hall.

CALDWELL, B.J. and SPINKS, J.M. (1988) *The Self-Managing School,* Lewes, Falmer Press.

CHARTERS, W.W. and JONES, J.E. (1973) 'On the risk of appraising non-events in program evaluation', *Educational Researcher,* November.

CLARK, D. *et al* (1984) 'Effective schools and improvement' *Educational Administration Quarterly,* 21, 3.

CLEMSON, D. and CRAFT, A. (1981) 'The "good" or the "effective" teacher', *British Journal of In-Service Education,* 7, 2.

COOPER, B. (1987) *Magnet Schools,* London, Institute of Economic Affairs.

CRANDALL, D.P. *et al* (1983) *People, Policies and Practices: Examining the Chain of School Improvements* (10 vols), Andover, MA, The Network Inc.

CUBAN, L. (1984) 'Transforming the frog into a prince: Effective schools research, policy and practice at the district level', *Harvard Educational Review,* 54, 2.

CUNNINGTON, B. and LIMERICK, D. (1986) 'The fourth blueprint: An emergent managerial frame of reference', *Journal of Managerial Psychology.*

DADDS, M. (1986) 'The school, the teacher researcher and the in-service tutor' in HOLLY, P.J. and WHITEHEAD, D. (Eds) *Collaborative Action Research,* CARN Bulletin 7, Cambridge Institute of Education.

DEAL, T.E. (1985) 'The symbolism of effective schools', *The Elementary School Journal,* 85, 5.

DEAL, T.E. and KENNEDY, A.A. (1982) *Corporate Cultures,* Reading, MA, Addison-Wesley.

DEAL, T.E. and KENNEDY, A.A. (1983) 'Culture and school performance', *Educational Leadership,* 40, 5.

DEPARTMENT OF EDUCATION AND SCIENCE (1977) *Ten Good Schools: A Secondary School,* London, HMSO.

DEPARTMENT OF EDUCATION AND SCIENCE (1987) *Education Observed 5: Good Behaviour and Discipline in Schools — A Report by HM Inspectors,* London, HMSO.

DRUCKER, P. (1985) *Innovation and Entrepreneurship,* New York, Harper and Row.

ETZIONI, A. (1964) *Modern Organisations,* Englewood Cliffs, NJ. Prentice Hall.

FENSTERMACHER, G. and BERLINER, D. (1986) 'Determining the value of staff development', *The Elementary School Journal,* 85, 3.

FULLAN, M. (1982) *The Meaning of Educational Change,* Toronto, OISE Press.

FULLAN, M. (1985) 'Change processes and strategies at the local level', *The Elementary School Journal,* 85, 3.

FULLAN, M. (1987) paper given at the SCDC Dissemination Conference, University of Leeds, September.

FULLAN, M. (1988) *What's Worth Fighting For in the Principalship?,* Toronto, Ontario Public School Teachers' Federation.

GADAMER, H.G. (1975) *Truth and Method,* London, Sheed and Ward.

GELINIER, O. (1968) *The Enterprise Ethic,* London, Institute of Economic Affairs.

GILDER, G. (1986) *The Spirit of Enterprise,* Harmondsworth, Penguin.

GOODLAD, J.I. (Ed) (1987) *The Ecology of School Renewal,* Chicago, IL, National Society for the Study of Education/University of Chicago Press.

GOODLAD, J.I. and KLEIN, M.F. (1970) *Looking Behind the Classroom Door,* Worthington, OH, Charles E Jones.

GRAHAM, D. and CLARKE, P. (1986) *The New Enlightenment: The Rebirth of Liberalism,* London, Macmillan.

GREINER, L.E. (1972) 'Evolution and revolution as organisations grow', *Harvard Business Review,* 4.

GUSKEY, T. (1986) 'Staff development and the process of teacher change', *Educational Researcher,* 15, 5.

HALL, G. *et al* (1984) 'Effects of three principal styles on school improvement', *Educational Leadership,* February.

HALL, V., Mackay, H. and MORGAN, C. (1986) *Headteachers at Work,* Milton Keynes, Open University Press.

HALPIN, A.W. (1966) *Theory and Research in Administration,* New York, Macmillan.

HALPIN, A.W. and CROFT, D.F. (1963) *The Organizational Climate of Schools,* Chicago, IL, Midwest Administration Center, University of Chicago.

HANDY, C. (1984) *Taken for Granted? Understanding Schools as Organisations,* York, Longmans/Schools Council.

HANDY, C. (1987) 'By way of encouragement: The path to a better society?', *Royal Society of the Arts (RSA) Journal,* 136, 5377, December.

HARGREAVES, D.H. (1982) *The Challenge for the Comprehensive School,* London, Routledge and Kegan Paul.

HARGREAVES, D.H. (1984) *Improving Secondary Schools,* ILEA Report, March.

HARVEY-JONES, J. (1988) *Making It Happen: Reflections on Leadership,* London, Collins.

HILTON, B. (1983) 'Towards a skills-based science curriculum', *Education,* 2 December.

HOLLY, P.J. (1984) 'The institutionalisation of action-research in schools', *Cambridge Journal of Education,* 14, 2.

HOLLY, P.J. (1985) *The Developing School,* TRIST working paper, Cambridge Institute of Education.

HOLLY, P.J. (1986) 'Soaring like turkeys: The impossible dream?', *School Organization,* 6, 3.

HOLLY, P.J. and WIDEEN, M. (1987a) *The Cultural Perspective on Institutionalisation,* OECD/CERI ISIP publication.

HOLLY, P.J. (1987b) 'Teaching for learning: Learning for teaching', *Curriculum,* 8, 2.

HOLLY, P.J. with JAMES, T. and YOUNG, J. (1987) *The Experience of TRIST: Practitioners' Views of INSET,* DELTA project report, Manpower Services Commission/Cambridge Institute of Education.

HOLLY, P.J. with MARTIN, D. (1987) 'A head start? Primary schools and the TRIST experience', *Cambridge Journal of Education,* 17, 3.

HOLMES, S. and JAMIESON, I. (1983) conference paper on the 'new vocationalism', mimeo.

HOLT, M. (1978) *The Common Curriculum,* London, Routledge and Kegan Paul.

HOLT, M. (1983) 'Vocationalism: The new threat to universal education', *Forum.*

HOPKINS, D. (1986) 'Recent developments in secondary education: Some premature reflections', *Cambridge Journal of Education,* 16, 3.

HOUSE, E. (1981) 'Three perspectives on innovation' in LEHMING, R. and KANE, M. (Eds) *Improving Schools: Using What We Know,* Beverley Hills, CA, Sage.

HUTCHINSON, B. (1986) 'The public image of a DES low attaining pupils' programme' in HOLLY, P.J. (Ed) 'Symbolism or synergism? Curriculum evaluation in the 1980s', *Cambridge Journal of Education,* 16, 2.

INNER LONDON EDUCATION AUTHORITY (1985) *The Junior School Project,* London, ILEA Research and Statistics Branch.

JOYCE, B. *et al* (1983) *The Structure of School Improvement,* New York, Longman.

JOYCE, B. and SHOWERS, B. (1980) 'Improving in-service training: The messages of research', *Educational Leadership,* 37, 5.

KANTER, R.M. (1982) *The Change Masters,* London, Allen and Unwin.

LEA, C.J. (1985) article on TVEI, *Forum,* 25, 3.

LEAVITT, H.J. (1986) *Corporte Pathfinders,* Homewood, IL, Dow Jones-Irwin.

LEITHWOOD, K. and MONTGOMERY, D.J. (1985) 'The role of the principal in school improvement' in AUSTIN, G. *et al* (Ed) *Research on Exemplary Schools,* Orlando, FL, Academic Press.

LIEBERMAN, A. (1986) 'Collaborative research: Working with, not working on . . .', *Educational Leadership,* February.

LIEVEGOED, B.C.J. (1972) *The Developing Organisation,* London, Tavistock.

LIGHTFOOT, S.L. (1983) *The Good High School,* New York, Basic Books.

LIKERT, R. (1961) *New Patterns of Management,* New York, McGraw-Hill.

LITTLE, J.W. (1981) 'The power of organizational setting: School norms and staff development', paper presented at the annual meeting of the American Educational Research Association, Los Angeles, April.

LORTIE, D. (1987) 'Built-in tendencies toward stabilising the principal's role', paper presented at the annual meeting of the American Educational Research Association, Washington, April.

LYONS, G., STENNING, R. and MCQUEENEY, J. (1987) *Employment Relations in Maintained Secondary Schools,* Bristol: National Development Centre for School Management.

MCCORMICK, R. and JAMES, M. (1983) *Curriculum Evaluation in Schools,* London, Croom Helm.

MCMAHON, A., BOLAM, R., ABBOTT, R. and HOLLY, P.J. (1984) *GRIDS Project Handbooks,* York, Longman/Schools Council.

MANASSE, A.L. (1985) 'Improving conditions for principal effectiveness: Policy implications of research', *The Elementary School Journal,* 85, 3.

MARQUAND, D. (1988) *The Unprincipled Society,* London, Jonathan Cape.

MEYER, J.W. and SCOTT, W.R. (1983) *Organizational Environments,* Beverley Hills, CA, Sage.

MILES, M.B. (Ed) (1964) *Innovation in Education,* New York, Teachers' College Press, Columbia University.

MILES, M.B. (1987) 'Practical guidelines for school administrators: How to get there', paper presented at the annual meeting of the American Educational Research Association, Washington, April.

MINTZBERG, H. (1973) *The Nature of Managerial Work,* New York, Harper and Row.

NAISBITT, J. (1984) *Megatrends,* London, Futura Books.

NIAS, J. (1980) 'Leadership styles and job satisfaction in primary schools' in BUSH, T. *et al* (ed) *Approaches to School Management,* London, Harper and Row.

PATTERSON, J., PURKEY, S. and PARKER, J. (1986) *Productive School Systems for a*

Non-rational world, Alexandria, VA, Association for Supervision and Curriculum Development.

PETERS, T. (1987) *Thriving on Chaos: Handbook for a Management Revolution,* New York, A. Knopf.

PETERS, T. and AUSTIN, N. (1985) *A Passion for Excellence,* London, Collins.

PETERS, T. and WATERMAN, R. (1982) *In Search of Excellence,* New York, Harper and Row.

PETTIGREW, A. (Ed) (1987) *The Management of Strategic Change,* Oxford, Basil Blackwell.

PLANT, R. (1987) *Managing Change and Making It Stick,* London, Fontana/Collins.

PRESSMAN, J.L. and WILDAVSKY, A. (1979) *Implementation: How Great Expectations in Washington are dashed in Oakland* (2nd edn), Berkeley, CA, University of California Press.

PRING, R. (1985) 'In defence of TVEI', *Forum,* 28, 1.

PURKEY, S.C. and SMITH, M.S. (1983) 'Effective schools: A review', *The Elementary School Journal,* 83.

PURKEY, S.C. and SMITH, M.S. (1985) 'School reform: The district policy implications of the effective schools literature', *The Elementary School Journal,* 85, 3.

RAGSDALE, R.G. (1987) 'Computers in the school of the future', OISE/paper presented at 'School Year 2000', Helsinki, September.

REID, K., HOPKINS, D. and HOLLY, P.J. (1987) *Towards the Effective School,* Oxford, Basil Blackwell.

REYNOLDS, D. (Ed) (1985) *Studying School Effectiveness,* Lewes, Falmer Press.

RUTTER, M. *et al* (1979) *Fifteen Thousand Hours,* London, Open Books.

SARASON, S.B. (1982) *The Culture of the School and the Problem of Change* (2nd edn), Boston, MA, Allyn and Bacon.

SCHON, D.A. (1971) *Beyond the Stable State,* Harmondsworth, Penguin Books.

SCHON, D.A. (1983) *The Reflective Practitioner,* London, Temple Smith.

SCHON, D.A. (1987) *Educating the Reflective Practitioner,* San Francisco, CA, Jossey-Bass.

SEDGWICK, F. (1985) 'Hammer heads', *Times Educational Supplement,* 9 August.

SEDGWICK, F. (1986) 'Master under God', *Times Educational Supplement,* 2 May.

SERGIOVANNI, T.J. and CORBALLY, J.E. (Eds) (1986) *Leadership and Organizational Culture,* Urbana, IL, University of Illinois Press.

SMITH, L.M. *et al* (1981) 'A longitudinal nested systems model of innovation and change in schooling' in BACHARACH, S. (Ed) *Organizational Behaviour in Schools and School Districts,* New York, Praeger.

SMITH, L.M. (1986) *Educational Innovators: Then and Now,* Lewes, Falmer Press.

SMITH, L.M. and KEITH, P. (1971) *Anatomy of Educational Innovation,* New York, John Wiley.

SOUTHWORTH, G. (Ed) (1987) *Reading in Primary School Management,* Lewes, Falmer Press.

STENHOUSE, L. (1975) *An Introduction to Curriculum Research and Development,* London, Heinemann.

TORRINGTON, H., WEIGHTMAN P. and JOHNS, S. (1987) *Management and Organisation in Secondary Schools,* Manchester, University of Manchester Institute of Science and Technology

US DEPARTMENT OF EDUCATION (1987) *What Works: Research About Teaching and Learning.*

WATERMAN, R.H. (1988) *The Renewal Factor,* London, Bantam Press.

WATTS, T. (1983) 'Redundant approaches to the world of work', *Times Educational Supplement*, 25 November.

WEICK, K.E. (1976) 'Educational organisations as loosely coupled systems' reprinted in WESTOBY, A. (Ed) (1988) *Culture and Power in Educational Organizations*, Milton Keynes, Open University Press.

WEICK, K.E. (1982) 'Administering education in loosely coupled schools', *Phi Delta Kappa*, June.

WEINDLING, R. and EARLEY, P. (1986) *Secondary Headship: The First Years*, Windsor, NFER/Nelson.

WEINER, M. (1985) *English Culture and the Decline of the Industrial Spirit 1850-1980*, Harmondsworth, Penguin Books.

YUKL, G. (1975) 'Toward a behavioural theory of leadership' in HOUGHTON, V. *et al* (eds) *The Management of Organisations and Individuals*, London, Ward Lock Educational.

Index

ability, 34
academic
  record, 3
  standards, 211
  success, 107
accessibility, 122
accountability, 123, 223, 224
accountancy, 227–8
acculturation, 144, 146
achievement, 43, 104, 134, 198, 210,
  257
Acorn, 47, 247
action, 115, 117, 150, 157, 203, 231,
  250, 251
  altruism for, 182
  images, 171
  implications for, 169–70
  learning, 184
  orientation, 169, 171
  research, 184, 263
active learning, 212
adaption, 150, 152, 179
administration, 118, 120
administrators, school, 114, 141, 171–2
adoption/initiation, 166, 190
advisers, 226
Advisory Service, 13, 14
aims and objectives, 36–7, 122
'A' level courses, 81
alternative schools, 224, 229
altruism for action, 182
America: principals and leadership, 110
analysis, 184, 250
ancillary services, private, 223

Andrews, R., 219
Apple, 49, 184, 189
'Applied INSET', 170
appraisal, employee, 257
approachability, 133
articles of faith, 139
assemblies, school, 35–6
assessment, 97, 198, 204, 207, 209, 212
'assumed': climate, 261
attainment levels, 196
attitudes/beliefs, 68, 150
Austin, N., 113, 122
  see also Peters
Australia: school self-management, 227–
  8
authoritarian regime, 186
'authority dependency', 129
autocracy, 110
autocratic phase, 128, 129, 174
autonomy, 113, 117, 132, 142, 154
  school, 172, 207, 221, 240
availability, leader's, 133

Baker, K., 3, 6, 221, 222, 227, 236,
  246
Barker, B., 202, 239, 265
Barnett, C., 234
basic skills, 89, 198
behaviour, 29–30, 104–5, 115, 150, 171
beliefs and attitudes, 150
belonging, sense of, 160
benevolent authoritative approach, 125
Bennett, W., 223, 238, 255
Bennis, W.G. (1969), 249

and Nanus, B. (1985), 110, 160, 161, 163, 178, 179, 182, 241, 251, 261
Berger, P. and Kellner, H. (1965), 140
Blake, R.R., Avis, R. and Mouton, J.S. (1966), 127, 174
Block, P. (1987), 133
Bloom, A. (USA), 238
Board of Governors, 41
 see also governors
bonding: school/community, 219
books/book shop, 3, 41
bottom-up/top-down decisions, 189
boundary spanning, 219
'Bourbon' type leadership, 122
Bracknell, 6–7, 17, 19–20
Bracknell College of Further Education, 20, 27, 64
briefings, morning, 112
Broxbourne school, 224
B/TEC
 see Business and Technician Education Council
budgetary control, 252
budget book, County's, 35
Buchanan, D.A. and Huczynski, A.A. (1985), 119–20, 248
'building block' terminology, 176
building improvements, 214
'Bullock Report', 84–5
bureaucracy, 83, 190, 249–50
bureaucratic phase, 128, 129
bureaucractic structures: inertia, 7
bursar, school, 228
business, education as, 242
business, school run as, 5, 26, 107, 112–18
business and information studies, 49
 course, 47
Business and Technician Education Council (B/TEC), 196, 201
Business Centre, 245
business consultant, 101
business culture/school culture, 141–2
business, small, 246
business interests, local, 80
Business Manager, 4, 42, 61–2, 98, 114, 152, 228, 246, 247
'business model', 223
business modules, 81

business objectives, 137
business office, high-tech, 47–9, 101
business technique, 14
business theory and practice, 171
'buying, in', 114, 137, 219

Caldwell, B. and Spinks, J. (1988), 227
campus management group, 73
careers, 37, 44, 68–9, 203, 204
Carnegie Task Force Report, 223
Carver (George Washington Carver High School), 116
CDT
 see Craft, Design and Technology
Central Advisory Council for Education: Report, 85
ceremonies, 141, 152
Certificate of Pre-vocational Education (CPVE), 81, 196, 201
CGLI
 see City and Guilds of London Institute
chairman of faculty, 70
Chandler, Sir G., 235
'championing behaviour', 251
change, 11, 143, 146, 152, 161, 163, 181, 207, 210, 260
 agents, 7, 8, 171
 approaches to, 175–7, 229, 249
 initiatives, 7, 150
 leader/leadership, 2, 119, **123–35**, 248
 managing, 104, 158, 163–90, 253
 resistance to, 70, 159–60
 scenarios, 218–19, 222, 254–5, 258
character-building, 238
charity work, 32, 43
Charters, W.W. and Jones, J.E (1973), 193–6, 198, 207
chief executive: leader as, 111, 124
choice, 222, 229, 232
'chunking', 151, 158, 167, 180, 182, 251
Circular 6/81, 222
City and Guilds of London Institute (CGLI), 201, 204
City Technology College (CTC), 100, 227, 228, 229–30
clarity, 171
Clark, D., *et al* (1984), 106
classroom, 3, 170, 178, 190, 262, 263

enquiry/observation, 194–6, 266
Clemson, D. and Craft, A. (1981), 200
climate, school, 138–42, 172, 178, 198,
    233, 261
    -setting, 152, 181, 188
cleaning, staff, 26–7
coaching, 130, 132
Cockroft Report, 196–7
coercive power: leadership, 119
Coleman, T., 131
collaboration, 107, 159, 176, 186–7,
    196, 259, 264–5
collaborative enquiry, 175, 178, 184–5,
    263
collaborative individualism, 149, 157–8,
    167, 183, 266
collaborative schools, 263
collective vision, 138
colleges, 37, 101, 236
    see also city technology
collegiality, 107, 198, 251, 265
commerce, 65, 69, 97, 111, 244
commitment, 118, 122, 189
communication, 83, 93, 119, 145, 161,
    251
community/school link, 32, 34, 39, 40–
    4, 80, 104, 113, 218, 219, 226, 244
    attitudes, 25, 28, 30–1
    sense of, 35–6, 107, 239, 256
    spirit, 177
'compact schools', 65
company culture, 145
competance, 209, 210
competition, 204, 210, 215, 229, 230–
    2, 252
    sporting, 67, 153
computer centre, 45–7, 245
computer innovation, 191
computerization of curriculum, 208
computer link: parents, 50–1, 245
computer technology, 65
conference centre unit, 60
conference room, 33
conflict, 67, 119, 142
confidence, 117, 133, 210
consensus, 27
conservatism, 186
consideration, 142, 167, 182, 188, 199,
    242

consultancy, 61, 119
contact ratio, teacher/pupil, 91
content and process, 180
    see also curriculum
contingency theory, 126
continuity, 132–3, 181, 182
contract, freedom of, 231
control, 151, 155–6
'control after the event', 150, 157, 167
conviction, 166
Cooper, B. (1987), 228–9
cooperation, 159, 209
Coopers and Lybrand: report (1988), 251
coping, 172, 209
'core' curriculum, 208, 212
core subjects, 230
core values, 152
'corporate culture', 145, 256, 257
costs, 190, 225, 226
counter cultures, 160
courses, 80
Cox, B., 142
CPVE
    see Certificate of Pre-vocational
        Education
Crandall, D.P. *et al* (1983)
Craft, Design and Technology (CDT), 86,
    204, 207
creativeness, 117, 151, 152
creativity, 185, 209
credibility, 22
crises/crisis, 112, 127, 129, 261
cross-curricular
    contact, 39–40
    initiatives, 212
    see also computers
CTC
    see City Technology College
Cuban, L. (1984), 253, 264
'cultural decomposition', 238
cultural mould, breaking, 181
cultural symbolism, 154
cultural vision, **163–90**
culturation, 143
culture, 106, 107–8, 112, 131, 134–5,
    137–61, 218, 219, 224, 226, 231–5,
    242, 256, 260
    -building, 251, 257
    and industrialization, 234

informal, 159, 215, 239
see also corporate; cultural vision;
   development; enterprise
Cunnington, B. and Limerick, D., 148
   (1986), 148–9, 157–8, 190
curriculum, 37, 68, 72–3, 88, 96–8,
   106, 190
   control, 222
   developing, **62–97**
   Garth Hill, 17–18, 191, 192, 193,
      198–9, 200–1, 203, 207, 208, 209,
      230, 245
   'pastoral', 80
   see also computers; core; enterprise
      hidden
customs, 148
   see also routines

Dadds, M. (1986), 177
Dalin, Per, 7–8
data, 138, 175, 184
Daily Mail, 3–4
Daily Telegraph, 124, 142, 192, 221,
   225, 235, 238
Deal, T., 141, 142, 153, 224
   (1985), 106–7, 134, 140, 141, 218,
   256
   and Kennedy, A., 143, 257
   (1982), 141
   (1983), 138, 141
decentralization, 132, 183, 229, 232
decision-making, 106, 110, 111, 113,
   232, 254, 259
delegation, 70, 129, 175, 188, 260
deliberation/action, 174
DELTA report, 182, 208
democratic/cooperative enterprise, 231,
   239
'democratic' leadership, 123
democractic self-help/responsibility, 232
denationalization of education, 223, 229
departmental liaison, 93–4
Department for Enterprise, 211
dependency, 213, 231, 238, 239–40
DES (1977), 129
   (1988), 226
   /HMI (1977), 142
desegregation: magnet schools, 229
DESSI reports, 187

development, 175–6, 177, 180
development culture, 146, 147, 150,
   151, 155, 219, 259
dialogue, 219, 259
differentiation phase of time, 127
direct grant schools, 222–3
directive initiator: Goodchild, 187
Directors of Study, 80
direction to delegation phase, 129
discipline, 3, 28–31, 32–3, 34, 43, 95,
   118, 217, 230
   and effective schools, 107, 117, 198
discontinuity/discontinuous change, 158,
   163–5
discontinuous incrementalism, 163
discussion: pupil/teacher, pupil/pupil,
   196
distance learning: industry links, 61
Doomsday Project, 58
drama, 59, 152
dramatist, leader as, 131
Drucker, P., 113, 148, 171, 183 (1985),
   118, 171, 233, 238
DTI, 210, 211, 232, 234
   White Paper, 236–7
Durham, M., 192
dynamism, 248

ecological approach, 219
'ecological niche', 160, 161, 252
economic philosophy, 230
eco-system, 218
education, 43, 117, 206, 221, 223,
   227–8
   change in, 7, 11, 143, 218–19
   higher, 236
   quality, 190, 225
   state: values, 142
Education Act (1980), 66, 22
   (1986), 222
educational institutions, 50
educationalists, 154, 253
educational philosophy, 230
education and business: theory and
   practice, 171
education and industry, 167, 134–5,
   236–7
Education Bill, 221
Education for Capability movement, 234

effort, personal, 37
effective schools, 8, 105, 106, 107, 141, 198, 256, 257
embedding, 190
employability, 210
employers, 37, 204, 228, 230, 236–7
employment, 3, 42, 63, 81, 116, 205
empowerment, 130, 133, 240, 250, 251, 260, 263–4
encouragement, 130, 132–3, 165
enculturation, 143, 258
endeavour, 43
English and literacy, 37, 82
enquiry learning
enterprise, 2, 41–2, 152, 211, 229, 231, 232, 236–7, 239
enterprise culture, 104, 147–8, 166, 213–40, 246
enterprise curriculum, 104, 190, 191–212
enterprise economy, 231–2
'Enterprise Initiative', 232
Enterprise, Ministry for, 232
enterprise philosophy, 239
enterprise training, 210
enterprising school, Garth Hill as, 103–266
enthusiasm, 117, 123, 170, 177
'Entrain', 211
environment, 34, 84, 115, 153
entrepreneural approach, 229
entrepreneuralism, 178, 210–11
entrepreneurs, 169, 170, 171, 233–4, 252
entrepreneurship, 117, 132, 150, 183, 233, 238, 242
equality of opportunity, 203
ethos, 139, 154, 199, 215–16, 217, 224, 257, 261
    and culture, 138–9, 142, 151, 155, 216, 256, 257
-making, 158–9
evaluation, 97, 122, 174–5, 177, 193, 196, 213
Evening Post, Nottingham, 4–5
Everard, B., 253
evolution, 148, 150, 151
evolutionary approach, 151–2
examinations, 201, 207, 209

examining bodies, 37
excellence, 6, 45, 114, 118, 229
expectations, 117, 122, 217
experience, 255
experiential learning, 208, 212
experimentation, 150, 151, 165, 179
expert power of leadership, 119
Etzioni, A. (1964), 120
exploitation, 125, 188
'extant': informal culture, 216
external advice, 259
external forces, 218, 219, 221
external ideas, 259
extra-curricular activities, 19
extrinsic motivation, 121

Facade, 215
facilitator, leader as, 131
factional collaboration, 265
failure, toleration of, 165
'familial approach', 114
feed-back, 119, 179, 192
Fenstermacher, G. and Berliner, D.(1986), 177
FEU
    see Further Education Unit
finance, 57, 61, 63, 64, 76–8
    see also funding
followers/followership, 119
forcefulness: leader, 188
'formal doctrine', 193, 215
founder/pioneer, 174, 186
fragmentation, cultural, 218
free enterprise, 116, 223, 225, 232
Friends of Garth Hill School, 41, 74
Fullan, M., 170, 171, 180, 215
    (1982), 167
    (1985), 106, 132, 164, 165, 166, 170, 182
    (1986), 189
    (1987), 167–8, 169, 170
    (1988), 141, 213, 239–40, 250, 256
    and Newton (1986), 187–8, 189
funding, 239
    see also finance
fund raising, 32, 43, 45, 243–4
Further Education Unit, (FEU), 200

Garth Hill School, 1–100, 182, 187, 227, 228
  aims, 36–7, 80
  background, 3, 16, 17–21, 23–4
  and community, 40, 65
  curriculum, 191, 199–200
  as enterprise school, 41, **241–51**, 226
  image, 38, 40
  and industry, 3, 6–7, 40, 57, 97, 114, 184, 246
  leadership, 130, 188, 251
  marketing and promotion, 39, 40–1, 51, 213–14, 216
  technology, leader in, 53, 65
  see also academic record; CTC; discipline; magnet schools; music; sport; teachers/teaching/staff; technology; 'UK firsts'
GCE courses, 80
GCSE, 196, 243
Gehlen, A., 140, 142, 144
Gelinier, O. (1968), 230–2
George Washington Carver School, 216
German industrial interest, 184
Gilder, G. (1986), 232–3, 234, 235
goals, 117, 119, 122, 137–8, 146, 150, 193, 198
Golzen, 257
Goodchild, Stanley, 43–4, 67, 152, 175, 188, 200, 244, 247–8, 252, 255, 266
  background/career, 1, 5, 12–17, 247
  business technique, 12, 14
  compare Harvey-Jones, 134
  industry/community links, forging, 40–1
  initiator/pioneer/founder, 186, 187
  leadership style: change in, 123–30
  quotations from, 213, 241
  school as business, running, 118, 246
Goodlad, J.I., 222, 259
  (1987), 218–19, 258, 263–4
  and Klein, M.F. (1970), 194, 198
government, 231
governors, 16, 41, 45, 77, 98, 221, 222, 226, 228
  function of, 73
  industrialist member, 65
  student member, 4
Graham, D. and Clark, P. (1986), 232

grant maintained schools, 223
Great Reform Bill, 222
Greenall, J., 214–15
Greiner, L.E., 129
  (1972), 127, 174
GRIDS, 174, 176, 178, 184–5, 227, 262, 263
  Handbooks, 197
GRIST
  see Grant Related In-service Training
guidance, career, 68–9, 203
Gusky, T. (1986), 166

Hall, G. *et al* (1984), 135, 251
Hall, V., Mackay, H. and Morgan, C. (1986), 110–11, 124
Halpin, A.W. (1966), 120, 142
  and Croft, D.F. (1963), 142
handbook, school, 81
Handy, C., 128, 129, 163–5, 167, 182, 253–4, 255
  (1984), 113, 117, 127, 150, 156–7
  (1987), 132, 133, 158, 163–4, 179
Hargreaves, D.H., (1982), 117
  (1983), 196
Harris, R., 143
Harrison, R., 128, 129
Harvey-Jones, J., 139, 140, 175, 181, 182, 183, 253
  (1988), 134, 137, 144, 146, 169, 170, 174, 184, 233
Hayek, F.A., 232
'headroom', 175, 183
headteacher, 35–6, 154, 222, 239–40, 247–8, 257
  and leadership, 104, 129, 217, 228
  roles of, 5, 26, 110, 111, 217, 224
    changing, 247
  training for management, 111, 253–4
  see also principal
Heckman, 258–9, 261–2, 263
Hewlett-Packard, 4, 65, 69, 152, 184, 247
hidden curriculum, 217
high risk strategies, 248
high-tech, 3, 192, 207
high-tech business office, 47–9, 101, 245
high-tech library, 56–8, 245, 246
Hilton, B., (1983), 203

HMI report, 106
HMI, 104–5, 106
  /DES, 196
    (1977), 142
Hogans, 116, 255
Holly, P., 108, 151, 174, 175, 185, 263
    (1984), 151, 178, 185, 262
    (1985), 123, 146, 166, 173, 176
    (1987b), 144, 156
    and Hopkins, D. (1988), 173
    and James, T. and Young, J. (1987),
      170, 182, 208, 254
    and Martin, D. (1987), 177–8
    and Wideen, M. (1987a), 143, 196
Holmes, S. and Jamieson, I., (1983), 204
Holt, M. (1978), 105
    (1983), 202
Hopkins, D. (1986), 200, 201, 202
House, E. (1981), 143
House system, 33–4, 74
Hume, David, 232
humility, 242

IBM, 184, 247, 257
ideology/guiding system, 190
IDPs
    see Institutional Development Plans
ILEA, 106, 125–6
image, new: marketing, 153
implementation, 135, 146, 147, 158,
    159, 166, 182, 190, 250, 251
    'black box', 180
    causal map, 172
    collaborative, 161
    'dip', 169
    enabling, 173
    as key concern, 167
    as learning process, 189
    management of, 188
    teachers' use of, 193
    stage, 132, 169
improvisation, 178, 183
IMTEC
    see International Movements Towards
      Educational Change
incrementalism, 158, 163, 252
independence, 195, 225
Independent, The, 232
individualism, 86, 150, 157–8, 159,

167, 183, 225
industry, 70, 144, 145, 231, 233–4
    and education, 14, 167, 235, 236–7
    and Garth Hill, 4, 6–7, 28, 39, 40–4,
      65, 97, 244, 246
      investment in 3, 5, 25, 57, 96
    and schools, 111, 112, 225
      staff, 65, 79
    see also governors
Industry-Education Liaison Group, 14
Industry Year (1986), 64, 235, 243
Information Technology, 45, 53, 65, 69,
    99, 207, 244–5, 252, 266
inertia, 152
initiation, 130, 131–2, 146, 147, 167–
    8, 190
initiative, 32, 132
initiatives, 132, 166, 177, 242
initiator, leader as, 187, 251
innovation, 7, 150, 152, 165–7, 170,
    171, 175, 183, 187, 189, 193–4, 199,
    231
    without change, 167, 218
    curriculum, 200–1
    and industry, 145
    phases/stages of, 191
    process, 168, 190
    and schools, 150, 238, 257
    and stability, 143, 144, 154
    theory, 165, 173
innovativeness, retaining, 151, 152
innovators, 7, 183, 234, 249
in-service, 13, 65, 67, 73, 80, 170, 182,
    191–2, 254
INSET (in-service), 73, 97, 191–2, 208
    'Applied', 170, 254
Institute of Economic Affairs, 230
Institutional Development Plans (IDPs),
    148
institutionalization, 144, 146, 152–3,
    155–6, 166, 172, 185, 190
insurance: letting out school resources, 42
interdisciplinary approaches, 212
interdisciplinary enquiry, 209
International Movements Towards
    Educational Change (IMTEC), 7
investment, 54, 231, 244
Italy: work experience, 69

Jamieson, I. and Watts, T., 211
Japan, 3, 53–4, 184, 243
job descriptions, staff, 19, 70
Johnson, P., 235–6
Joseph, Lord, 110, 232
Joyce, B. *et al* (1983), 146, 176, 196
   and Showers, B. (1980), 170, 182,
   191–2
Kanter, R.M. (1982), 138
   (1983), 260–1
Kemmis, S., 195
Kennedy, 143
Kettering Grammar School: astrology,
   101
keyboard literacy, 101
key persons in leadership, 119–20
key system, 55
key tasks/objectives, 77
knowledge, 37

language, 84, 85, 151, 169, 232
languages, modern, 17, 96–7
LAPP
   see Lower Attaining Pupils' Programme
Lea, C.J., 202–3
Leach, M., 207
leadership, 104, 106, 107, 110–35, 161,
   163–90, 228, 242, 249, 265
   change in, 2, 112, 123–35, 180, 187
   delegation of, 157
   functions of, 120, 134, 163
   and innovation, 145
   strategies, 251
   strong, 43, 111, 198, 223, 250
learning, 2, 7, 66, 107, 132, 151, 175,
   178, 195, 196, 197
   action, 184
   active, 106, 211
   approches to, 204, 207, 208–9
   and computers, 192
   difficulties, 87
   distance, 61
   and environment, **33–41**
   practical/experiental, 152, 208
   process, 37, 97, 156, 179, 228, 266
   organization(s), 161, 208
   research, 193
teaching, 49, 97, 164, 194, 228
'Learning School', 86–7, 188

Leavitt, H., 157, 158–61, 248, 261
   (1986), 120, 135, 137, 158–9, 178,
   250, 251
leisure pursuits courses, 204
Leithwood, K. and Montgomery, D.J.,
   (1985), 251
Lewin, K., 263
LFM
   see Local Financial Management
'liberal democratic' philosophy, 239
liberalism, 232
library, 3, 41, 56–8, 101
Lickert, R. (1961), 125
Lieberman, A. (1986), 164, 170, 175,
   263
Lievegoed, B.C.J. (1972), 127, 128–9,
   174
Lightfoot, S. (1983), 114, 115, 238
Limerick, D., 148
Lindley, R., 210
Listener, The, 210
literacy and English, 37
Little, J.W. (1981), 170
LMS
   see Local Management in Schools
local education authority, 25, 35, 39, 98,
   107, 226
Local Financial Management (LFM), 98
Local Management in Schools (LMS),
   225–7, 251
Local Resource Management (LRM), 225
'longitudinal nesting systems model',
   219, 220, 221
Lortie, D. (1987), 256
Lower Attaining Pupils' programme,
   196, 201
LRM
   see Local Resource Management
Lyons, G., Stenning, R. and McQueeney,
   J. (1987), 110

McCormick, R. and James, M. (1983),
   193
McMahon, A. *et al* (1984), 174, 263
magnet schools, 100, 227, 228–9
Makins, V., 227–8
management, 2, 43, 94, 106, 112,
   114–15, 119–20, 223, 226, 250
   for change, 163–90, 266

of change, 58, 119, 253, 266
and pupils, 134
philosophy, 230
roles, 77, 81, 149, 181, 233, 254–5
small business, 211
structures, 25, 72–5, 77
team, 69–79, 81, 97, 259–60
training, 111, 201, 256–4, 255
management culture in education, 251–6
managerialism, 248
Managing By Wandering Around
(MBWA), 120, 130, 131, 132, 133–
4, 248, 251, 260
managers, 26, 69, 126, 133
Manasse, A.L. (1985), 121–2, 217–18
Manpower Services Commission (MSC),
47, 63, 64, 200, 201, 210, 236, 237
/NED report, 253
Mansell Report (1979), 200
March, J., 148, 156
market, 47, 243
market forces, 145, 222–3, 224, 225
marketing, 153, 229
school, 39, 213–30, 246
Marquand, D., 234, 239
MBWA
see Managing By Wandering Around
MSC
see Manpower Services Commission
mathematics, teaching of, 13–14, 86
meaning, 118, 149, 161, 251
media, use of, 28, 34, 47, 154, 215,
216, 221, 248
Mercer, D., 257
merit system, 34
Meyer, J.W. and Scott, W.R. (1983),
155–6
Michael, D., 179
Miles, M. (1987), 142, 147, 171–3
mini-enterprise schemes, 41–2, 211
Mintzberg, H. (1973), 113–14
Modular Technology, 204
modules, 209
morale, staff 115
motivation, 119, 120, 134, 210
music: Garth Hill, 3, 36

Naisbitt, J. (1984), 110–11, 129–30,
189, 191, 219

National Council for Vocational
Qualifications (NCVQ), 209
National Curriculum, 211, 212
NCVQ
see National Council for Vocational
Qualifications
needs analysis, 174
needs assessment, 258
'neighbourhood schools', 223
Neo-Conservatives, 232, 236
networks, 149, 157, 158, 172
New Enlightenment, 232
Newman, 207
Nias, J. (1980), 122–3
Nottingham Evening Post, 242–3, 247–8

observation, classroom, 174
OD
see Organizational Development
office, high-tech business, 47–9
office maanger, 228
opportunism, 156, 171, 248
organization(s), 135, 141, 150, 161,
169, 174, 175, 178, 185, 187
adaptive, 151
and change, 2, 186
innovative, 184
learning, 151, 179, 182–3
school as, 86, 97, 157
organizational
change, scheme for, 248–9
chart, management, 71
concepts, 261
culture, 112, 138–9, 142, 250, 256,
261
development: group work, 180
effectiveness, 117–18
evolution, 148
health, 84, 105, 142
theory, 112, 150
Organizational Development (OD), 175,
176, 186
Organization for Rehabilitation through
Training (ORT), 210
ORT
see Organization for Habilitation
through Training
ownership, 183, 185, 199, 228, 232
see also 'buying in'

Papert, (1980), 192
parents, 3, 4, 21, 23, 27–8, 28–31, 38,
    43, 118, 217
    choice, 222, 225, 229, 237–8
    computer link, 50–1, 245
    involvement, 41, 45, 65, 74, 81, 98,
        107, 228, 244
    power, 221, 224, 248
participation, 115, 170, 250
partnership, 190, 219, 222, 224, 239,
    263
pastoral curriculum, 81, 206
pastoral policy, 18, 37, 72
pathfinding, 158, 159, 161, 178, 250,
    251, 261
Patterson, J. *et al* (1986), 250
people, 121, 133, 134, 181, 182, 233,
    253
persistence, 117, 150, 171, 179, 189
personal dimension, 117, 210, 211, 238,
    249, 251
Peters, T., 113, 122, 190, 252
    (1987), 189, 252–3, 254, 259–60
    and Austin, N., 139, 158,170, 176,
        183, 186
    (1985), 113–18, 130, 131, 132, 133,
        141, 167, 182, 183, 184
    and Waterman, R., 157, 170, 257
        (1982), 15, 116–17, 138, 141, 145,
        148, 150, 151–2
Pettigrew, A., 148
pioneering element, 127, 129, 128, 186,
    240
planning, 150, 151, 169, 176, 177, 179
Plant, R. (1987), 127, 128, 129, 171,
    173–5, 185, 186–7
Polanyi, 255
polytechnics: business/management
    training, 236
political philosophy, 230
positive elements, 117, 122, 133, 243
power, 119, 131, 160, 172, 221, 260
practicality: '*do-ability*', 118, 196, 206
pragmatism, 139, 158, 183
press, 3–5, 22, 28, 39, 47, 49, 65, 216
use of, 27, 43, 62, 67, 246–7
Pressman, J.L. and Wildavsky, A.
    (1979), 147, 166, 182
pressure (mandation), 121, 124, 170,

188, 199, 248, 261
Prestel, 3, 46–7, 247
pride in school, 4, 28, 34–5, 45, 116,
    198
principal, 72, 121–2, 124–5, 213, 156
    see also headteacher
Pring, R. (1985), 205–7
prioritization, 166, 169
privatization, 223, 225, 229
proactive leaders/heads, 121–2, 131–2,
    180, 187, 217–18
problem-solving, 119, 135, 158, 159,
    178, 179, 190, 197, 203, 208, 230,
    250, 251, 262
process, 180, 189, 206
proculturation, 143, 144, 152, 153, 166
productivity, 117, 206, 229
professional dimension, 86, 111, 170,
    255
profiling, 196, 203, 204
publicity/promotion, 116, 153, 214–15
    see also marketing
public relations, 39, 214, 216
pupils, 4, 41–2, 63, 80, 117, 141
    behaviour, 42, 104
    and computers, 192
    and industry, 65, 234
    learning, 87, 194, 195
    numbers, 68, 226
    in school organization, 74–5
    see also fundraising; pride; profiles;
        students; work experience
Purkey, S.C. and Smith, M.S. (1985),
    106, 107

qualifications, 37
quality, importance of, 56, 189, 190

Ragsdale, R. (1987), 192
reading/language abilities, 84–5
Reagan revolution (USA), 144
records, 37–8, 196
redeployment, teachers', 67–8
reform, 173, 175, 218
Reid, P., 86–7
Reid, K., Hopkins, D. and Holly, P.J.
    (1987), 86–7, 106, 108, 148, 175,
    176
remedial education, 17, 82, 91

reports, departmental, 77–8
research, 110, 184, 192–3
resources, 34, 113, 119, 145, 195, 196,
    207, 208, 226
    -led change, 249
    development, **45–62**
    use by outside groups, 98
responsibilities, 31–2, 252
restaurant, 59, 246
rewards, 119, 172, 190
Reynolds, D. (1985), 106, 111
risk-taking, 7, 132, 150, 164, 171, 179,
    234, 259
ritual/ceremonies, 141, 152
role-performance, 193, 225
Royal Society of Arts (RSA), 201, 204,
    209
Rowe, 253
RSA
    see Royal Society of Arts
Rutter, M., 142
    et al (1979), 106, 257

St. Andrews School, 224
Sarason, S.B. (1982), 143, 169, 257, 259
SBR
    see School-based Review
schemes of work, 82
Schon, D.A. (1971), 151, 255
school, 50, 114, 173, 185, 220, 238,
    257
    change initiative in, 150, 253
    and community, 43, 219, 228
    developing, 115, 180, 261–5
    effectiveness, 8, 26, 105, 106–7, 108,
        112–13, 129
    and industry/business, 65, 110, 236–
        7, 256
    as organization, 86, 157
    renewal, 218–19, 261–2, 263
    self-managing, 189, 227
    see also assemblies
School-based Review (SBR), 201
Schools Council Meetings, 74–5
Schools Industry Partnership, 40
Schumpeter, J., 249
Secretary of State for Education, 221
    see also Kenneth Baker
Sedgwick, F., 111

(1985, 1986), 110
self, 149, 251
    criticism, 84
    development, 252
    discipline, 32–3
    employment, 204, 210, 211
    evaluation, 185, 192–3, 199, 201,
        227, 266
    help, 232
    management, 32
    reliance, 32
senior management team, 81
Sergiovanni, T.J. and Corbally, J.E.
    (1986), 156
'shadowing' schemes, 69
Shell: enterprize schemes, 211
Shereded School, 224
sixth form, 31–2, 74
skills, 37, 90, 171, 198, 203, 210
skunk/skunkworks, 132, 167, 183, 184,
    185, 187, 252
small, 'thinking', 151, 169, 182–3, 190,
    252
small businesses, 246
small team work, 180, 184–5, 186,
    188–9
Smith, Adam, 232
Smith, L.M. (1986), 132, 139, 147 and
    Keith, P., 193, 215
    et al (1981), 219, 220, 221
social structure of organizations, 249–50
society, 142, 160
Sofer, A., 154, 229
Sony, 252–3
Southworth, G. (1987), 119, 154, 185,
    217, 263
special needs: gifted/low ability, 91, 97
    see also remedial
sport, 3, 33–4, 36, 43, 67, 153, 154
stability/control, 117, 142, 154, 161
staff, Garth Hill, 24, 205, 111, 138,
    140–1, 154, 178, 188, 191, 222, 225,
    263
    career development, 61, **62–96**, 107,
        182, 226
    effect on events, 113, 115, 174
    involvement, 45, 82, 97, 130, 145,
        172, 177–8, 196, 249, 265
    non-teaching, 73–4, 208

reactions to change, 39, 66
staff-
 briefing, 87
 college, 253–4
 conferences, **81–97**
 handbook, 37–8
 meetings, 74
 rooms, 112
standards, 37, 86, 96, 118, 122, 211
Stenhouse, L. (1975), 193
St. John Brookes, C., 224–5
strategic
 evaluation, 174–5
 planning, 135, 250, 251
structure, 150, 152, 193
student(s), 4, 34, 65, 212, 228
 see also pupils
Sunday Times, 145, 222, 224, 227, 257
support, 121, 132, 170, 175, 180, 182,
 187, 188, 199, 201, 240
 from leadership, 120, 122, 260
symbol(s), 115, 116, 122, 131, 134,
 135, 152
symbolism, 141, 149, 153–4

target-setting, 174
task, 121
task groups/teams, 157, 167, 170, 180
Taylor, C., 229–30
Taylor Report, (1977), 222
teaching, 4, 81, 104, 111
 -learning, 49, 96, 164, 194, 228
 styles, 204, 206, 253
teachers, 4, 83–4, 188, 194, 198, 203,
 222, 239, 259
 attitudes to, 112–13, 114, 115, 153,
 264
 autonomy, 117
 education, 111, 196, 153–4
 and industry, 61, 237, 246, 247
 part in innovation, 98, 146, 228
 -parent contact, 81
 -pupil, 87, 194, 195
 as researchers, 192–3, 263
 school values and culture, 141, 142–3
 'self-employed', 223
 types, 200
 see also reform; staff
teams, 157, 176, 178, 184, 188

teamwork, 132, 134, 154, 182
Technical and Vocational
 Education Initiative (TVEI), 47, 62–5,
 81, 101, 106, 196, 200, 201–12
technology, 37, 63–4, 65, 81, 207, 249
 colleges, 101
 courses, 230
 school, 99–101
 see also high-tech; information; Modular
television, 28, 41–2, 47, 216, 217, 246
TES, 236–7
testing, diagnostic, 90, 91
theory/theorists, 113–14, 150, 171, 173,
 188, 206
The Times, 4, 234, 246
3M, 65, 80, 184, 243
time, phases of, 127, 128
Times Network System (TTNS), 50, 245
timetabling, 14, 92–4, 207, 209
Times Educational Supplement, 64–256
 passim
Today, 4, 246
Tomlinson, J., 209
Torrington, H., Weightman, P. and
 Johns, S. (1987), 112, 142, 253, 256
tradition, 40, 116, 138–9, 141, 153–4
training, 65, 80, 116, 179, 206, 255
transfer of ownership, 176, 178
transformative leadership, 120, 161, 251
Trethowan, D., 253
TRIST
 see TVEI-related Inservice Training
trust, 179, 182, 251
TTNS
 see Times Network Systems
tutors, industrial, 65, 69
TVEI
 see Technical and Vocational Education
 Initiative
TVEI-related In-service training (TRIST),
 182, 201, 208

'UK firsts', 51, 58, 61–2, 98, 101, 216
UMIST, 112, 256
unemployment/employment, 3, 204, 205
uniform, school, 3, 20–1, 22–3, 28–31,
 33, 43, 153–4, 218, 225, 248
 shop, 41
United States of America (USA), 223,

229, 232
universities, 37, 236
USA
   see United States
US Department of Education (1987), 198

values, 117, 119, 135, 138, 147, 149,
   157, 217, 259
   core, 131, 132, 151
   and culture, 106, 140, 150
   school, 105, 114
   shared, 141, 142–3, 178
   traditional, 153, 205
vision, 117, 122, 124, 130, 131, 138,
   242
   attention through, 161, 251
   collective, 138
   creation, 7, 115–16, 137, 160, 174
   cultural aspects, 132, 163–90, 269–60
   metastrategic, 157, 158, 190
visitors, 42, 49, 98, 116
visits, interschool, 174
vocationalism, 116, 202, 204, 205
Vonnegut, K., 259
voucher scheme, 218, 222, 223

Waldren, G., 238
Walker, G., 239
Waterman, R., 113
Watson, 132
Watts, A., 205, 246
wealth, purpose of, 233
Weindling, R. and Earley, P. (1986),
   111, 187, 188, 213
Weiner, M. (1985), 233, 234
Wideen, M. (1987), 143
Wilby, P., 222–3
Wilson, J., 142–3, 153
word processor, 230
work, world of, 37
work experience, 68–9, 204, 212, 230,
   237, 245–6
   TVEI, 63, 64, 202
work shadowing, 69, 212

Yorkshire Post, 4–5
Young, Lord, 201, 210, 211, 232, 237
Young Enterprise Scheme, 65, 211, 246
Youth Training Scheme (YTS), 201, 210
YTS
   see Youth Training Scheme
Yukl, G. (1975), 120